Horn of Plenty

Horn of Plenty

The Story of Louis Armstrong

By Robert Goffin

TRANSLATED FROM THE FRENCH

BY JAMES F. BEZOU

ALLEN, TOWNE & HEATH, *INC.*
New York : 1947

Horn of Plenty

I

BETWEEN THE starting point of a man's life and its peak, there is often a middle stretch that reveals the secret of his career. We think immediately of Napoleon, climbing rapidly from a relatively low rung in the social ladder to become Emperor of the French; or of Hitler, starting from the very bottom, as the son of a humble customs inspector, and pulling himself up by his boot straps to a place of power above the thrones of the Hapsburgs and the Hohenzollerns. Thus does the enchanted realm of biography offer many a striking and romantic contrast. The life of Louis Armstrong, intensely fascinating in its play of light and shadow, is a case in point.

In the great cosmopolitan city of New Orleans, at one of the Mississippi's numerous bends, there is a street called Perdido, just a stone's throw from the Canal Street ferry. It starts at St. Charles Street and runs for some thirty blocks as far as Howard Avenue. In many respects, Perdido symbolizes the tumultuous past of the Crescent City.

We find it first recorded in the French colonial period, though it lies outside the limits of the Vieux Carré whose street names commemorate the great French colonizers of America, those who laid the cornerstone of France's power in the New World as in the Old—a splendid roll call: Bienville and Iberville, St. Louis and Conti and Dumaine, to mention but a few.

Horn of Plenty:

The street witnessed the epochal events of 1769, when Alexander O'Reilly—an Irish soldier who held a general's commission in the Spanish army—took possession of the city in the name of the King of Spain; and, as a consequence of the Spanish occupation, the street was thenceforth called Perdido. Some regard the name as that of one of the Conquistadores who blazed a fiery trail across the skies of colonial Spain; others believe it to be merely the Spanish word for "lost," since the street once disappeared for a time into the surrounding swamp.

Walk up Perdido Street in the evening when the rays of the setting sun cast a golden haze on the peaceful banks of the river and the skies above Gretna and Algiers turn crimson. You will cross many a street rich in memories of the past: Rampart, Loyola, Liberty, La Salle, Galvez, and—at the very end, where looms a sprawling factory bristling with smoke stacks—Jeff Davis Parkway. Whether or not you have sensed it, you have been breathing the warm and exciting atmosphere that envelops New Orleans after two centuries of vivid history.

Six blocks before the street ends, you reach an intersecting lane running from Perdido Street to Gravier Street. It is not a street but a cutthroat alley, ancient and squalid beyond belief. This is Jane Alley.

Standing here, in the mid-20th century, you are irresistibly swept back to the beginning of the 19th century. You see New Orleans as it was in the days of the French nobles, and of their successors and accomplices, the Dons and the Spanish Captains. There are old and nondescript frame houses; weatherbeaten hovels looking out blindly on the street through windowpanes stuffed with paper; open spaces where for two centuries broken bottles, discarded pots and pans, scrap iron, and miscellaneous junk have accumulated. In the alley itself, a series of other and smaller blind alleys are marked by shanties

[2]

still more ancient, dilapidated, rickety. One of these, near Perdido Street, is a sprawling frame structure—two floors of filthy rooms to which neither gas nor electricity nor running water has ever come. For here you are still in the year 1800.

Go into this tenement—it is to be the opening scene of Louis Armstrong's story. You reach the second floor by an outdoor staircase, whose landing is a porch that encircles the building. You enter one of the rooms, its only light furnished by an oil lamp, and you see an old table, a bed (or rather a straw mattress), a chest, two or three wooden chairs. The one relatively modern note is provided by the dazzling smiles of the movie stars whose pictures some tenant has torn from a Sunday Magazine section and fastened to the wall.

Some years ago, Jane Alley was truly a tragic and bloody lane—fearful hiding place for the dregs of the city's Negro population. On Saturday nights, when the Negroes—aching after their week's toil as beasts of burden—were inflamed by cheap liquor, Jane Alley would break out in a curious frenzy. The city police always knew what they would see then. Tipsy men and women are howling in a blind-drunk orgy; a few small children, frightened out of their wits, whimper near by; bullies are hurling insults at one another from house to house; a stone thrown through the darkness clatters against a rickety door; quaking women draw together in groups and sing hymns to banish the Evil One. Soon knives begin to fly from secret pockets; the flash of a straight razor appears in the shadows; all the tricks of street fighting at its foulest are used in brawls ranging from individual grudge fights to a general free-for-all, no holds barred. Women scream as they try to defend their men. Suddenly a rending cry ends in a gruesome death rattle; a man lies in agony, dying like a dog; and over the dark earth flows the dark blood of a dark man. Beads of sweat turn cold on shivering black spines as the heat of battle wears off. Unsteady men turn homeward still clutching their lethal razors. Sometimes the police stage a raid. They risk their necks only in large numbers and clutch their loaded guns with fingers nervous on the trigger. Usually a few policemen stand guard at each end, anxiously awaiting Sunday's dawn.

The uncertain light of the new day shows Jane Alley marked by a hundred sodden bodies in a drunken stupor, and malodorous with the stench of sweat, vile liquor, and abject poverty. The police come and remove the corpse, and the alley is silent.

Shortly before 1900, Jane Alley was the lowest Negro slum in New Orleans. Here dwelt the worst elements, vitiated by degrading vices and reduced to a bestial existence—truly a corner of Hell, where the old men and women toothlessly mumbled the Creole dialect and the young bucks spoke a drawling and musical English. For all of them, old and young alike, the word *Hope* had been stricken from their vocabulary, but the word *Resignation* remained.

Here had come one young couple, however, whose decent poverty challenged the alley's degradation. The man, Willy Armstrong, had been born nearby, and—until he met Mary Albert—had lived under his mother's roof. The Armstrongs, sprung from pure Negro stock, had grown up like wild plants. Willy's grandmother was still alive in 1919, and she was almost a hundred years old. In its lucid moments her uncertain memory could feebly trace back the stream of an unhappy life as she recalled the romantic years spent in the old French Quarter, where she had sold fresh water. Born a slave, she remembered the period of the curfew that obliged all the blacks to return to their kennels—that is, within the limits of their own district.

The Story of LOUIS ARMSTRONG

Willy Armstrong's great-grandmother, born during the period of French colonization, had seen many of the dramatic phases of the city's earlier history: man's struggle against the encroaching river, and the fight to save the city from the swamps, and the long series of wars—the whites against the blacks, the French against the pirates, the French against the French, the French against the Spaniards, the French against the English traders, the British against the Americans, and finally, the Americans against the Americans. But, however violently the whites fought among themselves, there was never any hope for the blacks, bent as they were under the yoke of slavery.

An old legend in the Armstrong family had it that one of their female ancestors had been a slave of the Noyans—perhaps the same Noyans of whom one had been arrested by order of the Spanish governor O'Reilly and tried along with a dozen other Frenchmen who had plotted against the Spanish rule. In speech and writing they had declared themselves for liberty and complete independence at a time when their brothers overseas were paving the way for the French Revolution. They were condemned to death. When, bound and handcuffed, they were brought before the Cabildo, a proclamation was read stating that the Governor had deigned to pardon Noyan. The lad, barely eighteen years old, looked up proudly and cried: "My comrades' ideals are my ideals, I fought with them, and with them I will gladly die!" An hour later he and his friends fell dead before the firing squad.

Willy Armstrong's great-grandmother knew little about her ancestors. It must have been four or five generations before her birth that the first of them left Africa in the pestilential hold of a slave ship. At just what period, or how, these forebears got the name of Armstrong cannot, of course, be

[5]

ascertained. The Cathedral's records of slave unions are scanty, and a Negro child nearly always bore his mother's name only—his father's was commonly unknown.

Some parts of this story of his slave ancestors in Louisiana came gradually to Willy Armstrong from his mother and grandmother. But his people had neither the time nor the ability to convey to him any real understanding of the past— of the river pirates long ago, of filibusterers with itchy trigger fingers, of owners of great plantations who lost them at cards, of low dives in which flashy prostitutes from the four corners of the earth plied their gold-digging trade. He might have learned, too, of the Negro's past—of the deep-voiced tomtoms rhythmically breaking the silence of the night, the wild jungle dances, and the awesome revelation of voodoo worship with its age-old rites centering on the snake.

But Willy Armstrong knew nothing of such things. For him there was little else in life but the hard bread of poverty which he shared with his black brethren after wearing the harness thin at the meanest kind of work. Nominally, the Negroes of his day had their "freedom," but the real meaning of the word was far from clear in their minds. All they knew was that they built up the levees along the river, carried milk, sold charcoal, swept chimneys, pushed carts, acted as scavengers—were, in short, jacks of the lowest trades because they had learned no other.

Willy himself was illiterate; he could barely sign his name. And his young wife, Mary—later called May Ann—was no better off. When they married they had nothing except their love and the hope of getting along—somehow and somewhere —more happily than their Jane Alley neighbors.

Soon there was the promise of a baby. With the obstinate courage of the simple-minded, Mary worked until the very last as a servant for a white family living near the cemetery. Willy had a job in a turpentine factory—twelve hours a day. They lived in one of the dead-ends midway in Jane Alley. The building was the dreadful shack we have already looked into; and their single room, for which they paid fifty cents a month, combined the functions of kitchen, dining-room, parlor, and bedroom. Across the alley was a vacant lot that was the local junk heap—a graveyard in which came to rest old wagon springs and shafts, axleless wheels, rusty stoves, odd lengths of piping, broken furniture. . . . It was here that the Jane Alley pickaninnies played cowboy and Indian while their parents were away at work.

On Saturday evening, when the weekly carnival of vice and crime swooped down like a tempest on Jane Alley, young Willy and his wife would huddle in the shadows, promising each other that some day they would get away from this foul hole; and Mary carried her child hopefully, as pledge of a better future. By working hard, by pinching and scraping, they were saving their pennies. On their table there was neither fish nor meat; for their evening meal all they ever had was red beans and bread.

Summer—the summer of 1900—set in with its relentless heat. Inside the wooden shack the air was stifling. Springtime, always early in Louisiana, had brought out the grape clusters, the azaleas and camellias. By late June the camphor tree and the bougainvilleas on St. Charles Avenue were already scorched and faded. The only tree growing in Jane Alley— it looks like a blue acacia and the Negroes call it the China-ball tree—wearily spread its barren limbs, reaching for the roof of a shanty.

July came, and Mary's time was near. She was staying at home now, hardly moving from her bed except to prepare food. After their meal, Willy would go out and sit on the wooden staircase. A slight breeze stirred the night. Above the city the purple sky caught the last rays of the sun sinking slowly behind roofs, gables, and chimneys. He stared at the clouds with their lavender linings, and every now and then he would glance at the door, left ajar so that he could hear Mary.

Had Willy been blest with imagination his thoughts might have ventured into the land of make-believe that was Perdido Street. But they would hardly have ventured farther; what lay beyond Perdido was almost beyond Willy's ken. For him and for his kind, Jane Alley was itself one veritable dead end. The human beings here were barely out of the beast's cage of slavery, and here they must remain. Jane Alley hung between night and day, beast and man, Africa and America: a short passageway from the Congo forests to the white man's house —and the cesspool in which he would drown if he did not escape very soon. But where could he and Mary go?

Beyond, along Perdido and Gravier, stood houses better built and more comfortably tenanted by a higher class of Negroes, relatively peaceable and industrious. They wore decent clothes, and they looked with contempt on Jane Alley. And still farther away was the even more "exclusive" district at Perdido and Liberty where—behind rigid caste barriers— lived the more refined Negroes. It was perhaps of these quarters that Willy Armstrong dreamed; but, if he did, he realized that his ambition must stop here. Perdido Street was the highest to which he could aspire—Perdido, the battlefield of the city's Third Ward, a kingdom inhabited by the Negro aristocrats: pickpockets and pimps and gamblers, porters and waiters, dancers and prostitutes.

True, some distance away there was Rampart Street, where the real nobility lived; here were the barber shops, the beauty parlors, the funeral homes, the Jewish pawnbrokers, the clothing stores. The Negroes of Willy's class, however, had only a vague idea of what went on in the unattainable reaches of Rampart Street.

On the downtown side of Canal Street, you entered the land of enchantment, the French Quarter, territory forbidden to the blacks, accessible only to those who came to serve as waiters, or to play the part of singers, clowns, or domestic drudges. A sort of earthly paradise where the white folks sat around drinking delightful mixtures, cool and yet fiery sweet, poured by beautiful, languid ladies. Through the doorways of the cafés you could glimpse the multicolored bottles filled with beverages that brought rapture and forgetfulness. On the upper side of town, in the Garden District, there stood stately mansions, half hidden in a semitropical setting of smooth lawns, shrubbery, and trees. Inside, the doors opened to a twist of their gold handles; the portraits on the walls had gold frames; the plates gleamed with gold. Studded with precious stones, gold rings encircled the pale fingers of mothers and daughters who rested on silken couches, and made love according to a complex code that blended the scent of alluring perfumes with the pungent odor of incense. Tales of all this splendor were brought to Jane Alley by the Negro servants, faithful watchdogs, who themselves belonged to a special and secret fraternity. Of such stuff are dreams and fairy tales spun. . . .

New Orleans, the dream city! And, if geography was not an invention of the rich and powerful, beyond the city Louisiana and America spread for many miles. Great buildings of cement and steel towered in other cities—in New York, Chicago, and Boston, where life was pleasant and smooth. And beyond the seas, far, far away, as distant as that Africa from whence the Negroes had come, there was Europe. London and Paris, magic and fantastic place names!

Horn of Plenty:

Another hot day, and Mary knew that her time had come. The noise of pickaninnies at play in the yard was more than she could bear. Her mother, Joséphine, was hurriedly summoned; now that her daily chores were done, she could sit at her daughter's bedside. There would not be long to wait, for the pains came faster and faster. It was high time to send for the old midwife who had brought all the neighbors' children into the world. Yet her services must not be engaged too soon, because her rates were high—she charged twenty-five cents for a day's work. And so on July 4, 1900, Mary Albert bore a tiny black baby whom the midwife pronounced strong and healthy.

On the following Saturday, Mary went back to work, the baby being left in the care of a friend. That evening Willy and Mary were visited by neighbors who came to congratulate them, and afterwards they sat listening for hours to the shouts of the drunken brawlers in Jane Alley. Suddenly a crash was followed by the tinkle of falling glass; another window pane had been shattered by a brick. The baby woke up crying, and groped for his mother's breast.

"Willy," said Mary suddenly, " 'tain't no two ways 'bout it—we's gwine leave dis heah mizzable dump!"

"Yo' sed it, May Ann."

"Yo' makin' nuf money now, an', ah kin wohk. We saves up and mebbe fin' us a place on Perdido Street."

The next day little Louis was taken in his grandmother's arms to Sacred Heart Church to be christened. As the family followed Perdido's sidewalk toward the church they were greeted by groups of black men and women going in the opposite direction.

"How come yo' all ain't comin', Willy boy?" cried one of these.

"Wheah dey gwine?" Mary asked of her husband.

"Ain't it Sunday aftehnoon? Dey gwine down tuh Congo Place."

When the family returned home after the christening, the great-grandmother—who had stayed at home—took charge of little Louis while Willy and Mary, with his brother and her grandmother, went off to Congo Place to watch the open-air dancing. The music was a new-fangled kind, full of rhythm and syncopation. In the center of the band a burly cornetist was blowing ragtime, and the hundreds of black spectators beat time with him, clapping hands and tapping feet. Tipsy black women gurgled in rapture. Warmed by the applause, the band blared forth a raucous tune that throbbed with the beat of the drum.

"Play it some mo' Buddy—play it some mo'!" chorused the children.

And the band obligingly repeated the novel music, which was as sultry as an African night. For the outgoing 19th century had given birth not only to Louis Armstrong but also to a new type of music.

"What yo' call dat?" Mary was asking.

"Wha' dat?"

"Dat music wif dem ragged tunes."

"Don' know 'zackly, but let's dance!"

And the old grandmother, swaying happily against a camphor-tree, said as the two young people got up:

"We's bohn nekkit, ain't we? Ef'n we die in rags, dat's more'n us had to staht wif!"

2

THE FIRST year of little Louis Armstrong's life was spent in Jane Alley, where he was looked after by his grandmother while Willy and Mary were off at work. As soon as he could walk, he joined the swarm of neighborhood pickaninnies who passed their days in a sand lot playing cowboy, climbing fences, fighting—and running home when another of the gang hit them too hard.

Saturday night was a special night for all the family. Louis's parents, their week's work over, would fetch the child from his grandmother's and the three would go off together. While husband and wife sought to forget their troubles by drinking at one bar after another, Louis was left outside to shift for himself and he would play with similarly stranded youngsters. Their greatest pleasure consisted in gathering at the candy-shop showcases and rolling their eyeballs at the fairyland display of chocolates and gum drops.

The Armstrongs led a humdrum existence: hard work all day long, and in the evening—stale bread and red beans. Mary, her dream of leaving Jane Alley no nearer realization, came to accept her lot. Now her only ambition was to be an honest servant and a good housekeeper, even if she could not call herself a happy wife. In that day as now, the domestic virtues were rated higher among the Negro families of New Orleans than good looks or charm. Life went on day after day, folks got hungry, and everybody had to get out and earn the few cents by which body and soul could be kept together. Eating was always a major concern—that, and fun whenever they could get it, especially on Saturday night, to the accompaniment of the bootleg liquor that stiffens the joints, dulls the wits, and produces a terrific hangover.

Three years after Louis's birth—years of increasing discord between Willy and Mary—another child was born. Taken to the Baptist Church, she was christened Beatrice. She looked strikingly like her brother, having the same wide nostrils, thick lips, and bronze complexion. Their father, tall and thin, was never particularly robust. It is the mother who seems to have had the stronger constitution, and the two children apparently "took after" her.

The arrival of the second child did not draw Willy and Mary closer together. The two were by now completely estranged. Willy had several times threatened to leave his wife, deterred only by the thought of the babies. However, it did not take him much longer to make up his mind. One night— it was when Louis was four or five and his sister was beginning to toddle—they came in from play to find their mother alone in the room, Willy had gone uptown. May Ann dished out the red beans but ate nothing herself, and the children saw that she was crying. Little Louis ran to kiss her and ask what the matter was. She did not reply, but just sobbed and hugged the boy tightly.

The next morning Jane Alley buzzed with the news that Willy Armstrong had moved out and was never coming back. Mary made her plans quickly: during the day the children would stay with their grandmother, as before, and she would hire herself out as cook to a French family and at night she could bring home the leavings from their kitchen.

Horn of Plenty:

But every night she felt more and more disgusted with the sordidness of Jane Alley and with the room that had seen the beginning and the end of her marriage. For a while she would spend the evening hours on the doorstep, hoping for the impossible; she would tell herself that Willy, driven either by remorse or by passion, might perhaps come back, at least for a few days. But she hoped in vain, and presently her dream faded away.

Another year went by. All of Jane Alley, including May Ann, realized that things would never, never again be the same for the Armstrongs. Willy, settled uptown for good, was living with another woman whose neighbors reported her as being with child. It was at about this time—probably in 1905— that the deserted wife left Jane Alley, taking her children to live at a place some eighteen blocks away, near the corner of Liberty and Perdido.* Although little Louis carried with him only a hazy memory of the Jane Alley years, it was some time before the new neighborhood seemed like home to him. Their room was not notably better than the old one, the tiny back yard was gloomy, and he had lost his friends of the sand lot; but the move was unmistakably upward, none the less, for the district offered a welcome change of scene. Left behind were the misery and the degradation and the horrible promiscuity, the desolation of empty lots and crumbling shanties around the turpentine factory. Just a few blocks from Liberty and Perdido the tall buildings in the center of the city reached toward the sky. Here one could breathe a cleaner air. This neighborhood—with whose every aspect Louis was

* Perdido Street runs parallel to Poydras on the one hand and to Gravier on the other. Going up Perdido, away from the Mississippi and in the direction of Jane Alley, you cross the streets that successively intersect the city's Third Ward in a series of right angles: Dryades, Rampart, Saratoga, Loyola, and La Salle.

to become familiar as he grew up—would exert a tremendous influence on his career and on the development of jazz, an influence whose full significance has not even yet been grasped.

From now on, Louis Armstrong lived sometimes with his mother (who soon remarried) and sometimes with his grandmother, according to the family's available accommodations and their current fortunes. But the heart and center of his childhood was always the intersection of Liberty and Perdido. It was here that he would begin to think, begin to fan that faint ancestral spark entrusted to him by his race. At Fisk School, just a block away from his house, he met many of his boyhood companions such as Sweet Child, Coochie, and Henry Morton, who grew up with him and are still his faithful worshippers.

For the white sightseer in New Orleans, the Kingdom of Perdido is a strange district. If by chance he hails from New York or Chicago, it will seem like the end of the world. Jane Alley itself has not changed much in appearance since 1905. A few frame houses still stand; the oldest crumbled into dust and were replaced about twenty years ago. For the past decade a municipal ordinance has prohibited new construction; when the weatherboards are sufficiently worm-eaten and the steps quite rotted, the demolishing crews take over, and very soon nothing remains but a vacant lot where little Negroes play hide-and-seek in the weeds.

Perdido, too, has its rows of wooden houses, but these—though crude and old-fashioned—are mansions compared with the hovels of Jane Alley, which Perdido natives call "back o' town." The average house bears traces of yellow or gray paint, and at the side there is a wooden gate opening into the yard. On the ground floor are several apartments of one or two rooms, each with its latched door; and a flight of stairs runs up from the yard to a porch giving access to all the second-story rooms. Each of these tenements shelters eight or ten families, whose offspring swarm through the yard when they are not fighting pitched battles from house to house or from street to street.

As a general rule the Negroes of Perdido Street are full-blooded, owing to intermarriage, half-breeds being the exception. Those who fall into the category of "high yallers" frequently migrate to the Creole districts on the other side of Canal Street. Louis Armstrong and his sister Beatrice shared the characteristics of the blacks who inhabit the Deep Congo, where they enjoy an enviable reputation for intelligence and docility. If on any afternoon you were to stand at the corner of La Salle and Perdido at the hour when school is dismissed, you would see hundreds of little Negroes of six or seven who look just like the small Louis of years ago; and the school itself is the same one that he attended, though it is no longer called Fisk School.

Not far away was a huge structure of red brick—the Parish Prison; and every time a Negro mother passed it she would glance at the right wing, in which the white man's justice held hardened criminals for the hangman's scaffold. "If you ain't a good boy, I'll send you to Parish Prison," May Ann would scold when little Louis had played too long in the empty lot between Liberty and Perdido.

On the other side, toward Jane Alley, Perdido's perspective was blocked by an immense gas-storage plant. In Perdido Street proper, between Liberty and La Salle, on the site now occupied by a concrete church, there once stood a dance hall—Funky Butt Hall of unsavory memory, where a few tattered musicians played ragtime melodies by ear, punctuated by the beat of the drum. Here assembled all the toughs and lazy sluts of the locality. To this day the denizens of Perdido have not forgotten that ill-smelling establishment. Its very name betrays a wanton etymology, graphically characterizing the awful smell that always pervaded the air after the dances were over. They were totally unrestrained in their lewdness, and the black dancers' sweaty bodies heightened the general atmosphere of depravity. So much for "Funky." As for "Butt," the word is the diminutive applied to the posteriors that shook so vigorously during the gyrations of the dance; indeed, the very name advertised the spot.

At the corner of Perdido and Liberty there was a honky-tonk kept by an Italian, one Matranga, whose name was notorious at the time of Louis Armstrong's birth. During this period, the New Orleans people were aroused by the outbreak of vendettas among the Sicilians of the town, who practically terrorized the whole place and killed Hennessy, the chief of police. Among those who were arrested was Charles Matranga, father of the man who kept the honky-tonk. After a sensational trial that created great excitement in the city, Charles Matranga was acquitted, but several of his accomplices were hanged in the Parish Prison. After the Maffia's power was thus broken, the members of the gang scattered, and Matranga found a convenient place of exile in the tavern on Perdido.

A little farther on there were two grocers, Segretta and Gaspar. Over their counters Louis and his sister would often thrust a penny for candy when their father could afford to give them one, and receive in return the precious licorice or gum drops.

Louis's small world was bounded at its four corners by the School, the Church, the Dive, and the Prison—all of them symbols of the black man's existence on the fringe of the white man's city. Though when he spent a few days with his grandmother on Dupré he would meet his little Jane Alley friends, he felt that he no longer belonged there and he was always anxious to return to the center of his universe. After school, when he sat at the top of the outside staircase, he would look into space, gazing at the mysterious roofs and gables of the white man's city. Occasionally he would venture as far as Rampart Street, stopping to look into the pawnshop showcases that displayed clocks and suitcases and clarinets. But as soon as he left Rampart's sidewalk he entered another world, mysterious and wonderful—Canal Street, main thoroughfare of New Orleans. Here he would be caught in a stream of white pedestrians dressed in the finest clothes. The traditional attire of the black man consisted of duck trousers, faded cotton shirt, and sandals. But on Canal Street the gentlemen wore collars and gay-colored neckties. Some of them raised strange-looking hats—high beavers straight out of the previous century—but most wore black derbies.

Gradually, Louis was learning the distinction between the black child and the white; but when he shut his eyes he had visions of handsome young men with wing collars and ties in which jeweled stick-pins sparkled, and he wondered if the time would ever come when he—just a black nonentity—would sport these signs of elegant superiority.

On the other side of Canal Street lay the French Quarter—romantic old houses whose galleries drew and held the rare summer breezes; exciting streets full of dens whose windows were draped with plush curtains; cabarets, their long, polished bars guarded by white-clad employees. Behind swinging doors you caught glimpses of card players intent around the tables, and of painted women who knocked on the window glass and winked. Carriages drawn by sleek trotting horses stopped before massive gateways, and sounds of far-off music floated through the air. When a little Negro boy would open a carriage door, a perfumed lady would drop a coin into his hand. In front of some restaurants whose ventilators blew whiffs of the choicest foods into the street, black doormen stood as stiff as ebony gods, resplendent in uniforms heavy with gold braid. These were the ambassadors extraordinary, the aristocratic emissaries of the race swarming at Perdido and Liberty. What incredible contrasts, what unknown stepping-stones mark the social distinctions from Jane Alley to Perdido, from Perdido to Rampart, from Rampart to the French Quarter, from the French Quarter to the fabulous boulevard—Canal Street, that fairy-land of marble and stucco, of lights and flowers and shimmering draperies.

What talisman had enabled the little Louis to escape from Back o' Town to the Third Ward? And what clue would guide him later from Matranga's domain to the colorful streets of the Vieux Carré where life was wonderful and fun was widespread, there at the very gates of the White Man's paradise? His mother and the kindly Mrs. Morton, principal of his school, never tired of telling him that there was but one way to get ahead—to be honest and keep smiling; that there was no place for the Negroes at the top of the business world, and that they must stick to their menial jobs. True, some rebellious souls talked of liberty and of racial equality—that fanciful dream which the black race handed down from one generation to the next. But Grandmother Joséphine insisted that time was the important thing; the Negro cherished the idea of freedom, but he must make haste slowly.

"Them that kicks over the traces too quick," Grandma would say to the boy, "forgets that I seen the days when we was slaves, when we was sold on the hoof like dumb cattle. Them that goes too fast gets nowhere. Them that shines and makes a lot of fuss in Perdido are goners. Them gamblers, them drunkards, them no-good women, them pimps—they'll all be in jail before you grows a beard."

Little Louis was gradually learning about the members of his race who had established a reputation and won Perdido's respect. His father, whom he rarely saw now, still had his job at the turpentine factory, and his stepfather sold coal from a small mule-drawn wagon. Involuntarily the child would contrast the shabby clothes of those two—and, indeed, of all his kinsfolk—with the well-cut garments and bright ties of the young bloods who earned their living the easy way, by seizing opportunity's horns in barrooms and worse. Perhaps he secretly envied the strutting young bucks whose women wore the heaviest paint and the thickest powder. But for him there was no choice: he had to struggle if he was to survive.

It was at the age of seven that Louis got his first job. A news vendor called Charlie ran a stand at St. Charles and Canal, and the boy applied to him for work. The result was that every afternoon Louis—having taken his schoolbooks home to "Brick Row"—would run out to sell papers at the St. Charles corner.

"Times-Democrat! New Orleans Item! Daily States!"
The ambitious youngster, yelling with the best of them, could usually sell as many as fifty papers during the next few hours, so that he had earned some "four bits" by ten or eleven o'clock. By the end of the evening, when he went home, his parents and his sister had gone to bed, so he had no choice but to warm over his red beans and eat alone. Tired though he might be, however, he tingled with the proud knowledge that he was making a living.

One Saturday evening the sky above the city was clear and starry, and moonlight etched the chimneys of the white quarter. Louis was walking beside the prison walls and staring with fascination at the dreadful corner where criminals were hanged. He knew that only two weeks earlier a pimp who had stabbed his mistress to death had dangled there, and from Rampart to La Salle people had buzzed with stories of Big Mack's wild deeds.

As Louis followed Liberty Street, he passed a row of miserable dens that now no longer exist, the spot having been converted into a parking lot. Then, from a distance, came strains of music, and he paused for a moment to listen. When he reached the corner of Perdido he was caught between two swirling currents of sound: from Matranga's on his left, and Funky Butt Hall on his right, jerky and lascivious tunes reached his ears through open doors and windows.

Such music was the only music that Louis knew—low-down tunes throbbing with the rapid-fire strokes of the drummer, and fierce with an insistent rhythm. Frenzied feet shuffled on the crowded dance floors. As he stood listening, the playing stopped at Matranga's, but the dancers' yelling and clapping soon induced the players to resume almost mechanically. In Funky Butt, meanwhile, the music was being drowned by the clamor of voices. Louis whistled softly to himself the popular air that everybody was humming. Suddenly a husky cry rose above the rest:

"Oh, play that thing!"

Some girls went by, laughing shrilly, their skirts swishing as they continued to sway with the rhythm of the dance. It was very late. Louis visualized the wooden stairs at home, saw the red beans waiting on the stove, heard the soft breathing of "Mama Lucy"—his sister Beatrice. But he also fingered the silver dollar in his pocket—for he had sold every one of his Sunday papers—and he leaned against a railing, dizzy with the potentialities of his new wealth. From time to time there came over him a crazy impulse to yell with joy, to mingle his voice with the cries of the dancers in Funky Butt. His heart beat faster as a wave of nostalgia swept over him, stirred by the same remote call which had come from the depth of the African bush to quicken the pulse of his ancestors in some dim past. He could hear the thud of the tom-toms pulsating in the night. Louis Armstrong had never known Africa, but Africa was throbbing in his heart.

He crossed Perdido and stopped before Funky Butt's open door. A crowd pushed and jostled at the bar, with many a drunken and half-naked wench emptying her whisky glass at one gulp between puffs of smoke from a fat cigar. Louis hesitated; dared he go in? The jerky rhythm beat like his own pulse. A hulking Negro with shiny black face, white eyeballs, and glistening teeth, was hugging a "high yaller" who pretended to swoon as she crushed a camelia to distended nostrils. An old shrew yawned, displaying the pink and toothless cavern of her mouth. One of the dancers was banging his fists on the counter. Others were moaning a nameless, dragging chant.

Louis took advantage of an instant when the bartender's attention was distracted and scurried through the barroom into the dance hall. Then, in order to catch his breath, he sat down on a bench and leaned against the wall. On a platform at the end of the hall a five-man orchestra was going full blast. The cornetist under a white derby faced the dancers and blew a cascade of savage rhythm on them. The drummer pounded his drums unmercifully, whipping up the frenzy of the crowd.

Louis felt that he was dreaming. The band resumed its syncopation with incredibly wild and savage blarings. The couples seemed to go crazy, bumped into one another and jigged like mad. The stag line on the edge of the dance floor beat time with their feet. The clarinet burst into a dizzy solo. A sort of frenzy took hold of the musicians and spread like wildfire throughout the hall. Some couples were hopping like kangaroos. A tall Negro with broad, muscle-bound shoulders began to toss his partner about like a sack of oats. Soon a circle formed around the two, urging them on while clapping hands in time with the music. The clarinet player blew high and low notes in a brisk medley, and in the semidarkness the women's eyes shone with passion and longing.

One tune followed another in rapid succession. Blues were followed by shouts. Couples moving almost as if in a trance were replaced by wilder couples shaking with a kind of frantic exultation. The music stopped abruptly like a wave breaking on the shore, and Louis had the sensation of teetering on the edge of a cliff. A female voice shrieked out:

"Oh! Shake that thing!"

Then the rhythm began again, implacable, steady, deafening. Women dripping with sweat mopped their arms and shoulders. Some young girls munched peanuts. A thunder of applause greeted the end of a cornet solo. Now the shirt-sleeved player took a bow on the platform. Women gurgled in ecstasy:

"Hurrah, Buddy! Hurrah! Play it again!"

Buddy grinned from ear to ear, and his booming voice stilled the noise of the crowd:

"It's gettin' late. All good gals done gone home to sleep. Now the stinkers can get ready to dance. I hopes that they ain't left their behinds at home, 'cause they got to shake 'em plenty for to keep time with this here music."

Buddy swung his trumpet back to his lips. The women howled with joy. Every corner of Funky Butt Hall was bursting with ragged rhythm. Little Louis had shut his eyes and was listening raptly. A shout in his ear broke the charm:

"Ain't you 'shamed, you little brat? Don't you know it's two o'clock in the morning? What you doin' here listenin' to that raggedy music?"

[23]

"I won't do it no more, Ma."

May Ann had grabbed him by the arm and began to thrash him with vigor.

"So you likes that there ragtime! I'll give you all you wants. *Here's* some ragtime! *Here's* a shout!"

"Don't beat me no more, Ma—I'll be good!"

He proffered the silver dollar. Instantly placated, his mother took it and impulsively kissed the boy. They left the hall and turned the corner of Liberty and Perdido. As they went through the yard they could hear the snores of the tenants through the open windows. A pale moon drifted slowly behind swift clouds. While his mother turned the key in the lock, Louis listened to the dying bursts of the trumpet and the clarinet. A train whistle blew a haunting note through the night. And before he fell asleep little Louis felt welling up in his heart the bewitching tunes that gave meaning to his life.

3

LOUIS'S LIFE was no different from that of his playmates. Left to himself during the day, he seldom saw his mother, except at night. She was cook to a family in Conti Street. Sometimes he grew bold enough to cross Canal Street and then pass idly by the cemeteries with their high white washed brick walls until finally he reached the house, set back from the street, where his mother could be found working in an inner courtyard. Behind the mosquito netting a wave of the hand which he could not fail to recognize would be the signal for him to wait awhile; it meant that the white masters were too near for safety. Then another sign would beckon, and Louis would squeeze through the fence with the greatest possible caution.

Moving on tiptoe, he reached the kitchen, which seemed to be the acme of a luxury not meant for the blacks. He was acutely conscious of something else: he had crossed the line of demarcation between the two races and found himself in the white man's paradise; but he had attained that goal only by sneaking through the back way. He knew that his life as a black boy was subject to the unwritten law of segregation.

May Ann would kiss him tenderly and, seating him at the kitchen table, would let him finish off the remnants of fine Creole dishes that she had prepared for her masters. These

[25]

moments were rays of happiness in the little boy's somber existence, as he contrasted this shining kitchen with the dingy room in Perdido.

One day when the family was absent, his mother took him upstairs with her. He went all through the house, and saw the dining-room with its mahogany furniture and its gilt-framed photographs of white ladies smiling from beneath plumed hats; the drawing-room, where an armchair upholstered in garnet velvet beckoned invitingly; a sort of wide veranda furnished with many swings; a library whose thick carpet deadened footfalls and whose shelves housed hundreds and hundreds of books; the white-tiled, gleaming bathroom. And he went back to Perdido with his heart full of happiness, the happiness of the elect upon their admission into Paradise. Thenceforth he could summon from his memory the mysterious beauty that surrounded the lives of those who belonged to a race of men set apart between the blacks and God.

Louis found the time spent in school tedious and long, from eight o'clock in the morning until two in the afternoon. He had to bend over copy-books in which he scrawled laboriously. There were words to spell, phrases to remember, sentences to construct. There was the map with the rivers marked in blue lines which traversed the borders of countries shaded in different colors. Louis was not the worst student among the children of his neighborhood. At two o'clock, after Mrs. Morton had said a short prayer, Louis would leave with his friends. On the threshold of the rambling schoolhouse the youngsters played light-heartedly. The little girls stood apart looking shyly at the boys, whose kinky hair was close-cropped save for a little tuft above the forehead in the style of Perdido around 1907 or 1908. Merton Wade smirked at the girls, stole a kiss from them, or hit them as the impulse seized him. Orleania, Mrs. Morton's daughter, would take Louis's hand and they would go off together to look at the good things displayed in Segretta's window. Fights would break out as Red Vanzan's gang bullied the smaller boys and threw rocks from the shelter of a stronghold where they were entrenched behind Matranga's.

Louis had half an hour to wait before the evening papers came out. How he would have liked to play until dark!—to shoot marbles under the shade of the tree where blue flowers were starting to bloom! Sometimes he would stop to talk for a few minutes with Little Mack or Inkspot or Georgie Gray. But when half-past two struck, all the little Negroes ran off to the odd jobs that served as introduction to a life in which hard work and submissiveness were the unfailing rules.

This was when Louis would take up his papers at Charlie's newsstand in St. Charles Street. He was always happy in the midst of the human flood which all but submerged him in its infinite variety. Bareheaded, his papers tucked under his arm, he waved a newspaper in his little black fist.

"*States* or *Item! States* or *Item!*"

And the passers-by would be astonished to hear such a deep voice coming from such a little black boy. They would laugh and buy the newspaper. Louis would scream:

"Read all about the horrible murder in Girod Street! Yessiree—read all about it!"

Every time a coin was dropped in his outstretched hand, he earned a penny. And so it went on for hours until dinnertime. Usually there was a lull which gave Louis a chance to leave his spot and run off to buy some cookies two blocks away. There he would meet all the newsboys and bootblacks of the business district who had left their work to eat and gape at the showcases. Pennies jingled in their pockets, and the thought of red beans would drive them to buy another cookie which they crunched greedily.

His little friends would laugh at the sight of Louis Armstrong stuffing cakes between his thick lips. "Come on, Dipper!" they would cry. And so "Dipper" became his nickname at school. It had begun when someone applied the term "Dippermouth" to Louis's lips, but the name was soon shortened. In later years, when he wrote his first musical piece, he recalled this transition, as well as the one that followed: from "Dippermouth" to "Satchelmouth." This last was to stick, in the form of "Satchmo'." His schoolboy retort to such nicknames was to describe the other boys' lips as "Gates"—that is, loose and swinging.

"All right, Gate!" he would fling back at some boy whose teeth spread like pickets in a fence, and all the kids would howl with joy.

Sometimes on a Sunday morning Louis would visit his grandmother. By now his father was virtually a stranger to him. He used to see Willy once or twice a week, but presently Louis never saw him at all. One day he learned that he now had a half brother, Henry. In any case, he preferred his grandmother, liked to sit beside her at the top of the shaky stairs during the soft days of spring when the weather is so mild in the South and the trees in St. Charles Avenue wear their tenderest green. In the distance they could see the city's skyline, the tall buildings in the heart of town. Good old Joséphine related stories of the days of slavery. Sometimes her own mother would toddle out to stand beside them, her elbows on the railing. She was a very old woman with white hair and a soft and peaceful look in her eyes. Caressing the rough and wrinkled hands that worked so hard, Louis would tell her all about the music at Funky Butt Hall, especially the trumpet playing of the famous Buddy and the continuous beating of the drums.

"Oh," his great-grandmother would sigh, "I remember the time when all the slaves would gather in Congo Square on Sunday afternoon. It was a long time ago; all the black folks still spoke French. Things would start around two o'clock under the trees on the square. All the slaves came in their finest clothes—not much to look at, when you see what our people wear now! The women mostly had on calico dresses, and their hair was bound tight in bandannas. Some colored musicians played African music, and we would dance the Bamboula or the Conjaie until we had to go back to our quarters.

"Grandma, tell me how they played!"

"There would be six or seven of them. One would beat the drums, another would scrape a cow's horn with a key, a third would blow into an instrument with slides, a fourth sat on his haunches and rang bells, and . . . and I've forgotten what else. But it was the same rhythm of the drum that you hear today. Nothing changes, son. The blacks carry that noise in their heartbeat."

There came a time when the family decided to send Louis to live with his grandmother for several months; it was when he was about seven. Mama Lucy was growing up, and—in addition to having to watch her—May Ann went out to take care of two other children. But as long as Louis was away from Perdido, he felt like a fish out of water He pined for the motley crowds on Rampart's sidewalks. He pictured the shoeshine stand in a doorway just after you passed the corner; he thought about Charlie's newsstand in St. Charles Street. From time to time he met Redhead Happy or Orleania at some street corner and plied his former companions with eager questions as if he had been a total stranger to the life of Perdido. Sometimes in the evening he would walk the whole length of the street and stop in front of Funky Butt Hall. The minute he reached Rampart and turned the corner he felt exhilarated. In the warm night air the passing blacks exhaled odors of heavy perfume stolen from the lush vegetation of the South. The gurglings of a cornet would burst forth, and Louis could visualize the motion of the hand or of the derby clapped over the instrument's mouth, throttling the notes to a shrill whisper, then pulled away for more strident effects.

On the thresholds or under the windows, in chairs tilted back against the house fronts, the Negroes peacefully listened to this far-away and soul-stirring music. At the edge of the sidewalk little boys, long past their bedtime, danced with girls in pigtails. Their dancing gave the illusion that they were dislocating their bodies from the hips up and they moved their legs in a jerky rhythm. Old black women smoked their pipes and spat deftly between their teeth. Stars twinkled in the magic sky. Somewhere in a yard, a young Negro woman followed the outburst of the pistons in a succession of wild steps. At the next corner Georgie Gray's grandmother puffed steadily on a huge cigar. The darkness was warm and inviting. From Matranga's open windows the clarinet's sound gave a musical meaning to the silence of the night, and the rapid beating of drums made the heart beat faster.

"That must be Creole Picou playin' Jack Carey!"

Jack Carey was a popular black musician who had transposed the air of a quadrille and given his name to the new version. The steady shuffle of feet ceased, and there was loud applause.

"*Play it again! Shake it up! Give us another ragtime, Picou!*"

For Louis there was no music except ragtime. Of course

he had heard that at the French Opera stately music was played by white musicians dressed up in stiff fronts and black ties; but for Louis all the music in the world was contained in ragtime throbbing rhythmically with the beat of the drum.

A few short steps from Matranga's brought him within the orbit of Funky Butt Hall, where the orchestra was larger and louder. But when one night Louis discovered that big Buddy was not playing the cornet, he decided not to stay. At the door, black men were squabbling and the women were leaving with shouts and in tears. He had a long way to go before reaching Dupré. Louis passed the dance hall and, near the next street, he saw some pickaninnies playing in the dark. Redhead Happy, little Mack, and Georgie Gray were trying to play ragtime. Redhead Happy beat on a dish pan for a drum while Georgie Gray was blowing a crude tin horn.

"Hello, Dipper."

"Hello, Gate."

Louis watched them awhile. The little musicians had broken off their playing and were looking in the direction of Funky Butt Hall from whose lighted windows a flood of rhythm poured into Perdido Street.

Louis went on. He slowly walked block after block. He was tired and the brick pavement was uneven. Yet he was buoyed up by a dream that somehow lent rhythm to his walk. Picou's clarinet blew exasperatingly in the back of his head— a tune that had no set form, no words. Humming it, he would mark with a little caper the sudden stop when the clarinet paused long enough for a doube step. And when he grew tired of humming in his deep voice, he whistled the syncopated bars of the hot tune that Buddy aways played in Funky Butt. Later on, it was titled *"Knock On the Door and Come In."*

It would be late when Louis reached Dupré. His grandmother was still up and about. The red beans were being kept warm over a slow fire. As soon as he had greedily gulped down his share, the youngster would fall exhausted on his pallet and sleep with clenched fists.

On the following day, having turned over his day's earnings to Grandma Joséphine, he was rewarded by a slice of watermelon.

"Where was you last night, Louis? You came in mighty late."

"I came around by Perdido."

"You'll go crazy listenin' to that blind man's music."

"I'm crazy 'bout Picou with his clarinet an' Buddy with his cornet."

"That won't do you no good, my boy That music's only good for trashy women or for them no-good loafers. Oh! I knows all 'bout it. Your grandpa was just like you, crazy 'bout the drum. He'd stay out all night, dancin' and listenin' to the noise of the Bamboula. In them days they call that music the Hoodoo's noise."

"What you calls Hoodoo, Grandma?"

"That's a African god, mighty powerful and terrible, an' all the blacks of New Orleans was scared of him. He had a sort of queen who was called Marie Laveau. Your grandpa did some of her dirty work at more'n one ceremony."

"An' they all played the drum? Come on, Grandma, tell me 'bout it."

And Joséphine explained the powerful and evil sorcery of the Voodoos carrying the box containing the sacred snake. Her husband had gone off several times on expeditions—always in mid-June—with the queen of the Voodoos to the shores of Lake Pontchartrain. There, in a clearing where the moonlight filtered through the hanging moss, the savage, hallucinating ceremony threw the few initiates into a rhythmic frenzy.

In picturesque words his grandmother described the strange ritual. She related how once the queen of the Voodoos, Marie Laveau, brought dead people back to life. Marie was the most powerful woman of the black race, and had many white followers who worshiped her like a goddess. Every year on a clear summer night all the votaries would meet in a clearing. During the first weeks of June it was very dangerous; all the blacks of New Orleans looked closely and fearfully at their doorsteps to see whether the hands of the Hoodoos had thrown the salt and the gris-gris powders that would bring death to all the inmates. The only way to avert an evil fate was to buy charms from Marie Laveau.

She lived in a little wooden shack on one of the streets bounding Congo Square. Through a latticed gate the blacks filed into her yard. There, towering among the religious trappings of her African royalty, she sold charms. Each was a collection of good-luck powder, cayenne pepper, dried frog-legs, chicken bones, and graveyard dust. It was all mixed in a little red sack, and it was all-powerful.

"An' what happened in the clearin', Grandma?" Louis would interrupt.

And the tale would continue. In the swamps near Pontchartrain there was a spot called "Fig Place." Near it the queen, Marie Laveau, owned a piece of land on which stood an evergreen altar. On St. John's night everybody would meet in the moonlight and they would boil the gris-gris in a big cauldron over an open fire. While the cauldron was bubbling the queen's black bodyguards held out torches. The others would throw in lizards, snakes, aromatic herbs, bananas; and, as a crowning touch for the *mamanloi*, a live black cat was tossed into the pot.

"A live black cat?"

"Just like I tells you. Your grandpa was there. After the

gris-gris charms was all handed out, the drum beat the Bamboula just like they plays it in Funky Butt, and all the blacks sang the songs you loves while the queen danced in the moonlight with the sacred snake. She went 'round and 'round an' when she look' at somebody straight in the eye, that person was lucky in love and ever'thing else for the rest of their born days."

"An' where's Marie Laveau now, Grandma?"

"Some say she dead, but us fait'ful ones we knows she still livin' in St. Louis Cemetery. Sunday we goin' pay her a visit. But keep yo' mouth shut."

On the following Sunday, when a rosy dawn was breaking on the horizon, little Louis was ready and waiting to set off with his grandmother. Thus they came to old St. Louis Cemetery where so many of New Orleans's historic dead rest —in raised tombs and not in the ground because of the extreme dampness of the soil. Within its precincts there are uneven rows of gravestones spelling the names of governors, generals, adventurers, Creole youths killed in duels, notorious Madams who ran brothels famed for their lavish settings, professional gamblers, cutthroat pirates. But Louis, not yet old enough to have learned anything of his city's history, walked at his grandmother's side obsessed by a single thought—that of worshipping at the shrine of the Voodoos who caused the Bamboula to resound, each night, in Funky Butt.

They went through the cemetery; at the very end, toward the left and against the wall, there was a brick tomb with cement facings. The mortal remains of the queen of the Voodoos were interred there, awaiting the homage of her followers. Grandmother Joséphine crossed herself several times and, with a piece of stone which the faithful always used, traced one cross on the tombstone, so that Marie Laveau might send

good luck to her, and then another for the future happiness
of little Louis.

Standing with clasped hands and filled with emotion, Louis
also pretended to mutter a prayer. Before leaving, his grandmother deposited a dime on the edge of the tombstone. A multitude of crosses, scratched on the same stone, gave eloquent
testimony that the ritual of the Voodoos was still observed in
New Orleans.

Slowly they retraced their steps, their hearts filled with the
tragic memory of Marie Laveau. They believed that, the moment no one was in sight, she would rise from her tomb to
pick up the coin offering. Louis for a moment thought of
hiding behind a grave to catch a glimpse of the great spirit;
but his grandmother, reading his mind, warned him that it
was impossible to deceive the queen of the Voodoos.

After they had gone from the cemetery they met some
gravediggers. Had Louis been hiding, he would have been
mortified at the sight of the gravediggers pocketing Marie
Laveau's dime and sauntering off to the corner barroom for
a quick toast to the queen of the Bamboula.

A little farther on they passed through the notorious red-
light district. The doorsteps were being scrubbed with great
splashes of water. A drunken woman, emerging, seemed suddenly blinded by the rays of the rising sun. She stopped short
and, leaning against the doorway began to sing:

> *"Love, O love, O careless love,*
> *You flied to my head like a wine!"*

And Louis walked on with his grandmother, humming
Buddy Bolden's favorite song.

4

NO ONE knows who gave the name of ragtime to this music which was still in its infancy. Doubtless the name originated in New Orleans, but when or where no one can say exactly. Those who created the first ragtime are still alive. They admit that it was born among them, but they have nothing to say when questioned about the circumstances surrounding its extraordinary gestation.

Though ragtime really began to take shape at the time that Louis Armstrong was born, it cannot be said to have assumed a concrete form on a certain day in a known dance-hall. Rather, there was a slow and gradual evolution. The survivors of that period—Emmanuel Perez, Alphonse Picou, Albert Glenny, Big-Eye Louis Nelson—none of these players can give a coherent narrative of the strange developments they witnessed. Nevertheless it seems probable that ragtime arose through the combination of such varied elements as the tom-tom, the French songs, and the romantic folk lore of the Crescent City. In any case, the consensus is that ragtime and jazz are of Creole origin. As a matter of fact, the first orchestras of Robichaux, Celestine, Petit, Papa Laine, and Bouboule Augustin, were marching bands that played at picnics near Pontchartrain, and at funerals; at night they enlivened the balls of the Creole section "downtown."

The Story of Louis Armstrong

Creole music evolved rather slowly into ragtime. The blues were already part of the local traditions. But it is safe to say that syncopated music really got its start when a youth usually called Deedee Chandler introduced a new conception of percussion and played the bass drum and the small drum at the same time. This took place at Creole balls such as the Francs Amis and the Indépendants, where at first the musicians executed quadrilles and polkas, mazurkas and the Highland Fling. Later in the evening, after the better elements had withdrawn and the rough crowd that remained began to feel the effects of the liquor, and even the musicians had imbibed freely, all the occupants of the hall succumbed to the frenzy of excitement and clamored for their strange brand of music. The musicians threw away their scores and improvised on the airs they knew by adding the element of syncopation which the Negroes had introduced.

By degrees this distortion of familiar tunes became popular. It spread uptown into the Perdido section where the Negroes, more excitable, more savage, feeling in their hearts the satanic beat of the African tom-tom, adopted it and carried it to the extreme. There developed an intense rivalry between the players on either side of Canal Street.

Little of this, however, came into Louis Armstrong's ken. He was growing up, and his passionate fondness for this new musical expression which he heard at Matranga's or at Funky Butt Hall kept pace with his physical growth. Now and then he would march in a parade or funeral procession. He was also learning gradually about the rhythm kings of New Orleans. Creoles like Emmanuel Perez or Alphonse Picou or Papa Laine would sometimes bring their bands to play in Perdido's black belt, and their music sounded far sweeter and more meaningful than the wild tunes that filled the honkytonks of the Third Ward.

Horn of Plenty:

A big dance was held in Funky Butt Hall every Saturday night and it is here that we probably find the birthplace of jazz. Not that it was then called by that name; the word itself did not come into existence until later, to be widely popularized during the First World War.

About seven in the evening, on the eve of every holiday, the atmosphere in Perdido became charged and tense. The blacks began to spruce up a bit. The young bucks had all arranged to meet in the very heart of the quarter. The late-rising strumpets had their alcoholic "breakfast" at Funky Butt's bar or at Matranga's on the corner before launching their nightly activities, and all the street urchins danced in vacant lots.

The appearance of the musicians carrying their instrument cases was greeted by the ecstatic clamor of all the denizens. Frantic women blew kisses at them and extended brazen invitations in the plainest language.

"I lives over there—third house, last room on the second flo', I'll be waitin' for yo' after the dance!"

"Lay off my man, you no-good wench!"

"Can't be your man, 'cause he's got a married wife!"

Somebody spied Bob Lyons, his double-bass slung over his shoulder, and the children flocked to cheer the popular musician who lived in the quarter nearest Rampart.

"Look—here comes Bob with his doghouse!"

But the crowd was now venting its feelings in an admiring murmur directed toward still another notable.

At last, Louis knew that the irrepressible cornetist who had filled his early life with stormy melody, and who was called Buddy for short, was none other than the famous black musician whose reputation had won for him the title of King Bolden. He was a giant of the brass instrument, this barber in Franklin Street. He would drop his scissors at a moment's no-

tice to play music at neighborhood dances, invariably drawing crowds of admirers. Any social club that engaged Buddy
was sure of doing a first-class business, and his name appeared
frequently on Funky Butt Hall's billboard.

All during the week, a huge poster had announced in bad
grammar and worse spelling that King Buddy Bolden and his
gang were to be the main attraction. Already the other musicians were drinking at the bar, invited by their friends who
stood treat after treat of whisky and gin.

Then the dance ushers would clear the floor. An indescrib-
able mob filled every inch of space between Liberty and
La Salle. The musicians sprawled in the doorway facing the
public. In the front row stood the hoodlums and their women.
Gold rings and diamonds flashed in the dying rays of the sun
which reddened the sky's rim out there by Ol' Man River's
banks. The hussies smoked long cigars with flashy hands.
Children fought and scrambled closer to the orchestra.

Louis Armstrong, Redhead Happy, Little Mack, and
Georgie Gray were handing out programs on this particular
Saturday. This brought Louis a few pennies and broke the
monotony of selling papers.

Buddy Bolden sat on the sill and put his cornet to his lips.
The women shook, the mens' hearts beat faster, the children
jigged. The first note broke out, long and passionate. Buddy
played in the evening shadows, seeming to double in size as he
filled his lungs and blew like mad. Back of him, Bob Lyons
was slapping the double bass while a razor-sharp clarinet added
its modulations. A fiddler scraped as if possessed by the Devil.

Moved by the aggravated ragtime rhythm, the entire crowd
of blacks began to sway. Buddy in his shirt sleeves seemed to
dominate the audience from an exalted throne. With the
sound of the first measures, all the windows of the neighborhood had been flung wide open.

Horn of Plenty:

"Ho! Ho! King Bolden is callin' to his brood!"

Even the oldest Negro couples, thrilled to the depths of their beings by this call, went down to Perdido and Liberty. And this brought on the climax. Then Buddy had to blow like one possessed so that all within earshot might know that Buddy Bolden was playing at Funky Butt Hall.

In the meantime a dozen scalawags, including Louis Armstrong, were fanning out in all directions to distribute the tempting little red handbills, Louis staying on Perdido Street as long as he could hear Buddy Bolden's cornet. For a half-hour, keeping time with the melody, the kids danced in the street and handed out the dodgers. The blacks on the side streets, drawn by the sound of the cornet, would flock to the corner of Perdido to find out what the attraction was. Buddy Bolden was playing at Funky Butt Hall!

At the stroke of eight, the parade would disband and Buddy Bolden would invite his fans inside to hear him play. Since he was parched by his strenuous efforts on the cornet, he stopped at the bar and drank down several hot Tom-and-Jerries, double size.

In a short while he had to break away from the women who clung to him.

"So long, Buddy, we's goin' uptown to work. We gets through at one o'clock, 'cause it's Saturday, so we'll see you, huh?"

Some strikingly handsome mulattoes turned soulful eyes on him. He kissed two or three of them and made a path through the crowd in order to reach the bandstand. Louis Armstrong had a free pass because he had distributed handbills and, as he leaned against the stand, he gazed raptly at Buddy Bolden.

The air was heavy with the stench of sweat and cheap perfume emanating from the hundreds of bodies swaying with the jerky melody. After every piece a thunder of applause rewarded the orchestra, and Buddy—getting tipsier by degrees—exaggerated his syncopation to the utmost.

The crowd clamored for a piece, stressing every syllable: "Play *Jo-sé-phine!* Play *Jo-sé-phine!*"

Buddy picked up his cornet and another storm of rhythm swept the frenzied crowd. Even the floor seemed to rise and fall with the syncopation of the orchestra. Toward one o'clock in the morning, when the respectable people had left, the young bucks who had been uptown came back with their women; eyes circled by dissipation, faces streaky with powder, lips heavily smeared, and as drunk as fiddlers, these wenches began to stir up a rumpus and to clamor for Buddy Bolden to play their favorite tunes.

"Play *Jack Carey*, King Buddy! Play *Careless Love!*"

And the strumpets vied with one another to see who would display the greatest generosity. They tied coins in their handkerchiefs and tossed them up to the orchestra, where Buddy Bolden caught his share and threw the handkerchiefs back at their owners. All the habituées had arrived: Mary Jack the Bear, Queen of Vice, fighting woman who carried a razor strapped under her garter; Jupee Bleeding Heart—she had killed a man in Gretna; Redhead Jane, for a brief but glorious space a reigning belle of Memphis's Beale street; Alberta, the youngest of this unsavory pack, battening on the lust of men by night and earning more than the rest, so that she could shower Buddy Bolden with greater largesse than her hated rival, Mary Jack the Bear.

The hoodlums and the professionl gamblers and the pimps were there, too—highly regarded and paying no admission if only their ties were loud and full enough and their stickpins sufficiently sparkling.

At two o'clock the bouncers of Funky Butt Hall began to

round up the kids who were sleeping against the platform.
Worn out, drunk with rhythm, Louis would stagger into the
night. As he turned the corner of Liberty the open windows
of Matranga's were still pouring forth their cacophony. The
stores kept by Segretta and Gaspar had long since closed.
From the Eagle Saloon at the corner of Rampart came the rant-
ings of brawling drunkards.

The next day was Sunday, and everybody slept late in Perdido. Toward noon the charwomen descended on the dance
halls and babbled about the previous night's performance. In
the afternoon, if all went well, whole family groups would
go off to Lincoln Park where Buddy Bolden could be heard,
while on the other side of the road, in Johnson Park, either
Emmanuel Perez or Freddie Keppard led his band. And many
would recall the Sundays long-ago in Congo Square and those
wild dances, the Bamboula and the Counjaie.

That Monday when Louis arrived at the newsstand in St.
Charles Street he found his spot usurped since the previous
Saturday evening by one of his little comrades. Going back
gloomily toward Perdido, he stopped at the employment
agency on Rampart Street. Redhead Happy was selling papers
in the vicinity.

"You on strike, Dipper?"

"Somebody done took my spot."

"I heared my paw say they was a job at Konowski's, the
coal man."

Louis was given an address and lost no time finding the
place.

"Got any work for me, Mister?"

"How old are you?"

" 'Leven!"

This was not true—Louis was adding two years to his age.

"Yes, I do need a little boy like you to ride on one of my coal wagons in the daytime."

"How much you pay?"

"A half-dollar, not counting tips."

"All right. When does I start?"

"Tomorrow."

On the next day, a Tuesday, Mrs. Morton missed Louis at school—which did not strike her as strange since many little Negroes started to work young. Louis had climbed on a coal wagon driven by an older Negro. Their itinerary covered the section between Tulane and Rampart. Rolling slowly from block to block, the wagon stopped before every second or third house. Louis's job was to fill up the buckets between stops and starts.

The well-trained mule would halt of its own accord, and Louis, standing on his chariot as proud as a Roman dictator, would chant between cupped hands:

"Stone coal, ladies, five cents a water bucket!"

The seventy-five cents or a dollar that Louis earned each day he faithfully took home to his mother when five o'clock came.

Toward six, his stepfather came home from work and May Ann got supper ready. At this time the family was faring a little better; though Mama Lucy was still in school, the other three members were self-supporting. And Louis was growing up—he now wore a colored shirt tucked into long pants tied with a leather belt.

After supper he would run off to meet his three buddies—Redhead Happy, Little Mack, and Georgie Gray—in the vacant lots of Perdido. They played marbles, or staged battles, or sat down near a fence, or sang or danced. At this period

Louis knew only one kind of dance. He would buckwing his way into the center of the group of kids, and imitate a hunchback or a lame man, then straighten up abruptly and dance a lively jig. In order to excite him to greater efforts the other kids sang ragtime songs, clapping their hands so as to stress the rhythm. Then another would take his place and Louis would join the singers.

Presently these haphazard performances led the four singers of the group to an important decision. On his rounds with the coal vendor, Louis had noticed groups of three or four Negro children who sang and danced for the amusement of the public in well-to-do sections, and then passed the hat.

Louis was an expert at jigging, and little Mack had no rival when it came to somersaults and contortions. They practiced for a week. Immediately after supper, telling no one what they were up to, they would meet stealthily in a deserted yard on Freret Street. Then they would sing together the tunes they had heard, Louis singing bass and leading the other three. One of them had brought a soap box and Louis beat out the rhythm on it with a stick. After rehearsing for about a month, the boys set out on their experiment. They walked as far as Poydras and stopped before Maylie's Restaurant. All four of them lined up against the wall and began to sing, beating time with their right heels. Even in those days Louis sang with his eyes closed, in a sort of ecstasy, his mouth wide open, much to the enjoyment of the passing public.

Soon about twenty idlers had gathered to listen to Armstrong's warm and deep voice contrasting with his pals' higher pitch, and the women, softened by their singing or by their youth, threw coins at their feet.

The songs the quartet knew were not complicated. There were some plantation airs; *Swanee River*, of course; then *Jack Carey*, which was to become *Tiger Rag*. In this song Louis took the part of the clarinet by whistling through his fingers to the great amusement of the crowd.

Already those kids had a sense of contrast, and after a ragtime they would play sweet music. Louis Armstrong was at his best in *My Brazilian Beauty* and *Mr. Moon, Won't You Please Shine Down On Me?* But the quartet's big hit was a side-splitting scene in which Louis Armstrong made passionate love to Redhead Happy. While the three others were blowing a discreet accompaniment. Louis declared his love in passionate terms and rolled his eyes in a simulation of desire. With shouts of laughter and approval the audience would demand an encore and Louis would break forth in his low voice, his lips drawn back to show the pearliest set of teeth in Dixie, and sing his biggest hit: *"Everybodys gal is my gal, and your gal is my gal too!"* And as soon as Louis had ended his song and Little Mack had finished his somersault, the quartet would be showered with pennies.

From Maylie's, which was their favorite spot, they usually went down toward Canal Street. At the corner of Gravier there was a point of vantage where the quartet could strut as though on a stage. Business was good, and at night they would divide the money and go to Gaspar's or Segretta's to eat their fill of cakes and candies.

Little by little, the quartet enlarged and improved its repertory, and within a few weeks it was functioning regularly every day. Presently the boys recruited two friends whom they would post at each end of the block in which they were playing, so as to be warned if the police were approaching. Whether they were playing in front of Maylie's, or opposite the barber shop on Poydras Street, or near the loan office on Gravier, the sudden sound of a shrill whistle would bring them to a stop automatically. Then each little Negro would lose himself in the throng until nightfall, when they would rejoin one another and slip into a dance hall, there to listen raptly to Perez or Picou improvising nameless melodies.

One bright day the sun shone with unusual brilliance, and newsboys were screaming headlines from the *States* and the *Item*. In front of the pawnbroker's window, Bob Lyons was lighting a cigarette. A police van clanged to a stop at the corner of Rampart. It had just left the Parish Prison and the Negro onlookers on the sidewalk stared curiously.

"What's up? What's goin' on?"

"They draggin' away some crazy man, gonna send him up to Jackson, to the nut-house."

It was not until dusk, shortly before going home, that Louis learned that never again would he hear Buddy Bolden play; the cornetist had been sent to the mental hospital.

"He blowed hisself cuckoo," asserted Redhead Happy. "This mornin' I seen one of his women cryin' like a fool."

And Henry Morton declared solemnly: "Women and drinkin'—that's what turned his head!"

Another swore that a Voodoo spell had been cast on Buddy's cornet. Sweet Child, however, believed that King Bolden had blown too long and too hard. Good-bye to the brood who ran to his call on Sunday in Lincoln Park! New tunes were sweeping Perdido. That evening, on his way back to Dupré, Louis immersed himself in the heady atmosphere which had pervaded his childhood. Buddy Bolden was gone forever. And Louis hummed the tune of the King of Perdido:

> *"I think I heard Jack Carey say:*
> *'Funky Butt, Funky Butt, take it away!'"*

5

DURING THE July of 1912 the New Orleans heat was almost
unbearable. In Perdido's highways and byways the darkies,
stripped to an untidy minimum, spent most of the night in
the open air. There was always a trumpet or two modulating
in the neighborhood, and those whom it kept awake went off
to try to snatch some sleep near the parks. Louis Armstrong's
nights were spent chiefly in search of adventure; he now
worked for Konowski, the coal man, only in the mornings,
and the afternoons were too hot for energetic pursuits.

One evening the Armstrong family were celebrating Louis's
twelfth birthday with a special dinner of pigs' feet, fried
chicken, and ice cream. As Louis was finishing his share the
gate below creaked loudly and a falsetto voice called: "Come
on, Dipper—we's waitin' for youse!"

Recognizing Little Mack's inimitable drawl, Louis quickly
swallowed the last spoonful of ice cream and morsel of cake
and dashed downstairs.

"Watch out for the cops," warned his mother. "Yestiddy
you was almost caught."

Redhead Happy and Georgie Gray were waiting at the
corner of Gravier not far from the Parish Prison.

"Where we goin' tonight?" asked Georgie.

"Where you thinks? In the districk."

Horn of Plenty:

The "districk" was Storyville, the section just outside the Vieux Carré which was set apart for bawdy houses. Past Canal Street, on the downtown side, there were a series of streets lined with houses that trafficked in vice. Following Rampart, they saw Bob Lyons arranging stock in the pawnshop window. When they reached Canal Street's wide expanse, crowds of white people in summer clothes were heading for the levee. A water wagon sprayed cooling jets on the hot asphalt, which steamed in its wake.

On North Rampart Street the large shade trees were bathing in a golden haze. People were sitting on their doorsteps, too listless even to talk in such stifling heat. The little darkies were drenched with sweat as they trudged along Iberville Street. Storyville was coming to life as night fell. Doors were ajar and some courtesans daubed like Indians were getting down from their cabs. At the corner of Crozat Street an open barroom flaunted rows of flasks reflected in the traditional mirror. Negro doormen in gaudy uniforms were beginning to take up their posts. Scrubwomen were busily polishing the brass rail. The syncopated tinkle of a piano sounded at the corner of Liberty. The kids halted for a moment.

"Who that is?" said one of them.

"Must be Jelly Roll; can't be nobody else."

Hearing the thud of hobnail shoes from the direction of Marais Street, the boys took Liberty Street on the right. In a ground-floor room a drunken woman was singing, her window wide open. In the house next door, behind transparent tulle curtains, in a sort of golden nimbus, the ladies of the evening smoothed their hair, sprayed their bodies with perfume, and smoked cigarettes. Few people passed by at this early hour.

The kids lined up and began to sing—in low tones at first. Then they launched into *Swanee River*, beating time with slaps of hand on hip. One of the women pushed the curtain aside and leaned languidly on the sill. She was red-haired and her dark eyelids were heavy with mascara. Next door an ancient harridan lounged against the door-frame and mingled her voice with the boys' singing. Above them, a frightfully ugly matron with blotched skin was opening her window on the second floor. In this section, they did not care to attract a crowd as they had before Maylie's Restaurant; their sole aim was to please the women whose generosity was a byword. Louis recalled a proverb which his grandmother never tired of repeating: "The drum catches everything thrown by the flute."

Little Mack danced a few steps; Georgie Gray started a lively jig, at intervals throwing his body over an outstretched leg. A good number of women were now looking out of their windows and doorways, diverted momentarily by this interlude in their sordid lives. Some of them urged on the performers. Louis flashed his teeth, tilted his head slightly, and stood with half-shut eyes. His three pals started to hum softly, and he broke into a passionate ragtime:

> *"There's a girl in Savannah—*
> *There's a girl in Savannah . . ."*

The women were laughing now. From the corner saloon a pimp had come out on the sidewalk to investigate the cause of a commotion that might interfere with his business. In a room facing the quartet two half-dressed wenches caught each other by the waist and began to dance. After the last tune Georgie Gray doffed his cap and went from door to door. The red-haired dreamer threw a coin into the cap and offered him a cigarette. The woman standing in the doorway raised her skirts high, revealing naked thighs. She slipped her right hand into a black silk stocking and extracted a roll of dollar bills. The kids stood open-mouthed. As she thumbed through her fistful of bank notes, she continued to blow smoke through the corner of her mouth. Finally she dropped a dollar bill into the waiting cap.

"Come here, darky!" cried the woman who had been listening to the quartet from the second story. She dropped a coin and it bounced on the pavement. As Louis, Little Mack, and Redhead Happy started to search for the coin in the warm darkness, a piercing whistle suddenly came from the direction of Bienville Street. In a twinkling, the women flew back into their houses, doors were slammed, curtains were drawn, and shutters were closed tight.*

Losing no time, the boys took to their heels and ran up Liberty toward Perdido. At the corner of Iberville they spied the looming shadow of a policeman coming from Canal Street. They ran back to Bienville and circled by way of Marais Street. Police whistles seemed to be blowing everywhere in streets that were now suddenly empty. At last they reached Canal Street and stopped on the uptown side to catch their breath.

By this time it was very dark. The street lamps cast ghostly shadows on the house fronts. It was senseless to go back to Storyville that night. The boys followed Perdido Street until they were close to the Parish Prison. There they sat down in a vacant lot to settle up. About ten o'clock, they decided to go off and serenade the wenches of the Black Belt. It was

---

* An ordinance issued by Alderman Story in 1897 had restricted vice to the district beyond Rampart, a district thenceforth called Storyville. Its strongholds were located in Customhouse Street and Basin Street. The law provided that any woman who sold her body would be condemned to pay a fine or go to jail if she showed herself in public or accosted a man in the restricted area; and it fixed the limits within which the black women could practice commercialized vice. This zone, called the Black Belt, lay between Perdido, Gravier, Franklin, and Liberty Streets.

understood that these dark-skinned practitioners could not afford to be so liberal to the boys as were their Basin Street sisters, due to the necessarily lower rates they charged their customers.

The four musical pals therefore went down toward Saratoga, where they knew they would probably get a little more than elsewhere. Here were no regulated brothels with several inmates each, as in Basin Street; instead, every woman—from the ever-desirable quadroon to the darkest skinned—shuttled from house to house in a merry-go-round of prostitution. Most of them occupied a single room each. The more favored ones could be found on the lower floor in a room that was bare, save for a mean iron bed and a wash basin. As twilight came on, they appeared at the windows or knocked on the shutters to attract the attention of passersby. As soon as they heard a man's footsteps they would run to their posts, eager to strike a good bargain. The men were invariably the dregs of the population. In this hopeless street, the riffraff of the port sought satisfaction, while the black customers—unable to spend so heavily—were content to visit the cut-rate establishments in adjoining streets.

Little Louis, with an eye for business, chose a spot where a dim light came through the windows. Total darkness indicated that the customers demanded the mystery of the night for fulfilling their dubious pleasures, and would regard the songs of the quartet as an annoying disturbance. In subdued tones the boys began *Jack Carey;* Louis's whistling served as accompaniment. Two or three heads appeared at a window, and an old panderess came to the door. Then they swang into *My Brazilian Beauty*. A wench struck a match, lighting up the shadows, and drew on her cigar. Men coming from Gravier or Perdido retraced their steps, distracted by this unusual ac-

[51]

tivity. Soon a group of curious women stopped at the yard gates. Those who had dens located in a near-by alley and who were obliged to solicit on the street started to form a circle around the four boys.

Louis noticed Mary Jack the Bear chatting before a trellised gate with The Killer. The crowd was increasing rapidly. Soon there was a stir of alarm among the denizens of the street. One by one the gates closed while the professionals of the "banquette" resumed their streetwalking. For a new group was arriving—the pimps—who had been drinking at Matranga's and who had heard of the disturbance from one of their spies. The wenches, these men knew, were far too inclined to waste time listening to the children's music; and they had to be "urged" to go back to work. Thanks to some sixth sense, they had foreseen the danger and returned to their trade before the men could vent their anger.

But the boys were not to get off so easily. Chuck Wade, one of the young sheiks of that period, caught Louis Armstrong by the arm and gave him a merciless beating. "If ever I catch one of you in this street again, I'll cure him of playing ragtime forever!"

Some disinterested spectators who observed this scene from their own steps, found nothing unusual in it. For this was but an ordinary example of the high-handed justice which hoodlums mete out impartially to unruly associates.

The other three boys had fled into an empty lot. Chuck Wade released Louis, who joined them, sought safety behind a fence, and then began to hurl insults at his tormentor.

"Yo' dirty whore-master! Yo' liver's rotten! You's gonna wind up on the 'lectric chair, an' your tail gonna burn before yo' goes to hell!"

It was now too late to visit another section. But it had been

[52]

a poor day. Mama Lucy, still up, took the forty cents that
Louis had earned that evening.

At six o'clock the next morning when Louis was awakened
by his mother he was so worn out by the night's escapade and
the short rest that he found it almost impossible to get up. Nevertheless he stretched his arms and went down the stairs rubbing his eyes. Reaching the large, communal bucket of cold
water, he washed in a perfunctory manner and gulped down
his oatmeal and fled, tugging at his pants and praying he would
be on time at Maurice Konowsky's.

The mule was already hitched, and he too seemed drowsy
as he pulled his dreary load. White children, Louis reflected,
were still fast asleep in spotless beds; but he forced himself to
stand up in the wagon and yell: "*Stove coal, lady, five cents a
water bucket!*" Trade was far from brisk during these dull,
hot summer days.

This morning the mule wandered into Storyville's streets:
Customhouse, Basin, Iberville, Bienville, Liberty, Marais,
Villeré, and Robertson, thus Louis returned in the guise of
charcoal boy, to the very spot where he had played the trouba-
dour the night before. At this hour all was very still and peaceful within the bawdy houses.

"Stove coal, lady, five cents a water bucket!"

The driver was dozing on the wagon seat. The mule had
stopped. A door opened and the woman who had taken the
roll of bills from her stocking the night before came out.

"Give me ten buckets of coal."

Louis picked up two full pails—the equivalent of ten
buckets—and followed the woman towards the rear of the
house. He went through a hall with brightly papered walls
and his feet sank into a carpet soft as down. The morning

light revealed paintings of nude women in suggestive poses. To his right the door was open and he saw a maid sweeping up countless cigarette butts and burnt matches near the white piano.

While he was refilling the pails the woman sat down at the piano. She put her cigarette on an ash-tray and haltingly played the plaintive notes of a blues song.

> *"Two-nineteen train took my babe away—*
> *Two-seventeen train brought her back today."*

The direct simplicity of the song's words twisted the boy's heartstrings. He stood still in the hall, feeling shy and guilty; but he was overcome by that intoxicating song which the woman kept repeating over and over again, while her clumsy fingers struck the burn-scarred keyboard.

He emptied the two pails and stood waiting near the door for his money. As he waited, he dreamed—dreamed about that sweet-sad melody, which was such a contrast to the ragged music of Emmanuel Perez or Buddy Bolden.

A loud voice brought him back to reality.

"What are you doing there, you rascal?"

It was the woman who had stopped singing and now held out a dollar bill. Louis, caught by surprise, stammered:

"I was listenin' to you, ma'am—only listenin', that's all. It's as fine as Buddy Bolden."

"Haven't I seen you before, darky?"

"Yas'm I was singin' *Swanee River* last night an' you give me a dollar."

"Do you know Funky Butt's tune?"

"Sho' 'nuf."

"Sing it for me. I'll play the piano."

She sat on the piano stool and struck a few chords. Louis was awestruck in the presence of this white woman who belonged to the category of superior beings revered by the denizens of Perdido.

"Why don't you sing? You aren't afraid of me?"

Louis's lips parted, his white teeth flashed, and the woman gazed curiously at his quivering chin as his voice vibrated with poignant feeling:

> *"I think I heard Buddy Bolden say:*
> *'Funky Butt, Funky Butt, take it away!'"*

She turned away, laughing, and lit another cigarette. Louis felt as if he had spent a lifetime of happiness in this paradise whose gates were closed to the black race. She laughed again at Buddy Bolden's refrain and handed Louis a dollar bill. "I owe you a half-dollar. Keep the change."

Louis thanked her happily. Life was sweet. The red and green flowers in the carpet near the entrance seemed to bloom in the morning light. He blinked in the bright sunshine, feeling as though he were leaving another world. His heart beat fast. On the threshold he drew himself up proudly and in a hoarse voice yelled: "Stove coal, lady, five cents a bucket," and at the end he added some improvised notes from the song he had just sung to the dark-eyed woman. The driver and the mule woke up and the wagon rolled to the next corner.

And so time went by. Perdido, the dark kingdom, was unchanging in its monotony. Louis sold coal, ate red beans, sang for the whores, and diligently attended Mrs. Morton's Sunday School classes.

A sultry Fall brought no relief from the hot summer. Sometimes Louis ran off to St. Charles Avenue and rolled in the grass for fun. The sweltering city was oppressed by leaden skies. People gasped for breath. The leaves hardly stirred in the shimmering heat. Sometimes thunder-showers would beat against the tin roofs. Puddles of mud and refuse would appear in Perdido's street, only to cake and rot in the blazing sun.

When the first north wind blew its cold breath on the city, Louis was still living in the narrow world of Perdido. He was now nearly thirteen. The coal business picked up while the profits of the quartet diminished. The shivering pedestrians would hurry by, paying scant attention to the vocal efforts of the little darkies.

Louis spent Christmas day with his grandmother Joséphine and his father. Willy's second wife was with him, as was their little boy, Louis's half brother, a tiny tot with thick lips. At noon they all feasted on chilli con carne and meringue pie. Louis was already tormented by the problem of finding a better means of livelihood, and his father advised him to take a job at the turpentine factory.

"Tain't 'zackly a gol' mine, but you'll eat reg'lar. An' then yo' can leave your Ma and stay here with Grandma!"

Louis imagined for a brief instant what life would be like away from the continuous circus of Perdido and Liberty. He would be lost without Segretta's, the best praline shop in the world. No more would he hear Freddy Keppard on Matranga's blooming porch, or lie in his lonely room listening to the excruciating lullabies of Funky Butt. And all this, he was convinced, was a basic necessity in his life. He did not answer his father, and as he started homeward he vowed to himself that he would never work in the turpentine factory.

That week the quartet rehearsed several times in preparation for the New Year's celebration. They decided that they would start on the Third Ward, continue by way of Poydras Street, and finally end up in the bedlam of Storyville where, toward three o'clock in the morning, rich topers gave away fistfuls of money.

So on New Year's eve Louis joined his pals in front of

egretta's grocery store. This was to be a day of unbridled
un and carousing, and the boys knew they would not be
othered by the police or by the pimps, who were shooting
raps in the Eagle Saloon and were much too drunk to give
hase. An organ grinder was playing for all he was worth at
ne corner of Loyola. Wreaths of holly and ivy hung in the
indows and on doors gave a holiday air to the shabby homes.
Vhisky, gin, and beer flowed freely. Already tipsy women,
naken with hiccups, staggered along the sidewalk. Innumer-
ple pickaninnies were setting off firecrackers.

In front of the Eagle Saloon the boys picked up a handful
f loose change when they sang. From there they went to the
ntersection of Perdido and Rampart. Just before they reached
ob Lyon's house, a little darky popped off his cap pistol in
ouis Armstrong's face and insulted him by calling him
Dipper."

Louis was blind with rage. He chased the kid onto a near-by
orch while his three friends roared with laughter. Redhead
Iappy urged his comrade on. "Go on, Dipper—yo' can't
vallow that!"

From the safety of the porch the little culprit had reloaded
nd again shot off his pistol in Louis's direction.

"If only I had my Pa's thirty-eight, I'd show yo' . . ."

"Go get him Dipper!" shouted Little Mack. "Yo' aint got
o guts?"

Louis, stung by the challenge, flew off for home. He ran
ast his mother, who was sitting on the outside steps, and
ooked for the gun. Finding it at last in the bottom of a trunk,
e thrust it in his pants pocket and left on the run.

The little darky on the porch, as soon as he spied Louis,
med at him again, and the three friends roared. Louis flour-
hed his gun.

"Get him, Louis—go get him, Dipper!' yelled the others.

[57]

Horn of Plenty

Louis loosened the safety catch, aimed at the porch, and pulled the trigger. He was stunned by the recoil and the loud report. With yells of rage he continued to press the trigger. The people of Perdido scurried to safety. A wench fled into the Eagle Saloon. Georgie Gray applauded wildly.

Suddenly Louis felt a hand on his shoulder. He turned quickly and recognized the stern face of a detective. His arm was sharply twisted, and the man's right hand swooped up the revolver. Louis fought back, but in vain. The rest of the quartet had melted away. A curious mob of Negroes collected at the scene of the shooting. Another policeman had come along. The two of them dragged Louis towards the police van which was stationed in Gravier in the shadow of the Parish Prison. As they went along Saratoga street they passed one of his schoolmates, who yelled, "So long, Dippermouth!" Louis was crying bitterly. He was shoved into the wagon, to stumble over the legs of assorted drunks and pickpockets.

At ten o'clock that evening, December 31, 1912, after a bumpy ride, the police let Louis out into a dark and dismal yard. He was still crying. An alcoholic floozy tried to console him. Then a voice boomed: "Line up, you all! Come here black boy—let's go to Juvenile Court."

As Louis Armstrong followed the officer his heart was heavy, for he knew that he had failed Redhead Happy, Little Mack, and Georgie Gray. The quartet would not sing in Storyville that night.

6

LOUIS'S MIND was in a whirl. He passed the night dozing on a bench, worrying about his mother, who might not know where he was. His childish imagination pictured Morris Konowsky coming to his rescue and putting everything to rights.

In this inauspicious fashion Louis greeted the New Year of 1913. Maybe they would let him go in the morning in time for him to enjoy the fried chicken lunch which his mother had planned. He remembered he had seen Mama Lucy dipping the wings and the legs of a chicken into the batter.

From time to time a turnkey passed by, but Louis did not dare ask any questions. At six o'clock in the morning there was a change of guards and the winter light streamed dully through the gratings.

Outside he could hear the distant cries of late revelers. From time to time the sound of a shot rang out. Louis had been left all alone and, exhausted from weeping, he had fallen asleep, his head against the wall.

A stentorian voice woke him up: "Come on, brat!"

A gigantic policeman filled the doorway, and Louis followed him timorously. The yard where he had stopped yesterday in the police van was wet and slippery and the wagon was waiting. The lad climbed in silently. Other boys were already seated on the inside; they, too, had probably been picked up the night before. Maybe he was being taken back to Perdido, the ride was so long. Finally the wagon stopped and the doors swung open. The children filed out and Louis got his first view of his new abode, a dismal sprawling building. At the entrance, the superintendent, Mr. Jones, stood waiting, flanked by his wife and the head warden, Peter Davis.

There was no choice but to make the best of this new situation. The boy was registered as a "transient" and remained with the group that was to be taken before Juvenile Court. He was given the inmates' uniform and on the first day he wrote a card to his mother and Mama Lucy begging them to come for him. But several days went by, and he thought he would die from loneliness and boredom.

A week elapsed before he was summoned to the reception room. In a dark corner, he made out the forms of May Ann and Mama Lucy, both tearful and frightened. He threw himself on his mother and broke into tears. Then it was his turn to console her, telling her that he was not mistreated, that the beds were clean, and the food was wholesome.

Another week dragged by and Louis left in the van to appear in Juvenile Court. He waited with other Negro lads and then, after a long time, his name was called by an attendant.

He shuffled forward and was shoved into the full glare of the court until he finally reached an immense desk behind which loomed the majestic figure of Judge Wilson. The detective who had arrested him was there. Louis turned slightly and caught a glimpse of his sobbing mother and sister who tried bravely to smile through their tears. The plainclothesman described the disturbance which Louis had created on New Year's eve. The big .38 was placed before the Judge and now and then His Honor would toy with it.

"Boy, did you know you could shoot someone with this gun?

"I wanted to celebrate, Yo' Honor."

"Your parents are to blame for leaving so dangerous a weapon where a bad boy like you could get at it!"

Louis's mother was called to the stand. She blurted out her story, frightened half out of her wits. The revolver belonged to her husband. More than once, Louis had played with the gun and she had scolded him severly. She hid it in a closet, then under a loose board in the floor. But Louis would always discover the hiding-place. The last time she had concealed it at the bottom of an old trunk.

"Case is tried."

His Honor's gavel came down on the desk with a bang. The spectators rose in the courtroom. Judge Wilson read a lengthy and unintelligible sentence. Finally he paused, out of breath and legal terms, and glared balefully at Louis.

"The Court has seen fit to be merciful. You will serve an indeterminate sentence."

The word "indeterminate" was the last straw for Louis. He fancied himself growing old in convict's stripes. The guard was already hustling him towards the door. He disappeared, blowing frantic kisses to his mother and sister. In the van his fellow-prisoners explained that he was going to the Waif's Home to stay until such time as the superintendent decided that his ways were mended.

This time Louis was registered as a full-fledged boarder. He had already struck up an acquaintance with several other unfortunate urchins whose ages ranged from nine to sixteen. His bed stood between Gus Vanzan's and Izzy Smooth's. Peter Davis, the warden, gave him final instructions. The familiar routine was starting all over again. Often Lou¹ thought of Perdido; on Saturday nights he went back in agination to Funky Butt, and saw the lighted windows through which came the low-down singing of Buddy Bolden:

> *"I think I heard Jack Carey say:*
> *'Funky Butt, Funky Butt, take it away!'"*

In the morning he could see himself on the wagon drawn by the drowsy mule. His ears would ring with the raspy urgings of the driver: "Go on, Mule," followed by a half-hearted crack of the whip. It was great fun to be free, to stand up in the wagon and bellow lustily: "Stove coal, lady, stove coal, a nickel a water bucket." What about the quartet? Who was taking his place when they sang in front of Maylie's? Who intoned the haunting melody of *My Brazilian Beauty?* And Louis had a vision of the lovely lady of Basin Street who played on the white piano and sang *The Two-Nineteen Blues*.

Peter Davis was well suited for his post of warden. He was young, a teacher by avocation, very dark-skinned, with eyes of slightly different colors, and his shiny black face radiated kindness. He used persuasion more often than force, although newcomers elicited the sterner treatment.

Louis Armstrong lost no time falling into the spirit of his surroundings and did not view his fate as a tragic one. In a few days' time he had become the leader of a little group, made up chiefly of several former schoolmates, among them Kid Rena, soon to become his close buddy.

His innate talent for acting soon made him popular with everybody. During the first month, every time he joined a group of inmates he was greeted with enthusiastic laughter. From the start, Louis had shrewdly made up his mind to become popular. During recreation, he would strut pigeon-toed, then limp along as though crippled, and finally imitate a nkard so well that the moment he appeared he threw the children into gales of merriment. He would dance, jig, recite, and sing. Not many weeks passed before he was acknowledged the uncrowned king of the Waifs.

Presently, however, Louis's early successes went to his head, and it was found that he had become a disturbing factor, threatening to undermine the discipline of the place. Peter Davis soon called his hand, warning him that the pranks must stop.

For some time, Louis cherished a secret desire to become a member of the Waifs' band. Izzy Smooth and Gus ("Red") Vanzan already played in it, and Louis envied their luck. The only hitch was that the privilege was granted only to boys whose good behavior was outstanding. So Louis's conduct became exemplary, and Peter Davis had no need to repeat his warning. The lad restrained himself at the recess period, and at all other times was tractable, attentive, and willing. Presently his reward came: one morning after breakfast, he was sent for by the superintendent, Mr. Jones.

"Armstrong, I've got good news for you. You've shown some musical talent, so we've thought about you for the tambourine."

This was a wonderful beginning. Louis was overjoyed. Naturally, he would have preferred to blow on one of the shiny brass instruments—cornet, trumpet, or bugle—in imitation of his idol, Buddy Bolden, or even Bunk Johnson; but the newly-instilled discipline of the place had ingrained a certain degre of philosophy in him.

Louis was in seventh heaven all that day! he had reached his goal; After classes, he ran to the music-hall, where he studied the charts of musical values and the positions of the instruments. Rehearsal was scheduled to start in half an hour. Peter Davis came in with the tambourine and showed him how it was played. At five o'clock, the rehearsal started and Louis did remarkably well, owing to his sense of rhythm and his strict attention to the business at hand. A few weeks later, when an older boy of sixteen left the Waifs' Home, the small drum was left without a player. Peter Davis immediately promoted Louis to this more powerful percussion instrument—which made the boy intensely happy. On this particular Saturday there was a full-dress rehearsal because the orchestra was to give a concert that Sunday. The crucial question was whether Louis was capable of rising to the occasion, so he was the center of attention when the players reached the main piece—*At the Animals' Ball*. This masterpiece contained an extremely difficult triple break on the drum which Louis's predecessor had taken a long time to master. Peter Davis voiced his fears and was almost resolved to omit the piece when Louis spoke up boldly:

"Stop worryin' 'bout me, Mr. Davis. They ain't nothin' June Cole could play that Satchmo' cain't do better."

Despite his bragging, Louis had to repeat the passage several times before getting the knack of it. The following day, Louis Armstrong was as serious as a pulpit-orator. The music of *Animals' Ball* was approaching its most sweeping passage and Louis felt his heart rise to his mouth. The tuba was speaking gravely and eloquently in the language of the wild animals of the jungle. Then came the critical moment, and all eyes were turned on Louis. Poised and tense, with an expression of utter seriousness on his ebony face, Louis Armstrong beat out a masterly triple break without a falter. Peter Davis cast a warm glance of approval on the boyish drummer, and Louis glowed with happy pride.

This musical phase lasted a month or so. Spring came, and the trees in the yard turned green and fragrant. Soft grass covered the lawns on which the children played. Frequent warm showers cleansed the air and the first buds broke out on the trees and bushes. Louis Armstrong saw many china-ball trees, bringing to his memory the forlorn and solitary tree that had spread its meager foliage over the vacant lot on Liberty Street.

One evening in May, Louis was summoned to the music-hall. Peter Davis was waiting for him.

"Armstrong, you've done a mighty good job in the band. How would you like to play the alto?"

"Yessiree, Mr. Davis, that's my speed."

When Peter Davis now talks about his most famous pupil, he never fails to assert that Louis was really and truly a child prodigy. Within a few days he had mastered the complexities of the new instrument, and played with such power, with so true a tone, and with such telling effect that he eclipsed those who had had several years' practice.

Then Louis Armstrong became the institution's official bugler. He gave up the alto and devoted himself to this new instrument. All agreed that they had never heard a more impressive performance on the bugle; Louis had no rival for sheer power of execution and steadiness in hitting the high notes.

Little Armstrong was a sight to behold as he marched in the band's lead, in his blue uniform, twirling his bugle and making it flash in the sun before gluing it to his lips. Sometimes the band went down to Canal Street for big celebrations. His mother and Mama Lucy would stand for hours on the sidewalk, waiting for their boy to strut by, proud as a peacock.

One day, at noon, all the children were assembled in the refectory. Louis was seated at a table busily addressing himself to a heaping plateful of red beans and rice. Peter Davis entered and the boarders rose to attention.

"My friends," Davis told them, "I am here to reward a hard worker. In a few months' time Louis Armstrong has proven himself capable with several different instruments. Now that Billy Ware is no longer with us, Louis Armstrong will inherit his trumpet!"

This was a red-letter day for Louis, and he walked on air. He took the old trumpet (which the Waifs' Home carefully preserves to this day) and kissed it in a simple gesture which he often repeated later on the stage.

At last he really owned the coveted instrument that had seemed so hopelessly out of reach.

"Now then, Dipper, you'll do your best, won't you?"

"So', sho', Mr. Davis. I'se goin' to play like Buddy Bolden!"

"Who the devil is Buddy Bolden?" exclaimed Peter Davis.

"He used to play the cornet at Funky Butt Hall, but they done locked him up."

All the children giggled, but Peter Davis looked grave.

"Listen to me, Louis Armstrong! I haven't given you the finest instrument in the band for you to play stupid ragtime on. The men you heard playing in the District are not men whose example you want to follow, and their way of playing is exactly the way you *mustn't* play! Those fellows are ignorant—a bunch of fake musicians. They don't know how to read music, they can't keep time, and they never hit the right notes. Forget all about them, Dipper!"

All that afternoon, Louis practiced so intently and patiently that his friends began to make fun of him. Kid Rena, who also played the trumpet, warned him that "he would blow himself out." But Louis was trying to smooth out his high notes. Despite all his efforts, the mouthpiece had an unfortunate tendency to slip from his unpracticed lips.

Next day Louis went off to the work-shop with his trumpet.

"What are you doing here?" asked the toolkeeper.

"I wants to borrow a file, please!"

Thereupon, much to the other players' surprise, he began

to scrape with the file on the trumpet held fast betwen his knees: the marks can be seen on the instrument today.

Ten days later, Louis Armstrong had taken the measure of all the trumpet players in the Home. Peter Davis had never met such an apt pupil. The superintendent, meantime, was sending in regular and favorable reports on the behavior of his charge.

Louis had now been an inmate of the Waifs' Home for a whole year, and he did not have a single black mark against him. Sometimes when he was practicing alone on the trumpet, the remembered glamour of Perdido would recur to him irrepressibly and he would try out some ragtimes, Funky Butt style, and this would infuriate Peter Davis.

Louis's big hit in a concert solo was indubitably *Home, Sweet Home*, which invariably brought down the house.

"That kid's playing is amazing," Peter Davis would comment. "I've never heard tones as true and ringing as he plays."

On one holiday the band went into town to march and play. It was Sunday evening, and Peter Davis swung them out in the direction of Perdido. Louis's heart was racing when they had crossed Rampart. In the twinkling of an eye, the whole section got wind of Louis's return and the sidewalks were crowded. The neighborhood bars were deserted by the customers who ran to the doors and windows. The band turned into Perdido. A warm burst of applause greeted one of Sousa's marches. All the pickaninnies of the quarter fell in and danced behind the orchestra. At the corner of Liberty, the boy's mother and Mama Lucy were shedding tears of joy. Once more Louis's happy gaze fell on Segretta's and Gaspar's storefronts, on Matranga's swinging doors, on the beloved sweep of Liberty. Little Henry Morton, holding his mother's

[67]

hand, waved to him. Sweet Child was cheering wildly from the top of a staircase. He saw the porch where the little darky had shot at him with his toy pistol. They came to a stop in front of Fisk School. Redhead Happy and Georgie Gray ran up to shake hands with him.

"How goes it, Dipper? Got a promotion?"

"It ain't bad, eh, boy?"

"Is you' really the secon' band-leader?"

"Nothin' else but."

They told him Little Mack no longer lived in Perdido. Then his mother and Mama Lucy caught up with him. They were still crying and Louis was ashamed.

"Stop that cryin'! Ain't you all glad? Satchmo' done got to be secon' band-leader."

Louis, who was close to tears himself, embraced his mother and sister. He held his mother close and whispered in her ear:

"I sho' wish I could come back to Perdido, Ma. You can trust me now, I'll be a good boy."

The spectacle of the street captivated him. The smallest details were suddenly clear to him. A house had collapsed in Liberty Street. A candy-shop now stood near the school. A new name showed on the barber's pole in Perdido. A poster at Funky Butt announced the coming of an orchestra which Louis did not know. It would soon be a year and a half since he had been sent to the Waifs' Home.

That night he dreamed about the sultry days of his childhood. He dreamed how pleasant it was to be able to loaf where the trees and the flowers threw off the odor of wet earth after a thunderstorm; he yearned for the Saturday nights at twilight when Buddy Bolden or Emmanuel Perez played at Funky Butt. The old syncopated tunes still lived in his memory and haunted him.

One day at the visiting hour, May Ann told him that perhaps he would be free before long. She had gone to see his grandmother in Dupré one evening and had met Willy Armstrong there. They had both decided to try to have the boy released. Willy was to approach his boss and ask him to put in a good word for his son. In order to obtain quicker results, his father bound himself to take him into his own home and keep an eye on him. On her side, his mother had enlisted the help of the good people for whom she worked as cook. Mr. Jones and Peter Davis had turned in very favorable reports. The matter was submitted to the Juvenile Court, and finally—on June 16, 1914—Louis was brought to the Superintendent's office.

"Louis Armstrong, you may pack your things. You'll be free after lunch. You've been a good boy. You must keep up the good work. You've got musical talent; try to develop it and you'll get somewhere."

In the refectory, Louis said good-bye to Gus Vanzan, Izzy Smooth, Kid Rena, and the others. Then he went off to take leave of Peter Davis, who was loath to part with his best musician. The trumpet lay on the table. Some other unfortunate child would now take possession of his cherished companion. Louis felt heartsick, but his mother was waiting in the parlor. He had grown a good deal and was wearing a new pair of blue denim trousers, the Home's parting gift. Louis drew near the trumpet, balanced it in his pink palm, fondled it, took a last look at the notches in the mouthpiece, and left sobbing.

It was a mild day out of doors. Mother and son boarded a street-car and sat down behind the screen marked "For Colored Only." In the distance the city's outline was dim in a cloudy sky. Louis was almost fourteen years old. How quickly time had passed! He felt that he was awakening from a dream

—or, rather, that he was caught up in a new dream. Far away, in Europe, there were rumors of war. But at such a distance this was no concern of the kingdom of Perdido, and Louis's heart was filled with great joy, now that he had regained the keys of the kingdom.

7

so LOUIS Armstrong went to stay with his father at Poydras
and Miro, which was some dozen blocks from Liberty. Gradually his adolescent mind began to brood on the tragic destiny
of his race. For himself, what was ahead in life?

He recalled Superintendent Jones's flattering remarks on
the special musical talent which was his to develop. Now that
he was out in the world, perhaps he would find in music the
answer to his problem. He soon discovered, however, that
there were no vacancies for an unknown and untutored player.
The organized bands wanted seasoned musicians, and not
even the meanest dives would consider a rank amateur. Moreover, at this gawky stage, his changing voice and awkward
manner made him the butt of merciless chaffing wherever
he went to look for work. He did not own any kind of musical
instrument and was too poor to buy one. The future looked
dark indeed.

The hopes he had built up while at the Waifs' Home
haunted him. How proud he had felt in the bright uniform
of the band! But that was all dead and gone now, and nothing
would come of it. Louis was just another black boy, fated to
eke out a bare existence at some menial task. There were but
few avenues of escape. Most of his kind were bound in the invisible chains of a perpetual and hopeless bondage, and those

who broke the fetters became evil characters like Clark Wade, always involved in some scrape or worse. Sometimes Louis was tempted to follow their example, but the solid training he had received at the Waifs' Home kept him from slipping into dangerous habits.

Until such time as he could decide what trade to follow, he played nursemaid to Willy and Gertrude's children. His step-mother worked out all day as a servant, so Louis became house-keeper and kept an eye on his two half brothers, Willy and Henry, and his half sister as well.

It was up to him to prepare the daily lunch of red beans and rice. The three hungry kids would pounce on the table like famished wolves, and Louis himself, when in a reminiscent mood, says frankly that they ate "like hell" and that when he sounded the call for lunch, he had to make a bee-line for the table so as not to go hungry himself. Such was the pattern of his life until 1915.

The dampness of winter yielded to the warm springtime. Louis gave little thought to music, except when he felt the urge to go back to the enchanted kingdom of Perdido and listen to some orchestra or other. The black belt was now raving about the prowess of a new trumpet player, Bunk John-son, who had inherited Buddy Bolden's mantle and was a sen-sation with his Eagle Band. Their springboard to fame had been the Eagle Saloon at Rampart and Perdido. Heaven knows, Bunk's playing fell short of Buddy's impassioned and powerful blowing. As an admiring gesture toward the old tiger who was now caged for good, the royal title had not yet passed to his successor. Sometimes, when Louis had saved a few pennies, he would go downtown to listen to the orchestra in Hope's Hall, Corporation Hall, or Economy Hall. But only the well-to-do blacks could consistently afford such a treat, the price of admission being twenty-five cents.

Louis paid frequent visits to May Ann in her old Brick Row tenement. And each time he went back he fell under the spell of his childhood influences. Life ebbed and flowed between the school, the dance-hall, the church, and the prison, and throughout his adolescence he often returned to the old neighborhood.

As the azaleas and the hyacinths burst into bloom, and the west wind dispelled the chill and dampness of winter, the blacks left the prison of their wooden shanties and sat on their front steps to enjoy the first breath of spring. Louis was now fifteen years old, and had grown tall and sturdy, even though he often went to bed hungry. He could stand it no longer— he would rather be last in Perdido than first in Miro! So one afternoon he packed his few belongings in an old box and quit the dingy, hatch lodgings. As he passed Fisk School, he saw Orleania Morton and her mother, and they smiled and waved at him. A new generation of kids now went to the school, and he did not know any of them. The quartet had given up singing, but Redhead Happy, Little Mack, and Georgie Gray had found a new outlet for their energy: they practiced on the drum. By degrees the simultaneous playing of both drums had become general, and the fad had spread among an ignorant class of musicians to such an extent that they honestly believed they could defy the law of the scale, thanks to the drums and traps.

At this time Louis tried earnestly but vainly to earn a living in a steady job. He went back to Charlie's and sold newspapers; but his earnings were very small and, after all, he could not sell papers for the rest of his life! He tried his hand as odd man in a dairy, doing all the heavy chores; but after a month of this he returned to Charlie's newsstand. One morning, driven to desperation, he stopped at Morris Konowsky's. Morris told him he was too big to be a helper and too young to handle the driving. So Louis lapsed into idleness and lived in haphazard style. His mother advised him to work with his stepfather on the coal wagon, but Louis could not convince himself that there was no alternative to that distasteful occupation. The encouragement he had received at the Waifs' Home had been enough to give him a certain amount of self-confidence and the hope that something in his make-up would enable him to escape the degrading trade of coal-boy.

One day Louis went out to the docks to hunt for work. He was hired for one day as stevedore, but he was too young for this back-breaking toil. At noon, while he was munching a sandwich and looking down at the muddy waters, he heard a group of longshoremen singing the blues. This reminded him of the old quartet. His romantic soul still loved the sound of music, but he thought that he had said good-bye to his dream of becoming a musician. His life had found its groove and the future was hopeless. He would be ground under the hard wheel of poverty. That evening he came home exhausted and bruised by the day's work, and at dawn the next day he was so tired that he could not get up. Finally, he went back to selling papers.

One evening, at the end of a day of intermittent showers, he counted his earnings and found that he had taken in just fifty-five cents. This would not even pay for his share of the family's food. He felt ashamed to face his mother and his stepfather. Even Mama Lucy, who now worked as nursemaid in a white family, was a better breadwinner! As he went up Perdido he heard bursts of ragtime, and he thrilled to the beloved syncopation. At home, he turned the fifty-five cents over to his mother, walked out of the room, and paused at the head of the stairs. What was the use of going down to the street to meet his friends? He did not have a measly nickel to

exchange for a glass of beer at Matranga's or Funky Butt. Yes
—he knew now why so many of his kind lingered at the bar
for one drink after another until they staggered home to find
in drunken stupor a release from their troubles, only to
plunge into deeper despair on the morrow.

Louis started aimlessly along the street. In the house across
the way a woman was puffing on a fat cigar. A crowd was hurrying in the direction of Funky Butt. He had never felt so
lonely. He turned the corner of Perdido, and taking a side
alley, reached the inky darkness at the rear of Funky Butt
Hall. He drew near an open window. Through a bluish fog
of tobacco smoke he saw the orchestra drawn up on the platform. A tall Negro was strumming his bull-fiddle violently.
In the front rank Bunk Johnson was playing ragtimes that
drove the dancers into spasms. Louis was very still, absorbing
this potent nepenthe, following Bunk Johnson's every motion, and with three fingers of his own right hand pressing on
the pistons of an invisible cornet. . . . But the next morning
he went off with his stepfather to become the driver of a coal-
wagon.

They gave Louis a mule hitched to a cart. At first he was
accompanied by his stepfather, who taught him how to drive.
Then, using a sack for an apron to protect his pants and with
a dirty old cap on his head, he started out as itinerant coal vendor. At last he had fallen into line and nobody could tell him
from the fifteen other drivers who worked for his company.
In a few days he had adapted himself to his new occupation,
and he acquired the knack of handling his sack and slinging
it over his shoulder when he had to fetch a new load.

Every morning the foreman assigned the wagons and
mapped out their routes. At noon the drivers, on their hour
for lunch, would meet in front of Segretta's or Gaspar's grocery. The mules would be tied to hitching-posts and be given

bags of oats; the wheel-brakes would be set; and the men would flock to the counter.

Everybody would order one of those famous "poor-boy sandwiches" which were a specialty in the poorer districts of New Orleans. For five cents you could buy a half-loaf of bread, sliced lengthwise and stuffed with ham and mustard. Then the drivers would go out into the sunshine, lounge in front of the store, and devour their "poor-boys" while exchanging news of the trade.

"My ole mule's a little balky today."

"Since yestiddy, I ain't sold two sacks o' coal."

"Satiddy that there Tuxedo Band is goin' to play at Economy Hall."

"Yo' know somethin'—that boy Henry what drives the lil' white mule done hooked up with lil' Daisy."

After the sandwiches had been eaten, each driver would go back into the grocery store to get his drinking can filled with beer—ten cents' worth. And when one o'clock rang out from the neighboring belfries the drivers climbed back on their seats, put away their beer cans, unhitched their mules, and went glumly off along their routes.

Louis was now a young man like the others. On Saturdays he visited Matranga's or Funky Butt or Economy Hall. And he learned how to dance with young girls of his age. He took particular notice of a certain damsel with smoldering eyes who lived above Gaspar's grocery store. Her rhythmic steps, as she danced to the ragtime tunes with a slick-haired nighthawk, fascinated Louis to the point of infatuation. But in those days he had neither the look nor the manner of a Don Juan and not enough money to compensate these lacks; and Nutsie disdainfully repulsed his shy advances.

On Sunday afternoon he would go off with a few comrades to Lincoln Park where the undying memory of Buddy Bolden was perpetuated by the ragtime bands. They were beginning to talk about a new trumpeter who could rival Emmanuel Perez, Bunk Johnson, and Freddie Keppard. He was a giant Negro with tremendous biceps, and one of his eyelids had been slashed in some battle royal. They called him Bad-Eye Oliver. It was at Lincoln Park that Louis heard him for the first time. He was thrilled to the core by the fellow's playing. Joe Oliver had recaptured Buddy Bolden's power, but he kept it under control. He played the current ragtime tunes: *High Society, Twelfth Street Rag, Panama, Clarinet Marmalade, Tiger Rag*—a new form of witchcraft to which Louis succumbed without a struggle. Joe Oliver had a novel way of interpreting a musical phrase: he improvised in the manner of Buddy Bolden but climbed the scale and held certain high notes for an incredibly long time, or repeated the same note several times. Louis realized that this utterance of prolonged sounds appealed strongly to the hearts of the blacks, who went wild with joy and swayed to the beat of the music, drunk with melody and noise. But Louis himself had not touched a musical instrument for a year and a half.

The family was now in easier circumstances, each member being a breadwinner. May Ann could improve their menu, giving them fried chicken once or twice a week, and Louis was able to keep some pocket money for buying a few drinks with his friends before bedtime. Usually he met them in Liberty at Matranga's, where they formed part of a group that frequented the honky-tonk kept by the good-natured Italian.

So long as the fading day afforded enough light to see in the empty lots, the boys would kneel in a ring and roll dice. They played craps with the same enthusiastic abandon that Negroes devote to all their pastimes. Louis would shake the dice interminably.

"Fade me for a dime!"

One of the gang would oblige; and Louis would throw the cubes, roll his eyes imploringly, and beg Lady Luck to bring up a "natural." If seven or eleven rolled out, of course Louis was the winner; but a deuce, a trey, or a double six was disastrous. These last were dubbed "snake eyes," "little Joe," and "boxcars," respectively. Howls of joy or disgust would rend the evening air and reach the barred windows of the Parish Prison.

When the deepening dusk made the dice invisible, the blacks went inside Matranga's. They would stop before the bar and drink a glass of beer before penetrating to a small inner room. In this room—which the habitués called the "cotchroom"— gambling went on. Beyond it there was a place to dance, and her a piano player, a trumpeter, and a drummer tried to entice the couples who could not afford the superior delights of Funky Butt. The music they rendered, vulgar and inept, could not be compared with the playing of Bad-Eye Joe. But, so far as Louis was concerned, it was still music. It touched off a feeling of sadness or of regret. His fists would vigorously rattle the dice and he would try to forget and submit himself to the universal law of his race.

One evening as he set out in search of adventure, he reflected on the framework of the society which held him in such frightful slavery. He thought about the stepping-stone from the life in Jane Alley up to Perdido by way of the Waifs' Home. Beyond Canal Street was the promised land that the whites guarded so jealously. On the outskirts of Perdido there was the quarter reserved for the black prostitutes. On the other side of Canal, organized vice took on glamour and power. Here he was dazzled by unfamiliar sights. He passed the saloon owned by Tom Anderson, king of the Tenderloin—

the District. At each corner there was a saloon with its orchestra, where the women, the pimps, and the white-slavers would meet. These resorts always harbored some human wreck, wasted by drink or disease, who ran errands for the harlots; though even this lowliest of all trades was denied to the blacks. A customer would enter the den of one of the Madams, and she would shout: "Joe, bring us two Tom-and-Jerries!" And the poor devil would rush to the barroom for the drinks, on which he got a commission.

At the head of Basin Street a riot of music created a lively atmosphere. Through an open door came the melancholy tinkling of a piano. Louis immediately recognized Jelly Roll's voice, singing a blues song. A little farther on a trumpet—doubtless Joe Oliver's was screeching ragtime. Around the corner a singing trio howled in unison, encouraged by the applause of the customers.

Near the saloon in Franklin Street, Louis was hailed by a policeman.

"What are you doing here, black boy?"

"I'se goin' home."

"Where?"

"At Perdido and Liberty."

"Good enough—but you didn't lose anything around here, so beat it."

Louis pushed on toward Perdido. It had started to rain and he walked a little faster, breathing the delicate fragrance which rises from the warm earth after a Spring shower.

He did not notice a fight that was breaking out near the Parish Prison. Louis felt crushed by the misfortunes of his race. What could he do to cross that insuperable barrier? By what means could he break into the enchanted circle? Though Joe Oliver and Jelly Roll Morton and a few others were admitted into the inner sanctum, they were barely tolerated.

[79]

Horn of Plenty

Would the time ever come when there would be but a single aristocracy, that of intelligence and of genius? What inspired Negro would definitely cross the infernal line and lead the way for his race along the road to freedom? Louis Armstrong burst into mocking laughter. His reason told him that the time was not ripe—perhaps after a few more centuries of suffering ...

Besides, why should a poor mule driver rack his brain about such things? As he pushed open the gate at home, he decided that it would take a wiser head than his to do the job, and his ears rang with the cry which identified him with the pariahs of his race.

"Go on, mule! Stove coal, lady, five cents a waterbucket!"

8

LOUIS BECAME an excellent driver, serious, punctual, and so willing that his boss preferred him to the others; and his stepfather congratulated himself on having brought Louis into the group. May Ann was pleased, too, and sang the praises of her big boy to all and sundry.

The family's finances had improved a little. Mama Lucy had changed jobs and was now working for a wealthy family on St. Charles Avenue for more money. The Sunday noon-time meal was invariably enhanced by the traditional fried chicken. Mama Lucy, who had been baptized in Mount Zion Church, said grace and they all sat down to an appetizing meal. May Ann, in her wisdom, found such simple pleasures sufficient to ease her hard lot. Sometimes she would say: "Louis, we had a hard time making you toe the line. A little more rope and you'd of hanged yo'self."

One morning a driving rainfall prevented Louis and his stepfather from leaving the house for work. The rain beat fiercely against the weatherboards and a curtain of water overhung the porch. Louis went out on the gallery and looked up at the leaden sky; he thought that the sun would come out later so that he could go to work; he was bored to death for want of something to do. In the rear of the yard, clumsy fingers were strumming a mournful banjo. Louis listened and leaned against the wall thinking of Bad-Eye Joe. From some recess in his memory an explosive melody burst forth, one that he had heard one night in the district—ragtime, the bewitching music created by those who could not read: the fakers, as they were called in New Orleans.

In the afternoon the rain abated slightly and Louis slipped out to Gaspar's grocery store. None of the drivers had worked that morning. Some who lived in the vicinity had come for lunch through force of habit and stood munching a poor-boy sandwich. Others were shooting craps at the bar. Louis joined them, made a few passes, won several dollars, and started to leave for the coal yard. But the rain beat down harder than ever and in the empty lot the dripping China-ball tree bowed to the fury of the wind; its blue flowers were withered, but the pervading moisture brought out the tender green of its foliage.

About four o'clock Louis ran to the nearest corner as far as Matranga's. Henry, the owner, officiated behind the bar. A sprinkling of whisky-drinking pimps were talking about the war and the condition of their business. The rattle of dice could be heard on the "cotchroom's" table. Clark Wade, who was known to the blacks of Perdido as a "broker" rather than a pimp, was talking loudly. For the last few days he had been flashing a huge diamond. Now he was smoking cigarettes daintily, crooking his little finger. He said to Louis: "How about a Tom-and-Jerry, old Dipper?"

"All right, Gate."

Clark Wade had not even offered his hand. He felt he belonged to a higher social category than that of his old schoolfellow.

The two fell to discussing ragtime. One of Clark's women had told him that Professor Jelly Roll was unquestionably the best pianist alive. Another pimp with a striking tie brought up Buddy Bolden and Emmanuel Perez. All began to sing the theme song of Funky Butt Hall. A mellow mood was settling on the gathering. From time to time Clark Wade would stroll out for a quick check on the activities of his crew and drift back to the bar; for every new visitor to Josie's he made a cross on his pad—at which the others roared with laughter. He raised his voice defensively. "That's right—split your sides. I gotta protect myself. When I count the chips, they better check even with my book."

Louis went on into the "cotchroom" and began to play and drink. He found a place among the crap shooters, who were all intently watching the roll of the dice. Two or three had lost their last penny and went off cursing their bad luck, but their places were quickly filled by others. This was Louis's lucky day.

"Seven . . . another seven."

"Yo' sho' is lucky, Dipper!"

"I ain't lucky—that's my natural style!"

Louis kissed the dice, rattled them, and called coaxingly as he threw them out:

"Yeah, dice, don't fail lil' Satchmo'!"

Shouts of delight and groans of despair would greet another seven on the first throw, and Louis's pockets were soon bulging with bills.

Then Nutsie came in, her head sheathed in a pink hood. The rowdies at the bar stirred and whistled admiringly. Clark Wade, as he showed her his flashy diamond ring, thought what a wonderful recruit she would be for his seraglio; and Louis, flushed with his winnings, made a gesture toward her.

"You know that black bitch?" one of the crap shooters asked him. "She don't want no mo' children to mind—she wants to play with the big boys!"

At the general mirth that this provoked, Louis flung down the dice, left the ring of players, and went over to Nutsie.

"How 'bout a shot of devil's brew?" he demanded.

"Sure. You got too much money?"

"Enough to make yo' eyes go dreamy."

"What you doin' for a livin'?" asked Nutsie.

"I works for the coal company."

"Ha, ha! What good is a man that gets up in the mornin' when I go to bed?" As she spoke, she looked toward the group of young bucks and noticed that they all addressed Clark Wade with obvious respect. Pointing at Clark, she went on: "*There's* a guy that knows the ropes." She yawned, and Louis thought he would like to close her lips with a hard kiss.

"We ain't made for your sort," Nutsie explained, not unkindly. "We belong to the tough guys and the dancers and the musicians."

"Well, I ain't in that class," he replied. "But I'm a hard worker, an' I kin support my wife so she won't have to work on her back. I makes a dollar a day. Let's get hooked up!"

To this, Nutsie made no answer, only telling him that she was bound for Rampart Street.

"I have to go to work, Louis. Come with me as far as the Eagle Saloon." And she took his hand in hers as they started for the door.

Out in the street the rain had stopped and the night was quite dark. But they saw lights breaking out near the Parish Prison. A distant cornet was blowing chords. The barber was closing his shop. A bootblack trudged homeward with his box. At the corner of Rampart, Louis kissed Nutsie and followed her with his eyes as she walked off, making eyes at the men she passed.

Louis was not quite sixteen years old and, if he had lost his

heart, he still had an appetite. He went into Segretta's grocery
and ordered a sandwich. By now it was about eight o'clock in
the evening, and he told himself that he ought to go home and
sleep so as to be fit the next morning at daybreak, since the
drivers were going to have double work. The windows in
Funky Butt Hall were lighting up, but their old attraction for
him was gone; he had no interest in music now. Nutsie had
said: A tough guy, or a dancer, or a musician. The little hussy
was making fun of him. Louis was nothing but a poor driver
with hands calloused from the pull of the reins and the weight
of pail and sack.

He walked along quietly, listening to his footfalls on the soft
earth. From Rampart Street came the sound of a band. For
a moment he was tempted to turn toward it—surely he would
see Nutsie there. But he shrugged his shoulders and continued
toward Liberty. As he passed Matranga's the door swung open
and Clark Wade came out. Little did Louis suspect that this
door was opening to admit him to a new life.

Wade, recognizing him, called out: "Where you goin',
Satchmo'?"

"To bed. I gotta get up at five o'clock tomorrow mornin'."

Wade grinned, flashing a row of white teeth in the shadows.
"You ain't goin' to bed with the chickens? Treat me to an
Old Tom-and-Jerry."

Louis had already reached Liberty Street. He had but to
take one step or say one word, and he would be rid of the im-
portunate Wade. But he feared that Wade would make fun
of him, so he nodded and joined the other, angry with himself
for having yielded. How much more sensible to have gone
home to bed!

After the Old Tom-and-Jerry, the two had a Bourbon each;
after the Bourbon they drank a rum-toddy, then another Old

[85]

Tom. By this time life seemed beautiful to Louis. The mirrors lining the walls glittered with gay reflections. He had given up all idea of going home. As eight-thirty rang, the pianist Boogers, and the drummer, Sonny Gaby, entered the saloon, showing Louis that the music was soon to begin.

Henry Matranga was waiting behind the bar "Where's Bunk Johnson?" he inquired.

"He can't come tonight. He's sick."

"The devil with his sickness! It's the same story every week, and I'm tired of it. My dance will be a flop without a trumpet player. Why, we might as well close down."

"You don't have a trumpet player? That's a shame. You'll make us go to Funky Butt," cut in Clark Wade. "Why don't you put somebody else in that fool's place?"

"Who, for instance?"

"Why not Satchmo'?"

Louis, guessing that they were poking fun at him, grinned diffidently. "Go on, Gate!" he protested. "That's a hot one. I ain't touched a cornet for the last two years. I'll have lips like a toilet bowl."

"Well, it's not a bad idea," observed Henry Matranga, swallowing a glassful of gin at one gulp "Weren't you band leader back of Jones? You blew a hot trumpet in the parades. Isn't that so?"

"I didn't play no trumpet. I played the cornet."

Clark Wade was insistent. "Henry, don't you let this chance slip by. He's just the man for you."

Matranga touched a match to his cigar, drank another glass of gin, and gestured the others into silence.

"All right. Here's my proposition—take it or leave it. Satchmo' will take over and start playing right now."

Louis was uncertain whether he should laugh it off or take

it seriously. He could not grasp the possibility that this was the golden opportunity he had been coveting for the past two years.

"I ain't got no cornet," he objected feebly.

"That's all right," Matranga told him. "If you're willing to get me out of this jam, I'll go with you right now to Jack Fink's. I'll buy you a cornet and it'll belong to you after two months if you don't miss a single night."

Clark Wade nodded in agreement and said: "It looks like a square deal. If Satchmo' accepts, I'll buy a round of drinks."

"What do you say, yes or no?" asked Matranga impatiently.

"I'll take it," Louis whispered.

Matranga was already filling the glasses and everybody drank a toast to the new cornetist. The boss told one of his bartenders to watch the shop, took a roll of bills from the cash drawer and left with Louis.

The night was entirely clear now, and a soft, warm breeze blew through the streets. The fat woman who lived next door to the barber's was enjoying her cigar. As they passed a dark corner, Louis felt a tug on his sleeve and heard a woman whisper throatily: "Come on, baby."

Louis turned quickly. It was Nutsie. On recognizing him she added a laugh to her invitation. But Matranga did not pause and Louis followed him without hesitation, thrusting off Nutsie with a vague gesture. At Rampart they turned to the left. The show-windows were still bright with lights. The barbers worked on under the flood of their ceiling lamps. Louis and Matranga crossed the street and stopped before a pawn-shop. Matranga halted before the window and pointed with his thumb against the glass. Louis saw a cornet lying between an accordion and a leather suitcase. His eyes lit up.

"How do you like it, Satchmo'?"

"It's real fine, Mr. Matranga."

They entered the shop. Behind the counter stood Budd
Bolden's former player, Bob Lyons, of double-bass fame.

"How much is the instrument in the window?" Matrang
asked casually.

"Which one, the accordion?"

"No, the cornet."

"That costs eighteen dollars."

Matranga flew into a rage. "Eighteen dollars for that piec
of junk? You're crazy!"

Louis was on pins and needles. What if all his good luc
ended before it had really begun? He told himself he woul
not go back to Matranga's—he would be ashamed to face Clar
Wade.

"I'll give you twelve bucks," Matranga offered truculently

The owner came out from a rear room to say, "Impossible!"

"Let's go, my boy," Matranga told Louis, and they turne
to the door.

The owner cried: "My last price—fifteen dollars! And I'r
losing money on it."

"It's a deal," said Matranga.

They picked their way among the trunks, the suits, th
sewing machines. Louis could not believe that it was reall
happening. He watched Matranga peel off fifteen dollar-bill
one at a time, saw Bob Lyons open the show-window, catc
up the cornet on the end of a pole—and hand it to Louis him
self. Louis wanted to try it right there and then, but Matrang
was in a hurry. Once they were outside, Louis lagged one ste
behind Matranga and in the dark kissed his new cornet.

When they got back to the saloon Boogers and Sonny Gab
were already busy playing. A few couples turned on the floo
Louis would have liked to dance and play at the same time

He sat next to the ancient piano and, dazed with happiness, tried in subdued notes to catch the piano's rhythm. At the end of ten minutes Louis Armstrong's lips were sore. He strained harder than ever, and hit so many false notes that even Clark Wade shuddered.

By midnight Louis felt in his heart that he had failed miserably. His mother was right. You can't chase two rabbits at the same time. He had better resign himself to driving his coal wagon. . . . Then he decided to start singing. He knew by heart the bawdy stanzas that were popular in all the dives of Perdido, and his warm and true voice offset to some extent the bad impression his playing had created.

At the end of the evening when he stopped before the cash drawer, Matranga paid off Boogers and Sonny Gaby and waited a few seconds for the pianist and the drummer to disappear.

"Here," said the boss, "fifty cents is plenty for your night's work, and you're lucky to get that much. If you hadn't sung the ragtime and the blues, I'd fire you. You play the cornet the way my aunt sneezes!"

Louis took the money, thanked Matranga, and went off with a heavy heart.

When he reached home everybody was asleep. He woke up his mother and sister, and showed them his cornet.

"Look—Matranga hired me and I played all night."

"How much did yo' get?" asked Mama Lucy, struggling to keep her sleepy eyes open.

Louis opened his hand and exhibited five silver dimes. May Ann and her daughter screamed with laughter.

"Half a buck! Are you crazy? Louis boy, you ain't got a bit o' sense. You'd do better sellin' papers for the rest of yo' life instead of tryin' to blow that thing."

"Fifty cents," said Mama Lucy, still laughing scornfully. "Throw that thing out the window and never leave that mule o' yourn."

And Louis Armstrong fell asleep with the thought that his mother and sister had spoken words of wisdom.

9

THE NEXT day Louis left with a light heart for his work.
When noon came—the time when all the wagons gathered
before Segretta's or Gaspar's—he reined in his mule at Liberty.
He took the steps two at a time and found himself alone in his
room. He ran to his cornet, sat down on the bed, and began
to practise running up and down the scale. He was trying to
recapture the classic touch that Peter Davis had taught him.
For almost an hour he blew without respite: then he hastily
grabbed up a crust of bread and left for his route with what
was left of his coal. And during the following week none of
the coal venders saw Louis during the lunch hour.

That evening he went back to Matranga's and slowly he
grew accustomed to the orchestra's routine. He tried to cut
his cornet playing by singing the blues more often. Gradually
he got back into practise. His lips ached no longer, and if the
applause for his playing was not exactly deafening, he succeeded in drawing some of the wenches and the rowdies from
Funky Butt to hear the new cornetist sing the ribald popular
songs of the day. Presently he got a raise to a dollar and a
quarter a night. And he earned it, for he worked until one
o'clock every weekday, and on Saturday until four o'clock in
the morning.

Horn of Plenty:

On his very first Saturday, as he was desperately pushing on the pistons, he saw Nutsie come in. At first she took no notice of him, but stood at the bar talking with another girl who was drinking and smoking. Suddenly her head turned toward the orchestra and she looked steadfastly at Louis. What was she thinking of? She drained her glass and, pointing to Louis—who was standing beside the piano—declared in a loud voice that there stood her man.

Immediately Louis launched into the blues, and the toughs and harlots in the audience swore they had never heard such a deep and vibrant voice. Nutsie was especially enthusiastic; she sent Louis a glass of whisky, and during the intermission she hugged and kissed him. Louis could not believe that his dream of happiness was coming true. Matranga called him and congratulated him warmly.

"Keep it up, Dipper, everything is fine. The customers are happy. In a week you'll be whipping the best of them."

That evening Louis blew as he never had before. He tried *Tiger Rag*, and the band followed him at full blast. Louis remembered Buddy Bolden and Emmanuel Perez and particularly Picou, who was the first to improvise the piece on the clarinet. The connoisseurs standing before the bar swayed to the rhythm, wild with joy.

"Give it to the Creoles!" Clark Wade shouted.

His suggestion needs explaining. The section on the uptown side of Canal comprising Perdido and Liberty was in those days called the Battlefield, so frequent were its fights and killings. Here were to be heard the savage and explosive rhythms of Negro music. Below the Vieux Carré—stronghold of classical music—and below the Tenderloin or red-light district, lay the Creole zone, called "downtown." And the old

French tradition of the Creoles made them the violent opponents of the "Battlefield" type of music.

One Saturday night a throng of women swarmed at the bar. Louis frowned questioningly. "What's that?" he asked "A female regiment?"

Without interrupting his beat, the drummer explained: "Them's the ladies from the District. The Law clamps 'em shut at one o'clock on Sunday, an' they takes their last fling out here on the Battlefield."

Louis watched them with curiosity as they shrilled loudly, swapped cigarettes, and drank gin. The pimps hung together and never missed the rounds that the women paid for, digging into their stockings for the money. It was a rare sight to behold, these strumpets, each dancing with her "Sweet Man," her stockings bulging with a roll of bills. Between dances they would try to outdo one another in their display of liberality to the musicians, thrusting bills and clamoring for their favorite tunes.

Louis recognized an old acquaintance, Alberta, who was very tipsy. A former lover of hers, Joe Bright-Eyes, was standing at the bar and had not given her even a passing glance. To show her disdain, she was buying drink after drink for the orchestra and kissing every black partner who danced with her. Drawing near Louis, she hailed him and coyly stopped the mouth of his cornet with her hand.

"You played divinely, Dipper!" she told him, "I just gotta kiss you."

And her painted lips deposited a resounding smack on Louis's cheek. He was somewhat taken aback, since ordinarily he kept to himself in some corner, observing and saying nothing. Yet he realized that this sudden and unexpected wave of popularity placed the seal of approval on his musicianship.

Alberta had returned to the dance-floor, and now Nutsie was pulling on Louis's sleeve.

"What right has that black bitch got to kiss you? You don't love me no more?"

Louis had recovered his cornet and was playing *Swanee River*. Nutsie looking up at him adoringly. Just then another woman approached Louis with a tumbler of gin and said: "Here you are, Dipper—blow it out, boy, blow it out."

As the plaintive melody drew to a close, Nutsie whispered in Louis's ear:

"I'll be waitin' after the dance, you know, upstairs by Gaspar's store."

Meantime, Alberta had saunterd uncertainly up to the bar, brushing against her sometime lover, who gave a marvelous exhibition of freezing contempt. She persisted, provoking him with meaningful glances and an occasional pat on calves that were thick with bills. On all sides, men and women swayed and stamped their feet, caught in the ragtime's rhythm. Through the thick bluish haze, black faces glowed indistinctly.

Suddenly the group at the bar shivered with emotion as Louis began to sing *Are You From Dixie?*, stressing the melody with compelling movements of his head. He saw Mary Jack the Bear make a grand entrance. The Queen of the Battlefield, now crowding forty, was at the height of her notoriety as undisputed champion of the Tenderloin prostitutes.

All eyes followed her as she swept regally through the crowd, calling the women by their first names and joking with the men, until she was face to face with Alberta. The two women looked daggers at each other, and offered at the same time to buy a round of drinks. Then Alberta said:

"Ain't nothin' tougher than a old hide, an' they ain't nothin' better than a tender beafsteak."

The mob howled with laughter. Mary Jack the Bear, her supremacy at stake, shouted angrily:

"I knows young sluts that only sleeps with po' white trash, while some old gals coins money at Lulu White's on Basin Street."

The taunt made Mary livid with anger. She drew away from Alberta's lover, slowly raised her skirts, tapped her bulging thigh, and screamed:

"Till yo' dirty hide gits you what I got here, you better keep that big mouth shut!"

Matranga, from behind the bar, tried to calm them, but Clark Wade poured oil on the fire:

"Come on, gals, let's have a show-down."

A momentary hush had fallen on the onlookers, broken by Mary's voice as she hurled a final insult, drowning out the melancholy melody of the blues:

"I ain't too old to take yo' man away from you, you low trash!"

Alberta stiffened as though paralyzed. Quickly her hand found her garter and out flashed the inevitable razor. The bolder spectators instantly formed a circle, so as to give the two adversaries plenty of room. When Mary pushed Joe away he did not seem to mind but wore a look of fatuous vanity: he was the prize of a battle that two famous women were about to wage. A second razor flashed out—Mary's; and she swung the blade wide open, ready for action. The noise and the tumult had attracted several customers who ran from the bar to investigate. Matranga made a vain effort to separate the bloodthirsty wenches, but it was too late. The women now faced each other in the center of the floor, and the crowd watched

[95]

expectantly as they sparred cautiously, each trying to outflank the other, just like two game cocks before the death blow.

Under the crush of the mob, the band had ceased playing. Matranga reappeared, and his right hand clutched a black-jack as he pressed through the crowd and reached the platform.

"Let's go, boys! Keep right on playing. We don't want the police to look in."

Boogers broke into a classic blues, then Louis stood on the edge of the platform and began to sing. The words poured out clear and loud in the silence of the hall as the fascinated spectators watched the skillful skirmishing of the razor wielders.

A muffled roar came from the crowd as Louis reached the end of the first chorus—Alberta had dealt Mary a deep slash on the shoulder and drawn first blood.

"Don't stop playing, boys! Hit it up!" exhorted Matranga, as he leaped from the platform into the arena and brandished his club at the panting fighters.

"Get the hell out of here, you black bitches! Go slit your throats somewhere else, alligator bait."

Louis took up the second chorus, improvising as he used to do with the quartet.

"And now we have Satchmo' Louis Armstrong doing the second chorus. Hit it, Boogers."

Mary had not waited long for her revenge. She feinted and found an opening as Alberta dropped her guard for an instant to be rewarded by a deep gash on the cheek. Blood splattered over her dress, and both women began a slow retreat toward the door as Matranga swung his club menacingly, forcing them back to the bar. They were breathing heavily, bathed in mingled blood and sweat, their dresses in shreds, but still with razors outstretched. Matranga's colorful invectives somewhat elieved the tension of the spectators, many of whom were rinning widely at his language. Now and again he would turn o the band and shout encouragement:

"Keep playing, boys. Don't stop!"

Louis had finished the blues and picked up the first stanza nce more. In the lurid semidarkness of the hall he felt Nutsie's and clasp his own and press it.

Matranga had finally succeeded in maneuvering the opponnts into the street. But his customers, having tasted blood, low thronged the sidewalk to watch the outcome of the truggle. A wave of curiosity swept over Nutsie and she lropped Louis's hand to join the crowd on Perdido, guided y the fierce howling which rose and fell with the intensity f the battle.

At last the orchestra could take a breath and Matranga leaved a sigh of relief. He had had a narrow escape. One false nove, and he would have had a free-for-all on his hands. He huddered as he thought of his place reduced to a shambles y such a battle royal. Grateful for the band's help, he ordered round of Old Tom-and-Jerry for all the musicians.

A half-hour later Nutsie came back, looking as if she had een a ghost. She paid no attention to a drunken man who was lumped against the bar, dead to the world.

"Alberta just got Mary!"

And she gasped out the tragic story. The battle had moved out into the night as far as the corner of Gravier and Franklin. At this spot, after an exhausting struggle, Alberta's youth had decided the issue. Her razor had bitten into Mary Jack the Bear's throat, and the death-rattle had sent the more squeamish element scurrying away while some of the others carried Mary off to Charity Hospital.

Matranga asked what had happened to Willy.

[97]

Nutsie replied that he had gone off with Alberta, as was fair and just. They had fought over him, hadn't they, and now he belonged to the winner. That was as it should be.

Only a few stragglers remained in the saloon. The night was warm, and Matranga suddenly felt very tired. He had weathered the storm, thank God and the band, and it was best to close up. Louis carefully wrapped his cornet in the lined sack which his sister had sewed for him. He went to the cashier and was paid off. It had been a pretty good night, after all; counting tips he had earned five dollars and fifty cents.

Nutsie was waiting, and her eyes spoke volumes. He took her arm and they walked down Perdido, occasionally meeting other late couples. The sky was gay with starlight, and Louis' heart was overflowing with exquisite happiness. Nutsie' warm palm snuggled confidently against his rough fist. As they passed the church, Louis crossed himself.

"I gotta get up real early to-morrow, an' I'll thank the Lord for all the good things He give me."

"Includin' little me?" asked Nutsie.

"Shucks, gal, I means my trumpet!"

Even at this early stage of his career, Louis's heart knew only one true love—a consuming, diabolical passion for this new music which coursed through his veins like fiery liquor and was destined to set the irrevocable pattern of his life.

IO

LOUIS HAD become the idol of the Battlefield. Each evening when he appeared with his cornet tucked under his arm, he was greeted warmly by the habitués. He now enjoyed a guarantee of one dollar and a quarter an evening, and, with the tips, he felt quite happy about his earnings. Thanks to daily playing, his mouthpiece gave him no trouble at all and he could hit dizzily high notes with ease.

He had definitely forsaken the coal-wagon and the mule, and his self-respect had grown immeasurably with the change of occupation. The very first time he was able to spare some money, he bought a handsome derby hat and a white shirt with wing collar. All day long, with the same bulldog tenacity that Peter Davis had discovered in him at the Waifs' Home, he practiced the scale, developed new arrangements, and tried to read various scores. He was burning with an exciting fever. Ragtime had become the focal point of his life. He breathed ragtime, ate and drank ragtime, and was always trying to improvise on the popular songs then current in New Orleans. Untiringly he searched for new musical themes; one of these arrangements was later known as *Dippermouth*, or *Sister Kate*.

Louis and Nutsie were in love. Often now he climbed the stairs that led to her room above Gaspar's grocery store. One day he got up almost at midday—he was a late riser, like all musicians—and went to see Nutsie, who was radiantly happy to receive the homage of Perdido's current idol. This time she had just gone out to buy some liquor. As she came back into her room she was humming gay snatches of song, and was about to uncork the bottle when a strange din rose from the street. Louis opened the window and saw at the corner of Rampart and Perdido, in the center of a motley crowd, two publicity bands parading through the streets on trucks and preparing to stage a contest.

Such affairs were common in New Orleans at this period. The two rival orchestras of the moment were those of Emmanuel Perez and Bob Lyons, who had met by chance and decided to settle their old scores. The Perez band had stopped their horses and truck in Perdido, while Bob Lyons and his musicians were perched on their wagon in Rampart; each truck holding five players. There were neither piano nor traps. The trombone players sat on the back of their respective wagons, legs hanging, so as to have plenty of elbow-room when poking full slides in the direction of the spectators. Hence they were called "Tailgate" players, and the rather primitive style of accompanying thus adopted was to be continued by others under this name. The customary procedure was for each orchestra to take a turn at playing a tune, and the reaction of the crowd determined the winner. This musical bout was long and closely fought.

All this time, Louis Armstrong did not leave the window, though Nutsie impatiently called him three or four times to take his drink. But Louis was too wrapped up in the music below to hear her invitation, and did not even answer.

The colorful spectacle of the street fascinated both his eyes and his ears. Louis saw Bob Lyons in a rhythmic rapture lashing the bull-fiddle with frantic fingers. At least half an hour had gone by since the wagon wheels had been hooked fast, and the crowd's enthusiasm had never flagged. Sweet Child waved to him from the opposite sidewalk, inviting him to come down. Clark Wade and Black Benny were hotly arguing the merits of the bands. *High Society, Panama, Twelfth Street Rag,* and finally *Tiger Rag* climaxed the musical contest. The throng was divided in its applause, however, and it was impossible to judge the winner. The hooks were unfastened on both trucks and they started off in opposite directions. This was the decisive moment when the entire crowd became judge and jury of the performance. Sometimes there was a clear-cut victory, as had happened in the celebrated duel between Joe Oliver and Keppard, when the crowd had been so worked up that they followed Joe's truck as one man and on the spot crowned him: King Oliver! But more often each band retained its loyal followers, who would follow it away from the scene of contest, carrying the players' coats. Such was the outcome of the present match. Emmanuel Perez' truck went off toward Matranga's, followed by a horde of tipsy women. The trombone player still poked into space, encouraged by the shouts of the rooters, all wildly hopping about and acclaiming their favorite.

Not once had Louis taken his eyes away from the picturesque scene beneath, and he did not hear Nutsie as she called him again, her voice thick with anger and gin. Her eyes wore an injured look as she began to hurl insults at Louis. He turned on her sharply and soon they were hurling bitter reproaches at each other. Louis grabbed his hat and made for the door, announcing that he wanted to get a closer view of Emmanuel Perez, now halted in front of Funky Butt. Agile as a cat, Nutsie had barred the entrance, spitting out vile words. Louis seized the door knob, shoved her aside, and—as he was pulling the door shut—felt a searing pain in his left shoulder. He reeled back, and Nutsie screamed as she dropped the knife and threw herself on him with sobs of remorse. But he shook her off and managed to stagger home.

That evening Louis did not play, although Matranga had come twice to plead with him to make an effort.

"Without you, Louis, my band's no good. You're the whole show!"

But Louis felt weak from loss of blood, though his wound was not serious, and he decided to obey the doctor who had left strict orders for him to remain in bed at least twenty-four hours.

One Saturday, Louis was blowing his cornet with truly explosive force. The strumpets from Storyville were already in evidence with their lovers when a flurry passed over the audience. All heads turned toward the door, which on this warm summer night was standing wide open. A huge man had just walked in and Louis could not quite make out who it was. Then admiring murmurs rose from the gathering:

"It's King Oliver, Pete Lala's trumpet man!"

Flattered by the visit of such a notable, Matranga was quick to proffer a tumbler of gin, which King Oliver graciously accepted. Leaning nonchalantly against the bar, he surveyed the women, who smiled coquettishly and admired his tuxedo and black tie. As soon as he had finished his drink, he went up to the orchestra and spoke to Louis:

"Swell, Dipper! They told me you was good and I just had to hear you. What you got, boy, brass lips?"

Louis was overjoyed. Oliver's words were a revelation, and he realized at that moment what a long road he had traveled since his mule-driving days. Those barely a year ago—and now the King of Ragtime had come out of his way especially to hear and congratulate him.

At intermission, Louis joined King Oliver for a drink. The

rowdies and the pimps looked on from a respectable distance and exchanged opinions on their talent.

"O' course, King's the head man," said Black Barney, "but Satchmo' is doggone good."

"An' can he sing? Oh, boy!" emphasized Clark Wade.

A clamor suddenly filled the hall, as the crowd began to chant in unison:

"*King Oliver! King Oliver! King Oliver!*"

But the star did not give in readily. His scarred eyelid fluttered with pride as he looked quizzically at the audience. He knew he was supreme and felt that a little suspense would not detract one whit from his glory.

The clamor grew in intensity as the frenzied crowd clapped with all their might and shouted: "We want Joe!" When the excitement had reached its proper pitch, the King strolled deliberately over to the platform, then leaped up to it at one bound. The feminine element screamed with delight. King Oliver held a short discussion with Boogers and launched into *Panama*. Louis had drawn near, anxious not to miss a note. With eyes and mouth wide open, he listened to his idol's playing and would willingly have knelt in adoration.

The throng swayed happily. Intoxicated couples danced crazily, exaggerating each step as their fancy dictated. The onlookers clapped their hands rhythmically. At the bar, the pimps twisted their diamond rings to catch the light and exchanged curt remarks on the quality of the playing and the dancing.

Seized by an impulse, Louis joined the players and, while Joe Oliver continued to blow the blues on his instrument, Louis sang and improvised to the greater delight of the audience.

When Joe Oliver finally left the hall, he told himself that this young cornetist was a musician who would bear watching. Soon he was a regular spectator on Saturday nights, sometimes performing with Matranga's small orchestra; and he never failed to express his admiration for his youthful colleague.

One evening, King noticed that Louis Armstrong looked unhappy. At intermission, he carried him off to a relatively quiet corner.

"What's bitin' you, Dipper?"

"Nothin', King."

"Quit stallin'. Somethin' I done?"

"Nosirree!" Louis rejoined quickly. "You're on the up an' up. They don't come no better."

"So what?"

"So nothin'. I got my troubles."

"Come on, maybe I can help."

"No, Joe, it's plumb hopeless. Las' year I was makin' a buck a day. Now I'm doin' twice as good, an' that's my limit. Yo' know, I wants to marry Irene, but she's pretty sick, Joe."

"Who's Irene?"

"A lil' gal they calls Nutsie in the Battlefield."

"You need some parsley—ain't that right?"

"I ain't askin'."

They stopped talking. The evening was drawing to a close. Couples were drifting off slowly and Matranga was counting the night's receipts. King Oliver squeezed Louis's arm and looked him straight in the eyes:

"Listen, Dipper, friends ain't jus' broomsticks. People has feelin's. Next week, I'm leavin' for Mobile. Be gone three days. Somebody's got to take my place at Pete Lala's. You know it pays good—plenty times you gets five-dollar tips. I'll fix it so's you'll get in."

Louis Armstrong could not believe that here at last was the long-awaited chance to cross the intangible line of Canal

Street. The tinseled splendor of the Tenderloin would now be his to see and enjoy. He glowed with pride. He grasped King Oliver's hand and thanked him with tears in his eyes.

Arm in arm they sauntered over to the bar. The last group of drinkers was on its way out. The sound of a noisy dispute at the door shattered the quiet. Matranga's bouncer, a brawny, square-shouldered man called Slippers, was trying to prevent two tipsy roustabouts from entering.

"Too late, I tell you; the place is closed."

Slippers was doing his best to keep his temper, despite the uncomplimentary language of which he was the object. The unbidden guests were pushing on the door and Slippers managed to shut it for a moment in their face. Meanwhile, Louis and King Oliver were sipping a last gin.

A violent push rattled the door and left it ajar. Louis caught sight of a hairy fist flourishing a revolver which began to fire at random. The two cornetists lost no time in vaulting behind the counter. Slippers had ducked behind the pianola, and Louis saw him draw his .38, a deadly weapon at such close quarters. Suddenly, the door was wide open and the intruders stood peering drunkenly inside. Louis watched Slippers apply a very slight pressure on the trigger from behind the pianola. Then came a series of ear-splitting reports. Matranga was quaking in his refuge under the sink. Suddenly all was quiet, and they heard the bouncer's voice state with calm finality:

"All right! You all can come out now!"

Joe Oliver, Louis, and Matranga emerged slowly from their hiding places. Slippers' gun was still smoking in his hand. On the threshold, two roustabouts lay grotesquely sprawled in death.

"Let's get out of here," Joe told Louis, "before they run us in fo' witness." So the two cornetists stepped gingerly over the corpses and hurried home.

Horn of Plenty:

On the following Monday, Louis was up betimes. He quickly dispatched a lunch of red beans and rice and made ready for Pete Lala's rehearsal. Joe Oliver had left for Mobile and Louis had to prove himself a worthy substitute. The weather was mild and a gentle torpor had settled on the dwellers of Perdido. On the doorsteps, the blacks had only one topic of conversation—the double murder at Matranga's. Screaming headlines announced the crime in sensational style, and news of war in Europe seemed very remote and unimportant.

Louis left on foot, his cornet in its usual place under his arm. He was dressed in his finest, sporting the gaudy sweater he always wore at Matranga's.

He found Franklin Street practically deserted at this hour. The rehearsal was scheduled for five o'clock and it was only four-thirty. As Louis strolled along slowly, his right hand caressed the dollar bills in his pocket—the money he intended to give to Nutsie so she could see a doctor. He stopped before the famous cabaret. He passed brothels that advertised their white and colored inmates by means of posters on the housefronts which proclaimed to the world what might be expected within. The club at 325 Franklin announced the competent supervision of Miss Maud Hartman. Next door, Miss May Evans's crib promised all comers "Pretty Women, Wine, and Song." Across the way, once Grace Lloyd made it known that her establishment, which had recently burned down, was now completely renovated and refurnished. Louis gazed wonderingly at the entrance of the celebrated Countess Willie Piazza whose placard boasted that she had what were "without doubt the most handsome and intelligent octoroons in the United States."

A sandwich-man was parading the life-size picture of Mademoiselle Rita Walker, the Oriental danseuse, famous for her Salome dance and her $5,000 wardrobe which she casually discarded in the course of her performance, in order to permit of a deeper appreciation of her Oriental charms

Louis paused for a moment before Ranch 101, at No. 206, where twelve passionate and desirable white ladies awaited the gentlemen of the evening. Pete Lala's saloon stood at No. 135, and was one of the few cabarets advertising colored prostitutes.

Louis was fascinated by the lengthy description of the physical attractions and erotic refinements of Sofronia Carter, Maudy Taylor, Jessie Barney, Jane Pinarba, and several other "high yellows," all first-class entertainers.

The appearance of the bull-fiddler brought Louis back to reality. He entered the hallowed precincts and walked into the main hall. A man who was tacking down carpets asked abruptly:

"Who are you?"

"King Oliver sent me to take his place."

"Are you crazy? Never in that outfit. Maybe you think this is Congo Square, eh? Go ahead and rehearse, but at eight you'd better get into a black coat."

Louis rehearsed for half an hour and left immediately for Fink's store, where he found Bob Lyons and bought his first tuxedo. The five dollars he had saved for Nutsie were gone, but at seven sharp, proud as a peacock, he arrived at Liberty and Perdido to show himself off to his mother and sister. They were struck speechless at the sight of their own Louis arrayed in such splendor. And it was only three days later, thanks again to Joc Oliver's generosity, that Louis had enough money to send Irene to the hospital.

II

AS TIME went by, Louis began to cut quite a figure in the Battlefield. But this was far from satisfying him. What he really wanted was permanent employment in the District; only there could he hope to find the recognition and the pay that he aspired to. He had no love for the District, true; nor for the Battlefield itself. Only Perdido claimed his heart. But the Battlefield was a step upward, a step that might conceivably carry him nearer to the District.

Several times he asked Joe Oliver for a frank opinion of his playing, and was assured each time that it deserved to be heard in the District. But there was a condition to be met: Tom Anderson's consent must be obtained. For ten years now this powerful politician had exercised absolute rule over the District—or Storyville, or the Tenderloin. He owned a saloon in Rampart Street, in front of which a slab in the sidewalk spelled out his name—a slab that might have been seen as late as January 1944, though it has now disappeared under a layer of cement, and gasoline is now sold at the place instead of liquor. But it will be long before the name of Tom Anderson fades from the citizens' memories as a classic example of the unholy alliance between crime and politics in New Orleans.

This saloon was the gateway to the District, dominating its activities much as a custom house controls the entry to a port.

And it was to this place that Louis went, one blazing July afternoon in 1917, knowing that Joe Oliver had already told Anderson that he was coming.

Tom Anderson, clad in light alpaca trousers and open sport shirt and wearing a derby tilted low over his eyes, stood on his threshold talking with a bejewelled and frilly creature holding an elaborate fan. Louis waited bashfully for a moment, afraid to interrupt. Then he blurted out:

"King Oliver sent me to see you."

Tom squinted beneath his derby and surveyed Louis with cold disdain.

"And who may King Oliver be?"

"He plays the cornet for Pete Lala!"

"So-o-o, Pete Lala's cornetist. And what do *you* want?"

"I wants to play in the Distric'."

"Oh, is that all? Go in and talk to my manager, George Delsa. You'll find him behind the bar, and don't forget to ask for a slug of gin."

Louis pushed the swinging doors and entered the saloon. In a far corner five or six card players sat around a table, busy with their chips and drinks. A few absinthe sippers leaned over the counter, each with a foot negligently resting on the brass rail. They were noisily discussing the trend of the war.

Louis found Tom's manager lolling near the till, and told him his story.

"So you want a job in Storyville? Well, maybe we could arrange it. Of course, I've got to have my usual cut."

"That's O.K.," replied Louis.

"In that case, everything's under control. Things are kind of slack just now during the summer, but in a few weeks business'll pick up—that is, if the war lasts long enough. Those soldiers and sailors keep things booming for us."

"When mus' I come back?"

"See me at the end of September."

But before "the end of September" something disastrous happened to the red-light district: in mid-July the City Council voted a new ordinance restricting Negro prostitutes within the kingdom of Perdido—forbidding them, that is, to ply their trade in the District.

The dog days that followed transformed New Orleans into a tropical city, its inhabitants stricken and listless with the fierce heat. Every night Louis played at Matranga's and saw the same old faces—the usual wenches and a few faithful comrades like Sweet Child, Clark Wade, and Henry Morton. One evening, Sonny Gaby was taken ill, and another drummer had to be found quickly—which was how Black Benny came into possession of Sonny's drumsticks. Benny was a sort of wild, savage creature whose greatest joy in life was to beat the drum, and he did so with a continuous grin which showed two rows of pearly teeth. Another time, Gus Vanzan, his old chum from the Waifs' Home, dropped in to see Louis. They had a long chat about old times and old friends. Izzy Smooth was playing for Kid René, who had become "Kid Rena." The Kid spent his daytime hours clerking in a grocery, but at night he still played the trumpet.

One day Irene came to tell Louis she had decided to leave town for greener pastures. She was heading for Mobile, whose bustling port offered numberless atrractive possibilities to an enterprising woman. Her announcement left Louis unmoved, for his passion for Nutsie had long since cooled and he worshiped at a single shrine, that of Ragtime. Briefly he recalled the bare room above Gaspar's and smiled at a dusky beauty who was dancing near the band.

Joe Oliver arrived one Saturday night, as was his custom,

and showed Louis a letter from Freddie Keppard. In it Freddie reported that the new music known as "ragtime" in New Orleans was called "jazz" in Chicago, where it was creating a sensation. The expressive new term soon spread like wildfire in New Orleans and was applied indiscriminately to the music played by white, Creole, and Negro bands.

As September drew to a close, Louis, recalling the invitation of Tom Anderson's manager, returned to the famous cabaret.

"You've come for that trumpet job, Dipper?"

"Yes, sir, you told me to see you 'bout this time."

"Bad news, kid."

"Sho 'nuff?"

"Well, maybe there's nothing to it, but the Mayor's got orders from the Secretary of War to shut down every last house in the District. They say it's got something to do with the Army's morale. You know about the new city ordinance, of course; but this here order really means business.

"Bad, ain't it, Mr. George?"

"I'm telling you. And mark my words, kiddo, if that happens the old town's gonna be a graveyard, and you might as well hang up your cornet on a nail for a few years."

Strange rumors spread quickly, to be magnified among the shady characters who operated profitably only under cover of darkness. Under this still indistinct threat, the panders and the prostitutes felt insecure and a pall of gloom settled on the Tenderloin. But they would not give up without a struggle. Strings were pulled by the big operators and the brothel keepers who had friends in high circles, friends who would surely use their influence before it was too late. Despite their vague fears, all were more or less confident that things would be arranged without undue difficulty. The ordinance adopted in

[111]

July might have been troublesome, but nobody seemed inclined to enforce it. And even this drastic Army order was surely not meant to deal a death-blow to the District.

Clark Wade stormed when he heard of the new ruling. Some of the women, following Alberta's prudent example, began to save their money against possible lean days. Sweet Child asserted that nothing would come of it all, there were too many fingers in the pie for it to be stolen away. An extraordinary aspect of the situation was highlighted by all this hubbub. Whereas the better white element heartily approved the lancing of this festering sore in the city's body politic, hoping that it would curtail the social evils of idleness and prostitution, from the Negro point of view, the abolition of the District would simply mean fewer jobs and more hungry mouths to feed among their kind. By October, however, residents and musicians alike suspected that the end was not far off. The petitions and entreaties presented to Mayor Behrman proved fruitless. Among the police speculation was rife; they trembled at the dismal prospect of finding their golden pool dried up at its source. During these October nights, they grew more and more exacting and the graft they extorted reached fantastic proportions.

On October 19, the situation looked desperate indeed. To Harry Gregson, the detective who twenty years before had gotten his start in life as a singer with the "Spasm Band" (a company of newsboys who were the first singing quartet or sextet in New Orleans), fell the task of going from cabaret to cabaret, from sporting-house to sporting-house, to announce that the City Council had voted the day before to enforce the July ordinance

In November, a momentary wave of hope swept through the red-light district Everything would be fixed up, now that Gertrude Dix had asked the Court for an injunction against the ordinance. She was the proprietor of a house at 205 North Basin that had once been the residence of Hilma Burt, a noted brothelkeeper of former days. But she could hardly be said to have come to court with clean hands, and her plea was summarily denied.

That night consternation reigned at Matranga's as the pimps and the wenches sought to drown their sorrow in alcohol. The great Tom Anderson was running frantically from pillar to post, but all to no avail. On November 12, flying squads of police swooped down on the Tenderloin like birds of ill omen, and passed the word that the death-knell would sound irrevocably at midnight. The remainder of the day was passed by the women in packing their belongings for the great exodus. The musicians who had come down for the last time thought that the air was particularly mild and sweet that night. Tearfully, the numerous "Professors" gathered their music-sheets and closed their pianos. In all the saloons, the pimps sulked and drank, served by melancholy bartenders who knew that their hour had struck. Here and there, the prostitutes gathered in small knots and discussed plans for the future. Linked for once by the bond of misfortune, the white and the colored prostitutes mingled to bewail their common fate. In the restricted area of Perdido the same excitement prevailed among the blacks. At Matranga's, the headquarters, the general uneasiness became so intense that it spread to the musicians. They left the platform and joined the crowd listening to Clark Wade. From time to time, a scout would dart in, merely to confirm their worst fears.

At half-past eleven, there was not a sober man or woman in the place. Storyville had but a scant half-hour to live, and the heavy tread of the police outside was punctuated by the clang of their nightsticks on the pavement.

Shortly before midnight, Clark Wade stood a final round.

They drank to all the poor wretches who had lost their livelihood, and went out on the sidewalk to watch the end of their world.

In the sky above, the stars twinkled as merrily as ever, casting a soft radiance on the sordid scene. In measured tones, the city's bells rang twelve times, north and south, east and west. Louis Armstrong smoked reflectively, his cornet secure under his arm. And from all the neighboring bawdy-houses there poured forth an endless stream of prostitutes, porters, procurers, bawds, and other assorted wretches, carrying valises, bundles, phonographs, and even mattresses. Some walked empty-handed, their useless finery packed in suitcases jealously guarded by Negro attendants. The mob took the form of a long parade on Perdido Street. Proceeding toward the District, they met along the way a white delegation which joined the blacks. The throng burst into song. All the musicians were sent ahead. Whites and blacks mingled freely in this bizarre march through the city. The luckless pianists walked behind their fellow-players—the latter could at least take their instruments with them! Here a drummer carried the big drum on his head, there a bull-fiddler had not abandoned his bulky "dog-house."

In the small hours of the morning the spent and disconsolate mob finally halted at Perdido and Rampart. This was the end! And on this spot, in front of the very house where he had fired the shots that had sent him to jail, Louis Armstrong raised his cornet to his lips. Some pious soul asked him to play *Nearer, My God, to Thee*. Louis complied, and without a trace of compunction or repentance, there in the open street the sin-soaked assembly began to pray, with folded hands and bare heads, as if it were the most natural thing in the world. In the eastern sky, the rosy streaks of dawn seemed to mock the despair and the wretchedness of the mob. Slowly at first, then more quickly and louder, a prolonged wailing rose to the heavens where the stars were gradually fading from sight.

A week later, Matranga's dance-hall was closed and Louis Armstrong went home, his cornet under his arm, and carefully hung it up in its accustomed place over his bed.

12

THE CLOSING of Storyville, considered a blessing by most citizens, was an unmitigated misfortune for the vice overlords and their numerous underlings. At one stroke all of these parasites were cut off from the only means of livelihood they knew or cared to know, and the life of the whole city was transformed. Unquestionably, this drastic measure deprived the Crescent City of much of its dash and color and plunged it into the dull routine of ordinary municipal organization.

The Tenderloin was deserted. Heartbroken, Tom Anderson had remained in his saloon until the bitter end, and now sat with two or three friends, mournfully reviewing the events of the previous night. Strange comings and goings stressed this unusual moving-day. The Madames who had heavy investments in furnishings and other stock-in-trade hurriedly sacrificed their carriages and trotting horses. Some few of these creatures, among them Gertrude Dix, made an attempt to carry on by bribing the police. A week later, they were arrested and sentenced to prison. The inferior category of common strumpets dispersed and went elsewhere to ply their trade. Others who depended exclusively on the activities of the underworld for subsistence were forced to toil like ordinary mortals to earn their daily bread. Even the "high yellows," dispensers of erotic favors that enabled them to live in luxury, were forced into drudgery. As for the pimps and other "fancy men," they disappeared completely from sight; they had put away their gaudy apparel for future use and were now unrecognizable in the rough garb of laborers and longshoremen.

Funky Butt Hall boarded its doors, and Matranga, who had closed his dance hall, was faced with bankruptcy. An era of fear and want opened for the musicians. In Mahogany Hall, the famous white piano on which Jelly Roll Morton had improvised so ingeniously and young Spencer Williams, another jazz addict, had tapped out his first compositions with one finger, was sold at auction.

More than two hundred musicians were thrown into the street. Some who had had other jobs during the daytime were now to depend on these alone for livelihood. Bob Lyons plied his trade of shoeshine boy with greater zeal than before. Once again Picou joined the ranks of the zinc-workers, and Emmanuel Perez toiled with his brother on a moving van. Willy Santiago turned porter; others, like Sonny Gaby and Boogers, were down on the docks unloading bananas; and the best drummer of that day, Black Benny, shifted as best as he could, drifting from one job to another.

A few of the luckier musicians found work in the French Quarter, where some forms of nocturnal activity had sought haven. King Oliver played in Kid Ory's orchestra, and his reputation was still growing. At this time, none dared dispute his royal title. The old-time star performers were all but forgotten. Buddy Bolden, finally released from the asylum at Jackson, reappeared one day in Perdido, but did not even recognize Bob Lyons. Younger rivals had completely eclipsed Emmanuel Perez and Bunk Johnson.

Some musicians exiled themselves to Chicago, a magnetic city which had fired the imagination of the musicians of New

Orleans ever since they had heard that ragtime had been legitimized there under the name of jazz. Stories were rampant too, of the huge success which the original Dixieland Band, a white orchestra, had obtained in the Windy City.

Just when the future had seemed brightest, Louis Armstrong was once again confronted with the old problem of finding an outlet for his musical talent. Only a few days before the fateful closing, he had received several flattering testimonials which had stamped him as a high-class performer. On several occasions he was asked to replace the absent cornetist in various bands—among them, Buddy Petit's, Roy Palmer's, Sam Dutrey's, and Bob Lyons's. But he had to eat every day, and after a few fruitless attempts to find a regular job as musician, he deposited his cornet at the bottom of an old trunk and began to look for any kind of paying job. His stepfather, who had once pointed out to him the uncertainty and dangers of a musical career, now gloated: Louis could not return to the coal company; for someone else had long since taken his old place. But he learned that Boogers had gone to the wharfs, where he unloaded bananas, and Louis decided to follow suit.

He found it a tiring business, this endless shouldering of heavy banana stems from the ships to the waiting trucks of the wholesalers or the railroad cars of the shippers. It meant a radical change in living habits. His working days now began at the time that he had formerly gone to bed. It was not strange, therefore, that Louis did not display the same enthusiasm over lugging bananas that he had thrown into the playing of blues on his cornet.

While unloading one Friday, he had several skirmishes with some hungry rats who leaped at the ripe fruit and even brushed against his face. An immense feeling of loathing and fatigue swept over him. Unaccustomed to great physical exertion, Louis ached in every muscle of his body. Toward evening, he had just slung another load of bananas over his shoulder when he felt a slimy and chill pressure on the back of his neck. Shouts of alarm rose from his fellow-workers. Louis hastily dropped the stalk and fled in terror—he had glimpsed the writhing shape of a snake intertwined among the bananas. He broke into a cold sweat as he realized how narrowly he had escaped a fatal bite. That evening, he asked for his wages and left for home with the firm resolve never to work again in the port.

Fortunately he had managed to save a few dollars and could afford to spend some time in job-hunting. Eventually, in March, he landed work as milkman and was due to start on the next Monday.

Early each morning he loaded his wagon with cases filled with bottles of milk, and set out for the State Street section, near St. Charles Avenue. But this job, too, proved exhausting; the work of delivering milk from back door to back door, taking out the heavy trays containing the full bottles and then bringing them back loaded with empties—it was too much for his strength. Valiantly he stuck it out, however.

Then one day he got a call from his draft board, for by now the United States had entered the World War. He was examined and classified fit for military service. The poor devil welcomed his registration, thinking that it would end the worry and struggle of breadwinning. But days and weeks passed and still he was not called.

By this time, Perdido had lost the character of nocturnal gaiety which gave it so much glamour in 1917 before the closing of the resorts. A few diehards still led the loafing existence they had always known. One night Louis was returning peaceably to his mother's when he was attracted by a milling throng at the intersection of Gravier and Franklin. He quickened his pace, thinking that the Battlefield was showing new signs of life. When he arrived on the scene, he saw women crossing themselves. A man was stretched on the ground, gasping for breath. It was Black Benny, artist of the traps. His assailant, still clutching a bloody knife, had just been arrested by the police: a strumpet called May Daughter, who was Black Benny's sweetheart. Louis elbowed his way through the mob and saw the ambulance waiting to carry off Black Benny. The luckless musician, who had caught a stab of the knife full in the chest, was retching bloodily.

The hospital to which Black Benny had been taken was on Louis's milk route, and next day he entered a rear hall and asked after his friend. The drummer was still out of his head and was singing blues in his delirium; a passing interne whom Louis questioned told him that it was touch-and-go. Black Benny's agony continued for a week before he died, and he sang the blues day and night throughout that week. He had met his fate on the identical spot where several years earlier Alberta had taken her razor to Mary Jack the Bear's throat.

One morning Louis was coming to the end of his milk route. He was growing accustomed to the hard work. The wagon was already in motion, for the mule was well trained and began to pull as soon as Louis came close enough to throw in the case. This time Louis lost his balance and the wagon wheel rolled over his big toe. Almost fainting from the pain, he climbed back to the seat with great effort, and returned at once to the warehouse. There he was told to go home and stay in bed. Of course, his wages stopped automatically. Ten days later he went back to resume his duties, only to learn that he had been replaced. . . .

The Story of Louis Armstrong

Louis was becoming more and more bitter; even his passionate fondness for jazz seemed to be dead and buried forever, like the cornet that lay lifeless at the bottom of his trunk. Louis was again sharing the harsh lot of the needy. One evening he met Louis Wade the pianist, who told him that his brother Clark Wade, Perdido's flashy "fancy man," who wore diamonds down to his garters, had been killed by a jealous wench. His funeral was to take place on the next day, a Saturday, and a great array of musicians would march with their instruments before the hearse, as befitted a man who had had the foresight to join four burial societies.

Louis witnessed the funeral—an event so sensational that it is still talked about in Perdido. Near the Rampart Street funeral parlor, four bands were lined up in uniforms and aprons blazoned with the emblems of the different organizations. When the coffin was borne out, the wailing of the women on the sidewalk was fearful to hear. An immense crowd had gathered to pay final tribute to the departed King of the Sidewalk. Kid Ory's orchestra led the procession. King Oliver came up to Louis and shook hands warmly, but Louis was shamefaced—he was nothing now but a common laborer and hated the calloused hands that betrayed it.

Imperceptibly, the funeral procession began to move with the conventional studied slowness. After marching for two hours, they reached the cemetery. Funeral dirges succeeded doleful marches. The bereaved family writhed with grief and sorrow, and scooped up handfuls of dust to throw on the coffin—the dust of oblivion. Then it was the turn of Clark Wade's numerous sweethearts, who shouted their despair for all to hear, groaning, weeping, and spasmodically distorting their features. After the throng's final burst of emotion, the bands left the cemetery and turned their aprons inside out.

Horn of Plenty:

Now that Clark's mortal remains had been duly laid to rest, it was fitting that the survivors should express their joy at being alive. The four orchestras burst out with the liveliest jazz. Urchins weaved in and out of the parade, gamboling and jigging in great glee. Quickly drying their tears, the female mourners lost no time in falling into the now joyful spirit of things. Louis Armstrong heard Kid Ory's orchestra break out into *Did He Ramble?* Walking backwards, King Oliver faced the orchestras and defiantly soared into a dazzling solo which went straight to Louis's heart. Right hand in his pocket, leaning against a wall, mute, he caught himself following the finger movements of an imaginary solo.

Now it was King Ory's orchestra's turn to sound forth. Louis fell into step. When they reached the next turning, the two leading bands ahead of Kid Ory lined up on either sidewalk and began to play while Kid Ory's band and the fourth orchestra marched past. The mob sensed the rivalry as each group sought to surpass the others, and conflicting shouts rose:

"Let's go, King Oliver! Kill 'em dead!"

"Come on, Bunk Johnson, knock 'em down!"

Suddenly, an extraordinary thing happened. The four orchestras began to play simultaneously with all their might, King Oliver's trumpet dominating the musical bedlam. Frantically, the crowd tried to pick the winner of this weird contest. During a brief lull, Kid Ory attacked *Tiger Rag*, having shrewdly held back this dizzily fast piece until the last. Its effect was startling. Men and women hugged and kissed one another, the children hopped about in ecstasy. Shaken by the exasperating power of this music, Louis Armstrong wept bitterly, mourning his vanished dreams and the passing of his most cherished ambitions.

Soon afterwards, the four bands dispersed in different di-

rections, and Louis followed the crowd that fell behind Kid
Ory as one man and thus signified the total and unequivocal
defeat of his rivals.

Having lost his job with the dairy, Louis returned to the
coal business. But things went from bad to worse, and by the
early part of November he was again desperate. The day before, he had not been paid, and that night he had gone to listen
to Kid Ory's orchestra with King Oliver, ashamed to be in the
latter's company, so conscious was he of his degradation. For
several months now, he had been expecting a call from the
Army; he even wished for it in his heart.

That morning, he left on his coal wagon and guided the
mule in the direction of St. Charles, stopping now and then
to unload his buckets of coal into the bins. He sat straight on
the front seat, his grimy sack tied around the waist and a dusty
cap covering his head. From time to time he chanted: "Stove
coal, ladies, a nickel for a waterbucket." As he halted his mule
and wagon on front of Fabacher's restaurant at St. Charles
and Perdido, he got wind of an extraordinary rumor. From
the direction of Canal Street he heard sounds of rejoicing.
People were dancing and leaping up and down. Urchins
wound in and out of the crowds, clasping hands to form a
chain. Standing on his wagon, Louis looked down on this incomprehensible scene of delirious enthusiasm. Lines of automobiles moved at a snail's pace, and their horns blared continuously, contributing to the general din. Apparently the entire city had gone mad.

He spied a black man who had stopped near the wagon.

"What's goin' on, old man?"

"Don't you-all know?"

"If I knew, I wouldn't ask, pops."

"The war's over—we's got peace!"

Horn of Plenty:

The contagion of the children's antics now caught hold of the older persons. The streets were soon littered with torn bits of paper fluttering down from the surrounding buildings. Louis stood silent for a minute, pondering the meaning of this sudden turn of affairs. A great decision was welling up in his mind, an impulse that he knew he would not resist. At this moment a white man hailed him from the sidewalk:

"Hey, nigger, where's your instrument?"

So Louis slowly loosened the bag tied around his waist, carefully adjusted the hook on the wagon wheel—and walked off. It was as though by this action he were leaving behind forever all the misery and privations of his youth. As he followed Perdido he said aloud to himself:

"The war's over. Good-by, ol' mule. I dig you another time!"

When he reached the black belt, the Armistice craze had already seized it. Hugging and kissing was general, and liquor flowed everywhere. Old mammies puffed reflectively on pipes and cigars.

"Peace at last. Plenty to eat, plenty jobs. Hallelujah! Hurrah for jazz!"

Louis went home. He opened the dusty old trunk, picked up his tuxedo, and took out his cornet. He sat on the doorstep and practiced all afternoon.

At nightfall, with a drummer and a banjo player, he played at the corner of Perdido and Liberty. As more and more women gathered around him, he knew that at last he was really living again. This intoxicating applause was what he had been craving! He began to blow *Tiger Rag*, vowing that, come what may, he would always be a musician.

Suddenly he felt the touch of a hand on his shoulder. He turned and recognized Irene.

"How goes it, Nutsie!"

"Louis, my darlin'! The war's over! Sing my fav'rite tune, will you?"

And Louis Armstrong lifted his voice in an ancient and bawdy ballad, mournful and sentimental, which the members of his race had been singing for generations. And as he sang, the blacks in Perdido drew closer and listened with pounding hearts to the deep tones of the musician who had found his soul.

13

DURING THE gay period that followed the Armstice, Louis Armstrong was able to devote his entire time to his beloved trumpet. For several weeks he played in Perdido, filling engagements in one orchestra or another whenever a trumpet player was needed.

One day he was asked to form a small band and play for a week in Gretna, at the Brick Hall, one of the lowest resorts on the west side of the Mississippi. On arriving there he was taken to a small platform on which he and the drummer and the banjoist were to play.

On the left there was a long stretch of bar, known to the patrons as the armored bar because the tavern-keeper, whose air suggested a piratical past, had concealed along its entire length an assortment of lethal weapons, handily reached when a display of firearms was needed to protect bottles or bartender. This was the favorite haunt of the toughest Negro river hands or "wharf rats" on the Mississippi, who spent money as fast as they earned it and who were wont, after the third round of gin, to wax sentimental and extremely sensitive to insults, real or fancied.

The Brick Hall was also the rallying-point for all the riffraff of Gretna. The immediate vicinity and every street leading toward the hall swarmed with wenches lying in wait for their prey—a score or more of loose women who depended for their living entirely on the tavern's transients. Every night some misguided fools were lured outside and taken to the adjoining empty lot; while others of the women, inside the tavern, having earned their "fees" earlier, could pat their stockings with pride and flash a roll of bills whenever they stood drinks. From time to time a drinker would be led away by one of the women, into a cubicle beyond the bar, where privacy of a sort obtained. Before they entered it, however, a fifty-cent toll was duly handed over to the vigilant host by the latest victim, drunk and hiccuping, who was never allowed to leave the clutches of his seducer until his last dollar was hers.

With this rabble Louis Armstrong scored an instantaneous hit, men and women alike going wild over his playing of ragtime and blues. On this opening night, in the midst of the music, the door flew open and a colored girl of uncommon beauty made a sensational entrance. The drinkers at the bar stared boldly at her, but the women eyed her jealously and made insulting remarks on her youth and inexperience; for she could not have been more than sixteen.

At the counter she called for a double gin, but did not raise the glass to her lips; she just stood there and smoked. A fierce-looking ruffian accosted her.

"What's yo' name?"

"Daisy."

"Daisy what?"

"Daisy Parker."

"Wanna drink with me?"

"I ain't thirsty. Maybe the band is. Go give 'em the dollar, you old tightwad."

She was leading him by the arm, and, hardly realizing what he was doing, the blackguard dropped a silver dollar into

Louis's outstretched hand. Louis grinned broadly, showing his dazzling teeth as Daisy spoke to him.

"What's that new tune you sang in Perdido las' Saturday?"

"Which one?"

"You know—the one about Basin Street."

"Oh! You mean them Basin Street Blues."

"That's it 'zactly. Play it, Dipper."

Under this cajolery, Louis felt his heart melt. Never had he looked into such coaxing eyes as these.

"Who is you, gal?"

"Parker's my name fo' everybody else, but you can call me Daisy."

The song she had asked him for was a recent work by his friend Spencer Williams, pianist and track-walker. The *Basin Street Blues* celebrated the street that symbolizes the notoriously voluptuous aspect of New Orleans life.

"An' now," began Louis, sending his vibrant voice through the hall in a sort of introduction, "here's the Reverend Satchmo' who's gonna preach a Lenten sermon. Oh, yea! I wants everybody to bow down and repent. Reverend Satchmo' is gonna to lead us into Paradise—yea, men, the Paradise o' Basin Street!"

The piano played a prelude, and the banjoist joined the syncopation. Then Louis broke into the song, and the words of the sentimental ballad reverberated throughout the hall. The men stared at him through bleary eyes. Daisy had released her escort's arm and stood alone at the end of the bar, wreathed in the blue smoke of a cigarette, her eyes fastened on Louis. As the piano repeated the opening bars, Louis sang on, his face tense and every fiber of his being quivering in unison with the powerful vibrations of his voice. Accompanied by a sort of unfathomable baritone from the instruments (something that has never ceased to astound the classical

critics), he intoned the verses once more, the orchestra giving
him perfect support:

> *"Won't-cha come along wit' me*
> *To the Mis-sis-sip-pi?*
> *We'll take the boat—to the lan' of dreams,*
> *Steam down the river, down to New Orleans.*
> *The band's there to get us,*
> *Old friends to dig us,*
> *Where all the light and dark folks meet—*
> *This is Basin Street, yea, Basin Street Blues!"*

Spellbound, the crowd was very quiet. Absent-mindedly,
the boss still held a tumbler in his hand—his imagination had
wandered off to "the lan' of dreams." Under the impact of the
song, Daisy was swept off her feet. She had closed her eyes
and when she opened them again at the end of the stanza,
Louis knew that she saw none but him. Then he intoned the
melancholy chorus:

> *"Basin Street is the street*
> *Where the elite always meet*
> *In New Orleans,*
> *The land of dreams;*
> *You'll never know how nice it seems*
> *Or just how much it really means*
> *Glad to be—*
> *Yessirree—*
> *Where welcome's free,*
> *Dear to me,*
> *Where I can lose*
> *My Basin Street Blues!"*

As the band picked up the melody, Daisy blew a kiss to
Louis, and he felt his heart bursting with happiness. Erased

from his memory were the grim days of toil; the coal wagon, the milk route, the banana boats were all forgotten now. A prolonged burst of applause, mingled shrieks of delight, hand-clapping and feet-stamping, marked the end of Louis's performance. He saw Daisy toss a half-dollar to the boss as she looked straight at the orchestra. Louis could hardly believe in his luck, realizing that he had a half-hour's intermission before resuming his stand on the platform. Then as Daisy opened the door behind the bandstand she winked slowly at Louis, and he was sure of her meaning. Unsteadily he left the orchestra and followed her into the back room where she stood waiting. She took his hands, held them tight and said nothing.

When Louis came out, he was in love, and Daisy, disdaining all the jeers and jibes hurled at her, sat on a stool and drank in the passionate music which spoke the language of the crowd and went straight to their hearts.

Toward the end of the night, under the spell of Daisy's beseeching gaze, Louis once more sang to the queen of his heart:

"Won't-cha come along wit' me
To the Mis-sis-sip-pi?"

He found Daisy waiting for him outside in the darkness. Silently they walked together, and slowly climbed the dewy slope of the levee. In the distance across the river, the city's myriad lights burned bright against the sky. Daisy pressed close to Louis, and he repeated, his arm clasping her waist, the haunting refrain:

"Won't-cha come along wit' me
To the Mis-sis-sip-pi?"

In the semidarkness the flowing river had a velvety sheen. Its waters lapped against a half-submerged stump and the sound fell gently on their ears. They looked down on Old

Man River and there, in the gloom and chilliness of early morning, they plighted their troth.

For a whole week, Louis was blissfully happy in Gretna. Every day, as he crossed the Mississippi on the Canal Street Ferry, he threw a dime into the water to placate the river's evil and redoubtable genie. And on the following Saturday, when he had to return to the city for a new engagement, his heart was sad.

As he was strolling along Perdido the next day, however, he saw Daisy Parker coming toward him.

"What you doin' in Perdido?" he asked her with delight.

"I'm gonna live here."

"What for?"

"I just can't live without you."

A few days later, Louis Armstrong married her and they set up house at Melpomene and Saratoga. Unfortunately, Daisy's love made her intensely jealous, and she followed Louis suspiciously wherever he went and waited for him until he had finished playing. He resented this, and bitter quarrels soon began. Sometimes Louis would pack his trunk and go off to his mother's at Perdido and Liberty. Then he would once more fall under Daisy's spell, and she would promise never again to provoke his anger. But her jealousy gave her no rest, and she would soon find a real or fancied occasion to unleash it.

One day Louis learned that Joe Oliver and Jimmy Noone had left for Chicago to try their luck. Later he stopped at the corner café and was told that Kid Ory had been hanging around in Perdido, hoping to see him. When he came home, his mother had a message for him: the orchestra leader was waiting for him downtown.

Louis tingled with anticipation. Was he about to force destiny's hand after so many years of seemingly hopeless struggle. A cold wind was blowing and people walked hurriedly, stamping their feet to keep warm. And tomorrow he had to brave the icy river breezes to keep an engagement in West-wego, worse luck! Louis crossed Canal Street and found Kid Ory waiting for him:

"Louis, you know King Oliver's gone to Chicago?"

"Yeah, I knows it."

"We need somebody to take his place. I thought about you."

"All right!"

Louis tried not to betray his joy.

"When does I start?"

"Day after tomorrow."

In Westwego the next day, Louis blew his trumpet like one possessed. It was true, after all: he was about to cross the invisible line. Tomorrow he was going to play with Kid Ory in a cabaret patronized by white people.

In this fashion, Louis climbed rapidly to the pinnacle of local fame. Soon he was acclaimed the best jazz musician of New Orleans. Well trained and wrapped up in his work as he was, he made use of his powerful lungs to play higher in the scale than anyone before had ever attempted. Kid Ory was astonished by this performance, and the other trumpeters in New Orleans quickly realized that Louis's phenomenal success was developing along a line that was possible only to the possessor of steel-hard lips.

And so Louis's powerful trumpeting grew in demand and he was hailed at the Country Club, at La Louisiane Restaurant and at Tulane University's dances. It was not long before Kid Ory was writing to Joe Oliver: "Dear Joe: You couldn't have a better man in your place. He plays higher than you do, and is just as popular."

Though Louis got great pleasure from the esteem of his

fellow musicians in New Orleans, his private life was still greatly disturbed by Daisy's unbearable jealousy.

His rise in popularity as musician was further stressed in February 1919, when he was elected to exalted office among the Zulus. This year especially the parade would take on added significance on account of the recent Armistice and the revival of the Mardi Gras Carnival after the temporary lapse due to the war. Everywhere in Perdido, Louis's election to the famed Negro organization was acclaimed with joy. This was indeed a fitting tribute to the prodigy of the trumpet, and the general impatience grew as Mardi Gras drew near, bringing the gorgeous pageantry of Rex, the white king who arrived on his yacht at the foot of Canal Street, and the gay buffoonery of his Negro imitator, the King of the Zulus. The latter would land on the banks of the Old Basin, followed by a retinue which had faithfully accompanied him aboard the battered watermelon barge that they would exchange for the tinseled glory of a papier-mâché chariot, drawn by gaily caparisoned mules and glistening with gold and silver leaves.

When the great day came Louis, resplendent in the costume of a court dignitary, complete with the sweeping ceremonial headdress, was waiting at the corner of Liberty and Perdido for the arrival of the retinue so as to take his place on the float which symbolized the grandeur of the Zulus. As the other courtiers came up, arrayed in similar splendor, they all began to discuss the day's program. Their group was joined by a tawny charmer named Rela Martin and they were soon bandying words in true Carnival style. The coquettish beauty flirted brazenly, first with one, then with another. Suddenly, Louis cut short the conversation:

"Rela! You better git. Daisy's comin'. She's passin' by Funky Butt right now and she's got a razor."

As Rela gave one look and fled, Louis assumed a carefree

manner, engaging his companions in animated talk. But Daisy was already on the scene, her lips twitching with anger and her right hand clutching a menacing blade.

"Ha! You Dipper! I'll learn you to trifle with them good-for-nothin' high yellows!"

Coming on like an avenging fury, she threatened Louis with her razor. He raised his arm to parry the blow, and jumped quickly to one side. To add to his distress, his plumed hat fell off and rolled in the gutter. One of the dignitaries tried to catch it as it fell, while Louis beat a hasty retreat from his wife's reach. As his friend stooped over to retrieve the hat, Daisy turned her attention to the unwary Samaritan and in her blind rage slashed him from the rear, inflicting a deep wound in a particularly tender part of his anatomy.

The bleeding and crestfallen courtier was rushed to the hospital, and Daisy was quickly arrested by the police. Meantime Louis had finally recovered his hat, but, alas, it was now bedraggled and covered with mud—a total loss.

Undaunted by these events, Louis appeared in his appointed place on the float, after having borrowed a hat several sizes too large for his head. Tired of having it slide down over his nose and obstruct his view at every jolt of the float's fitful stops and starts, he finally held it nonchalantly over his heart, when he was not bowing and scraping and waving it in joyous response to the enthusiastic acclamations of Zulu's faithful subjects.

14

THE TRAGICOMEDY of Mardi Gras was followed by many explosive domestic scenes between Louis and his wife. At eighteen, he had achieved the seemingly impossible through sheer will-power. He lived in a backyard at Melpomene and Saratoga, still surrounded by grim and abject poverty. Fortunately, his nightly excursions to the bright land of song and music broke the monotony and renewed his courage. Along about four in the morning, his homeward journey brought him back past the endless rows of frame shanties, and he had to step carefully to avoid tripping on the uneven rows of bricks that formed a precarious sidewalk.

At this dismal hour, the filthiest garbage lined the curb, clamoring odorously for the street-cleaner's broom. Often on these lonely homecomings, occasionally interrupted by the half-hearted solicitations of weary trollops, Louis ruminated on the fate of his miserable, downtrodden race. At last he had seen his former dreams merge into daily realities. But the immense weight of his past, the ineradicable color of his skin, held him fast in accursed shackles. There to his left dwelt his mother; his sister would never leave, that was certain; his father was little better than a slave in the turpentine works; all his friends were herded in this unbelievable ghetto of corruption, without a chance of escape.

And so sweet is freedom to primitive hearts that Louis was already nurturing the hope of leaving Perdido for good. How wonderful it would be to stay where he was, in those small hours of morning when the shadows trembled in expectation of the rosy dawn, with no need to recross the racial boundary of Canal Street, and find sleep in the enchanted land where gay spring flowers peeped through the lace of wrought-iron balconies!

At about this time, the Strekfus Brothers were the first to appreciate and recognize the influence of jazz. Their fleet of excursion boats, known as the Strekfus Line, made short trips up and down the river, loaded with pleasure seekers hankering for cool breezes, moonlight, and romance. Since their ambition was naturally to lure as many people as possible to their decks, the brothers were seeking some irresistible attraction that might draw the multitude.

Their choice was not long in the making. Jazz, the wild music which now thrilled whites and blacks alike, would be their talisman. They decided to give it a trial. The whole Mississippi Valley knew well the sound of the calliope which marked the arrival of the three stately steamboats, all snow-white: The *Sidney*, the *St. Paul*, and the *J.S.* Everybody knew, too, that the charitable Strekfus family had gone so far as to adopt a Negro boy to whom they had given a good musical education, Fate Marable. And they now decided to give their protege the concession of jazz music on the boats.

Louis had by now left his wife and gone back to live with his mother. He was playing in Tom Anderson's cabaret, the Arlington Annex, between Canal and Iberville, now the rendezvous of all the assorted characters who had sought entrance to the District in the good old days. After the closing, the

Mayor of Vice had vowed to himself that even if but one place remained open in the Tenderloin, that place would be his own. George Delsa, still there, warmly greeted the young trumpeter he had been compelled to send away more than a year ago.

The orchestra was not very good—a makeshift combination composed of a few players who were trying to weather the crisis: Paul Dominguez played the clarinet, and the pianist was Edna Frances, his wife; Albert Frances handled the drums; and Louis was always on his feet as he blew wild effects on his trumpet.

His stint at Tom Anderson's served to strengthen his popularity. Sooner or later, everybody who had ever been in the Who's Who of the red-light district could be heard at Tom Anderson's. Late in the evening jockeys and owners, trainers and bettors flocked here for a last drink and discussed the following day's races, while Louis sang the blues and gathered princely tips.

There even came a time when, at every break in the program, he would leave the cabaret and hurry over to play a few numbers with the Tuxedo Band, as a sort of guest star. As he started out, his lips parted to show his gleaming white teeth, Lulu White—yes, the celebrated Lulu White who would not have looked twice at him a year ago—would grasp his hand and exclaim:

"My sweet little Louis! Hurry back and sing me those blues. You're the only one that can make me forget my troubles. When I die of loneliness, I want you to sing at my funeral."

One day Daisy came and waited for him opposite the Arlington Annex. When he emerged, she heaped insults on him for having dared to exchange a few words with some of the women in the establishment. On her return the following day she was armed with a razor, throwing that section of Rampart

Street into a panic. On still another occasion, she behaved so outrageously that Louis chased her into the Melpomene backyard and up to their room on the second floor. Locking herself in, she appeared at a rear window and screamed for the police, yelling that her husband was threatening to kill her.

Louis was still pounding on the door when he heard the policemen blowing their whistles as they closed in on the yard. Then, as now, the New Orleans police force were anything but tender in their treatment of the blacks. Mindful of this, Louis scaled the closest fence and dropped silently into the adjoining garden. Hiding behind a convenient shrub, he heard the police vent their wrath on Daisy; and finally they led her away, under arrest for disturbing the peace.

Some time later Louis stole out cautiously, still wary and frightened. He learned that Daisy had been carted away in the patrol wagon and was now in jail. That evening, when he reached the Arlington Annex, a colored fellow was waiting, looking curiously at the mosaic of Tom's name in the pavement.

"You Louis Armstrong?" he asked.

"Who's you, Pop?" retorted Louis.

"Fate Marable. Look, I need a trumpeter on the *Sidney*. How's about joinin' my band?"

In ten minutes' time they struck a bargain, and three days later Louis was ready to leave. Luckily, Fate Marable had told the Strekfuses about Louis and Daisy, and a well-placed telephone call was quickly followed by Daisy's release. Hence, when David Jones, the melophone player, came for Louis on the morning of his departure, things went smoothly enough. David and Louis left on the train to meet the orchestra in St. Louis. Armstrong was in a turmoil of happiness and shyness. This was his very first trip far from home, and it had all the glamour of a wonderful expedition—he was out to conquer the world! Before leaving the city he went to Segretta's grocery, bought a fish sandwich and a bottle of olives, and took them away in a brown paper bag. Then—alas!—at the place where they had to change trains, as Louis was asking a white trainman which track they should go to, he dropped the brown bag and the bottle broke, splattering the trainman's uniformed legs with vinegar and olives. The man cursed him roundly, and Louis cast an imploring glance at David Jones. But David was suddenly engrossed in the scenery, ignoring Louis's predicament. So Louis, afraid to make a false move, boarded the train for St. Louis both crestfallen and hungry.

When David Jones finally spoke, he asked about Daisy. Louis said he was through with her and all other females—he had been burnt once too often. And he went on to describe his latest misadventure with them. Just before leaving New Orleans by the merest chance he had met Irene, his first love, who had briefly brightened the drab days of his struggling youth. Aware that Louis had come a long way since then, she had invited the newly famous musician to come up to see her. The prospect tempted Louis and one warm spring afternoon he arrived at Irene's address while it was yet broad daylight. Promptly admitted, he prudently locked the door before he went to the window, threw it open, and took off his coat.

Irene's tender smile was replaced by a worried frown as she heard a knock on the door.

"Who is it?" she asked.

"Cheeky Blake. Open up!" came the reply in a rasping voice.

"I got company!" was Irene's angry answer.

Cheeky Blake, who had undoubtedly seen Louis go into Irene's room, now redoubled his knocking, shouting that he was being cheated. Meanwhile Louis was hastily struggling into his coat. Then the door burst open under the impact of

Blake's weight—and Louis jumped out of the window. From the street he heard the ensuing brawl as he hurried away.

He was therefore doubly happy to go up to St. Louis and take the long boat-rides along the Mississippi. Fate Marable's sensational jazzband was lodged aboard the *Sidney*, which wandered from town to town, following the river's sinuous course. Louis himself tells the story of their adventures in his autobiography, *Swing that Music*.

These peregrinations lasted two years. He beheld with wonderment the carefree and prosperous ways of the teeming towns along the banks of the river. During this period he learned to read music, and he perfected his technique.

After many months, the steamer came down the river toward New Orleans. Summer was almost over. Already in the North the first brown leaves were appearing. An overpowering homesickness crept over Louis and nothing would cure it but the sight of home.

During this prolonged absence his reputation had become established. Standing on the forward deck, he would blare out with all his enthusiastic might and the excursion crowd responded with joyful shouts. At first it had been hard to catch the rhythm, and Strekfus recalls that things did not go smoothly until the right beat was discovered. But even at this early stage, the passengers stamped their feet with such energy to stress the melodies played by Louis on the trumpet that the boat itself moved jerkily on its course.

One more week, one more day, one more hour . . . then the Crescent City's buildings loomed sharp and clear in the morning sky. Leaning against the rail, Louis recalled the past and dreamed about the future. He knew that in New Orleans the fate of his race was harsh, but Perdido's image had not faded. His thoughts turned to jazz, born at the same time he was born, growing up with him between the School, the Prison,

the Church, and Funky Butt. How well he remembered those
who had created jazz from the obscure fantasies of ragtime!
In his mind he evoked the image of Buddy Bolden, the legen-
dary king who was now behind a madman's bars at the Jackson Asylum, but whose playing still lingered in the memories
of his loyal followers. He thought of other noted figures:
Emmanuel Perez, Freddie Keppard, King Oliver. And now
he shared the laurels of these champions!

He had at last, Louis realized, broken through the galling
fetters that had held him captive, he had stepped over the line
that neither his family nor hundreds of his friends would ever
cross. But—however happy he now felt—memories of the past
were potent. He yearned to mingle once more with those who
—from the distant days of the torrid Congo, from father to
son since—were writing in sweat and blood the heart-rending
epic of his race. He felt the urge to find out what had been
happening to the friends and associates of his earlier years.
He wondered whether Sweet Child's leg had been amputated;
whether Mrs. Morton's boy had really become a drummer.
Was it Detective Gregson who had arrested Red-head Happy
and then turned him loose when Red sang for him an old favorite which the Spasm band used to play? And Bob Lyons,
did he still wear his driver's cap backward, and work at his
shoeshine stand? What was Tom Anderson's status now in
the District? And Josie Arlington, was she truly dead and
buried. For he had heard bits of news about these and other
matters from time to time, but he had to talk them all over
with the old gang before he could really *know*. . . . Someone
broke this train of thought. It was Fate Marable who was
summoning him to play:

"Let's go, Dipper, for the last time before you hit Perdido!
Give it a solid lick!"

Erect on the platform Louis blew as he had never blown

[141]

before. His passionate intensity reached such proportions that the passengers thought his trumpet would swallow him whole.

"Won't-cha come along wit' me
To the Mis-sis-sip-pi?
We'll take the Sidney *to the lan' of dreams—*
Steam down the river, down to New Orleans!"

As the boat touched the pier, Louis stood waiting on the forward deck. Returning to the city of his birth, he was—in the minds of his race—the kingpin of jazz. Hundreds of handkerchiefs fluttered gaily in the breeze, and the women excitedly blew kisses in his direction. It was a mild morning; a gentle wind blew from Algiers over the river. A rhythmic ripple came from Gretna way, where he had first met Daisy. When the steamer was moored fast and Louis brought *Basin Street* to an end on a prolonged high note, bedlam broke loose. He saw his grandmother and Daisy, who were waving to him. Some distance away, May Ann and Mama Lucy were stretching their arms toward him. Then the gangplank was lowered and there was a rush to get ashore. As Louis set foot on the ground he was surrounded by excited relatives and friends. At length, when calm was partly restored, a white youth approached.

"I heard you play just now," he said to Louis. "It was wonderful, wonderful! You're the king of Jazz!"

"You a musician, Pop?" queried Louis.

"Yes, I play the trombone."

"What's yo' name?"

"Jack Teagarden . . . and say, I'd like to shake hands with you!"

And thus for the first time in his life Louis encountered friendly warmth from a member of the race that had never shown anything but contempt for his own.

15

IN 1921 Louis Armstrong left the *Sidney* and the Strekfus Line, owing a debt of gratitude to Fate Marable for the development of his polished style on the cornet. Moreover, the orchestra boasted a talented group of performers and Louis would later have good cause to remember the names of several players who had been his fellow-musicians for so long: Fate Marable, who sat at the piano and conducted with ever-watchful fervor, Baby Dodds (drums), Lorenzo Brashear (trombone), Johnny St. Cyr (banjo), Henry Kemble (bass), and David Jones (tenor sax). If Louis could now read music with far greater ease than at the Waifs' Home, he could thank David Jones for this accomplishment.

Louis wanted to stay ashore for at least this winter. Once again he put up at his mother's and the influence of Perdido and Liberty regained its hold. Though from time to time he would make up with Daisy, these brief interludes but stirred the ashes of a dead love.

Gradually, the face of Perdido was undergoing a transformation. The decrepit old houses were crumbling away and under the law rebuilding was forbidden. Behind Matranga's the vacant lot grew larger by degrees and a new generation of urchins waged mock war on a wider battlefield. But noontime still brought the usual quota of coal venders who came to order their poor-boy sandwiches and to throw a few passes with the dice between bites. Louis remained on the friendliest terms with his former companions and sometimes he joined them at noon, walking pigeon-toed and feigning total drunkenness while the drivers guffawed as they squatted and stamped one foot on the unpaved street in the peculiar Negro style now widespread in America.

Naturally, Louis was proud of himself when he thought of the successes he had scored in the past two or three years. He could afford to look back with amusement on the days of the white mule and on the dismal prospects which were his when he wore the coal sack tied around his waist. Now he was a musician and the outline of his future was clear in his mind. He would join the select ranks of those blacks—in all, about two hundred—for whom jazz was both an escape and a breadwinner. If luck were with him, this would be his livelihood. On the other hand, he might fall into the general pattern, and take up some side-line in order to play jazz at night. Bob Lyons had neatly solved the problem in just that way: every night he tackled his double-bass after he had shined shoes the whole day long. And Louis recalled that distant night which had been the turning-point in his life, the night he had brought back a half-dollar to his mother.

Louis's stepfather, still at his old job with the coal company, advised Louis to go back to work.

"You'll see," his mother would say, "you'll do like the others. You'll get plenty hard knocks in the music game. Plenty times you won't have no work, nothin' 'ceptin' promises. One day you eats, nex' day you liable to starve."

Louis did not have to wait long for work, however. Almost immediately he was hired by the Tuxedo Band which held forth under Papa Celestine's leadership at a cabaret called "The Orchard." The Tuxedo Band was an old-time orchestra which had started out as a brass band in the era of Buddy Petit and later had blossomed into a jazz orchestra. Its drummer was none other than the famous Ernest Trepiana, reputed to be the best drum-player that ever strutted in a parade or funeral procession and who had long been the mainstay of the Olympia Band.

Louis Armstrong was a dazzling success. On the river, he had perfected his style and attained a mastery over his instrument which found its expression in a sort of exaggerated poise. Even his most devoted followers were often astounded by the inventive genius of this fiery youngster.

About this time the orchestra introduced two new pieces which Louis had perfected aboard the *Sidney*. These were *Dippermouth* (later known as the *Sugarfoot Stomp*) and *I Wish I Could Shimmy Like My Sister Kate*. In those days most of the tunes played in New Orleans were more or less common property. But as jazz became more and more popular, some alert musicians dipped into their bag of tricks and turned out to be better conjurers than composers. When the original Dixieland Band was recorded by one of the music houses, eyes opened suddenly. An old quadrille, or rather its distorted arrangement originally titled *Praline*, was subsequently known as *Play, Jack Carey* and finally became *Tiger Rag*, whereupon it was copyrighted.

One day Louis met Piron who lavished praise on him for his *Sister Kate* tune.

"Tell you what I'll do, Dipper—I'll give you fifty bucks for it."

"All right," promptly agreed Louis.

At that time fifty dollars was a very tempting sum. Piron had Louis sign a tight little contract and told him that the money would be forthcoming during the following week. Needless to add, Louis is still waiting to collect.

From time to time some local musician would hear from King Oliver, who was leading the life of Riley in Chicago. From Louis's painfully scrawled replies, Oliver learned that a new star was rising in the musical firmament of New Orleans. And he remembered Matranga's, where Louis had taken Bunk Johnson's place four years ago. Sure, sure! That young fellow was pretty good then, but who would have thought that one day he would be spoken of as a possible rival of King Oliver?

Throughout the Mississippi Valley the spring of 1921 was uniformly delightful. Louis renewed his acquaintance with the half-forgotten wonders of his beloved city. Everywhere, plants and trees wore a soft, moist-green garb, and in the last days of March the azaleas started to bloom. Not long after, the heady fragrance of magnolia blossoms filled the air and the blue flowers of the china-ball trees gladdened the eye once more. Louis reveled in the romantic blend of a thousand scents and as many poignant memories.

One evening in early June, Papa Celestine announced to his musicians that they were to make preparations for four o'clock on the eighth. Eddie Vinson had lost his father, and the band would play at his funeral in Algiers. The elder Vinson had been a member of the "Fast Friends Society," and even at that time burials with music were restricted to those who belonged to certain exclusive organizations.

On this eventful day, Louis jumped out of bed earlier than usual. Stopping at the saloon on the corner of Rampart, he related some of his adventures on the river to Sweet Child and Clark Wade's brother, the latter a drummer at present. Bob Lyons was already on duty at his stand in a corridor of the Masonic Hall. Little Mack was a laborer somewhere in the suburbs; Louis had not seen him. Curiously enough, three of the former quartet had become devotees of the drum.

At half-past two, the Tuxedo musicians began to arrive at the barroom. One by one, they pushed the latticed door open and spoke to Louis.

"How are you, Satchmo'?"

"Awreet, ol' man!"

"Have a gin?"

"Oh, yea!"

As Louis talked with them, he was thinking with pleasure of the next day, a Sunday, and the fun he would have with his chums—they were all going for a cool dip in Lake Pontchartrain.

Papa Celestine and Trepiana were the last to show up.

"How are you, Satchmo'?"

"Perfect, Dipper!"

"It's about time to leave!"

Louis was wearing full regalia—a black suit, his best stiff shirt with wing collar, and a derby—for the proper respect due a musician's father demanded formal attire. Edmund Hall, a young clarinet-player, crossed the group.

"How d' you feel, Satchmo'?"

"I feel like a million."

They were headed down Rampart Street. Sweet Child stayed behind, unable to march with one leg, and waved good-bye from the doorway of the Masonic Hall.

"Don't forget, Satchmo'—two o'clock tomorrow. And bring yo' trunks," Sweet Child called after him.

On Canal Street they boarded a streetcar, and sat in the colored section, moving the screen forward a few seats so they could all be together.

At the foot of Canal Street, they climbed up the ramp that leads to the ferry landing. A cool breeze from the Mississippi brought welcome relief from the evening heat. In the distance, they could see smokestacks breathing darkly against the horizon. The ferry-boat pulled away from its moorings, straining against the undertow, and the musicians leaned on the handrail looking down on the turbid stream.

Suddenly Louis dipped into his pocket. "I'm lookin' for a dime to throw in the river, fo' good luck."

Though the others poked fun at him for being superstitious, Louis merely set his jaw more firmly and the small coin sailed into the air before disappearing beneath the muddy waters.

Arriving in Algiers, they set out at once for the funeral home, following a narrow canal. Black crape was hanging on the open door. The musicians donned the traditional apron embroidered with the society's emblem, and stood near the coffin in the center of the floor. Outside, a crowd was slowly gathering, while the official mourners worked themselves into a frenzy of hysterical wails and moans, chanting over and over again their rhythmic lamentations in the automatic cadences which were to develop into the blues and—much later —to inspire the systematic repetitions of swing music.

The master of ceremonies, standing as stiff as a ramrod, began to issue instructions, seeking to bring order into the proceedings. Having invited the mourners to leave first, he placed the orchestra just outside the doorway and then gave the signal for the coffin to be carried out, slowly and carefully. At a sign from Papa Celestine, the orchestra started to play the invariable overture to a dignified funeral: *Abide With Me.* In the front rank stood Louis, who had just placed his cornet to his lips when he saw a hand waving from behind the mourners and recognized Mama Lucy, his sister.

What had happened? She was beckoning to him and seemed out of breath as though she had been running very fast. When the hymn was finished and while the undertakers busied themselves with the casket, Mama Lucy pushed through the crowd and handed him an envelope.

"What's that?"

"A telegram!"

"A telegram? You mus' be crazy."

"Read it. It's from Chicago!"

Meanwhile the pallbearers were setting down the coffin in the hearse and piling it high with flowers. Louis opened the envelope, and handed the slip of paper to Papa Celestine, who read:

LOUIS ARMSTRONG
COME IMMEDIATELY LINCOLN GARDEN CHICAGO JOB FOR YOU THIRTY DOLLARS A WEEK.
KING OLIVER

The players gathered around inquiringly.

"What's the matter, Dipper?"

"King Oliver wants me to go to Chicago—right away!"

His heart was swelling with joy. Now he knew he had been right to throw a dime in the good old Mississippi!

Papa Celestine signaled to the band, which fell into step behind the hearse as it rolled slowly toward the cemetery. But every man in the band had got wind of the big news in those few seconds.

"Satchmo's goin' to Chicago!" they whispered to one another.

Before entering the cemetery the band halted for a few minutes. Papa Celestine turned to Louis.

"Well, Dipper?"

"Well, I'm goin' to Chicago."

"You gonna leave us flat?"

"Can't help it, Papa!"

"I knowed doggone well I couldn't keep you for long."
And Papa Celestine heaved a sigh and grasped Louis's hand.
But his comrades tried to discourage him from leaving.

"Don't go. I heard King Oliver's havin' trouble with the
Union."

"You can't quit Perdido like that."

Louis had made up his mind, however, and he called Mama
Lucy. "Run back home and pack my grip, the one that's tied
with a rope."

"When you leavin', Dipper?" asked Trepiana.

"On the first train, I guess. I hate to leave New Orleans—
an' I wouldn't go for nobody else but King Oliver."

It was time to enter the cemetery. The mourning women
shouted their final lamentations while the throng filed past
the grave and the orchestra played a last dirge.

They left the graveyard and met at the entrance. Already
Papa Celestine was turning his apron inside out, and Louis
followed suit. Then the orchestra went on ahead to lead the
crowd, playing *Didn't He Ramble?* The mourners, following
behind, began to dance and sing. The urchins took up the
chorus:

> *"He rambled all around*
> *Till the butcher cut his tail down."*

At the station near the ferry Louis learned that a train was
leaving for Chicago at ten. He was surrounded by admiring
comrades, many thinking how wonderful it must be to live
in the big city, up there in the North

"You sho' is lucky, Louis. There ain't no Jim Crow in
Chicago!"

Soon they were crossing on the ferry. As night fell, the
first lights flashed on over the river. They had gone to the
bow and their group was alone at the rail. The bell clanged a

final warning and the boat started. Louis's eyes embraced the purplish haze of dusk gathering on the opposite shore, the home of his past. In the middle of the river, Trepiana's hand went to his pocket.

"Pals," he said, "let's all throw a dime in Ol' Man River so Satchmo' can have good luck an' plenty of it."

As Louis saw the flash of the dimes flying downward to be swallowed by the night and the water, there was a lump in his throat. . . .

Reaching Canal Street, Louis hastened toward Perdido. The shop windows of Rampart were flooded with light as usual; Bob Lyons was dragging his stand inside as usual; the fallen women were walking the streets as usual. But for Louis Armstrong this was anything but a usual day. It was the greatest day of his life, and he felt like shouting to everybody he passed that he was leaving for Chicago.

His mother cried as he kissed her good-bye. Mama Lucy went along with him, carrying the valise. Near Franklin they saw a figure emerge from the shadows. It was Daisy Parker, out for a stroll. Louis quickened his pace to avoid meeting her. When he reached Rampart her figure had merged forever with the shadows.

At the station, he embraced his sister, and was startled to hear the sound of music. A band was playing *Basin Street Blues.* He left the waiting-room and saw his friends of the Tuxedo Band, waiting for him near the tracks. "Wontcha come along with me!" they played. But this time the "land of dreams" was not New Orleans!

The conductor cried: "All aboard for St. Louis and Chicago!"

And Louis left to meet his destiny, reflecting that Sweet Child and the rest would miss him tomorrow at Lake Pontchartrain.

16

THE TRAIN arrived in Chicago at twilight of a blistering hot day. Louis was wearing his best black suit, his derby and a wing collar that was anything but spotless after the long trip. As he followed the hurrying crowd toward the nearest station exit, a sense of power surged in him, tinged with a slight anxiety.

For he couldn't help feeling anxiety as his imagination sought to penetrate the unknown wonders that awaited him in Chicago. He had escaped from the ghetto of his race, was no longer bound by the immemorial servitude that burdened his brethren in New Orleans, and he felt the uneasiness of a dog that has lost its master.

He walked on, carrying his cardboard suitcase. Other blacks passed him, but none paid any attention to him. Reaching the waiting-room, he felt completely lost. For a moment he stood still, looking around at the newsstands, the hot-dog vendors, the florist shop, the colored bootblack. Through a megaphone came the blare of the train announcer's voice.

Louis searched in his pockets, found the telegram, and read it once more. Then he asked the bootblack: "Say, Pops, where's the Lincoln Garden?"

"Pops" looked blank, and Louis was dumbfounded. How

could any black man be so ignorant as not to know where King Oliver played?

"Don't you know King Oliver?" he asked incredulously.

"No, boy, never heard of him!"

Louis was seized with sudden panic. Here he was in Chicago on the strength of a vague address—merely "Lincoln Garden." Now he must find the place. Could he do it? Wildly he saw himself lost in the big city. . . .

Seeing the worry plainly written on Louis's features, the bootblack took pity and told him to look up the address in the telephone book. Clumsily Louis thumbed through the pages of the thick book, until finally a white man came to his rescue. Such a thing had never happened to him before—a white man helping out a black—and he was very grateful. He asked what was the best way to reach Thirty-first Street.

"That's on the South Side darky. Take the El!" And the white Samaritan went off smiling.

Then Louis spied a colored fellow near by and asked him how to get to Thirty-first Street on the South Side.

"You take the Elevated and get off at Station Eleven," he was told.

Louis was famished but did not dare go anywhere for something to eat. He scanned the establishments outside the station. White patrons were everywhere! Someone showed him the stairway, and he climbed a few steps up, then stopped to look about for a fellow Negro.

"What mus' I do, Pops?" Louis asked.

"Drop a nickel in that box there."

The colored man disappeared and Louis was alone on the platform. The train roared up and stopped with a grinding of brakes. Beyond the tracks he saw second-story windows bright with lights. A stream of passengers rushed out. Louis

[153]

followed the inbound crowd and boarded a car. Instinctively he looked around for the familiar sign "For Colored Only." He could not find it, and was frightened. This was unbelievable! He did not dare sit down. Holding his suitcase between his legs he stood uncertainly, swaying with the motion of the car; beads of perspiration broke out on his forehead. Then he saw a Negro take a seat and Louis subsided next to him, greatly relieved.

The train was rushing by long rows of houses. At every intersection, there was a dazzling display of electric signs, multicolored advertisements flashing dizzily on and off. Louis was counting the stations. At the eleventh he asked his neighbor, for greater certainty, and started downward. When he reached the sidewalk he caught sight of a newsboy.

"The Lincoln Garden? Never heard of it. You don't mean the Royal Garden?"

"No, man—it's the Lincoln Garden, with King Oliver."

"Never heard of no king in Chicago. Ask a cop."

The nearest policeman obligingly gave him clear directions. At last! Louis breathed a sigh of relief. Here was somebody who really knew!

As he walked among the anonymous throng Louis kept repeating the directions. Turn left, then right. Two blocks. A building with a large electric sign on the outside.

"You can't miss it," the policeman had said. Louis walked turned, looked. He saw nothing that answered the description. He was tired, his legs ached, and his stomach was empty. He set down his suitcase on the sidewalk and mopped his brow. Suddenly he spied a sign—red and green letters alternating in a stingy display of electricity. So this was the dream castle he had envisaged! Wearily he trudged up to the door. It was almost one o'clock in the morning. A few couples straggled out. Some drunks shouted abuse at one another. Then a black doorman, appeared, his uniform trimmed with gold braid.

"Is this the Lincoln Garden, Pops?" Louis queried.

"Yeah, man, but there's nothin' here for you."

"What you mean?"

"There ain't no jobs open in the kitchen."

A horrible thought crossed Louis's mind, and he felt a shiver crawl over his spine: somebody else had stolen his job as cornetist! He spoke again, timidly,

"The King sent for me."

"What king?"

"Oliver." But his soft southern pronunciation failed to show that the name ended in R, and the man did not recognize it.

"Nobody here by that name!"

In desperation, Louis caught sight of a poster on a near-by wall. "That's him—Joe Oliver!" he cried.

So now at last Louis was admitted to the sacred precincts. His eye fell on a series of arches overhanging the stairs. Respectfully he doffed his derby and held it in his hand. Already his ear was catching the distant moan of the trumpet. Without a doubt, that was Bad-Eye Joe! There was a pause, then the piano's prelude. A clarinet slid off an improvisation strewn with breaks. The doorman took Louis into a large room where soft lights glowed dimly. It took Louis a few moments to become accustomed to the semidarkness, and then his eyes found the black faces of the orchestra, barely noticeable against the dark backdrop of the platform. Without realizing it, he reached the door.

"You can undress here, darky. And then you'll sit at the orchestra's table."

Louis recognized Joe, who was looking his way. He was

smiling reassuringly without interrupting his trumpet-playing and continued to sway to his own rhythm.

Louis sensed the excitement of the crowd under the spell of the music's rhythms. The scraping of feet formed a sort of undertone for the orchestra. The music stopped for a brief moment, then started again. That was a wonderful take-off, so smooth, so sure, thought Louis, and he grinned happily. The notes of the trombone stretched into seemingly endless effects. How well Louis knew the piece, *High Society*, which they were playing in his honor! In a flash his mind evoked Pete Lala, the Orchard, Matranga's, Funky Butt! Truly he had been touched with a magic wand, that he should be here tonight! He felt like pinching himself to make sure that it was really he, Louis Armstrong, the wretched kid of the Waifs' Home, the cornetist of Perdido, sitting here in Chicago at a table right next to other tables where white folks laughed and clapped their hands.

Now the orchestra was playing the last piece before the rest period. All the musicians were smiling at him and he grinned widely in response, his thick lips curled over gleaming ivory. Bill Johnson, whose nimble fingers rapidly plucked the taut strings of his double-bass with the dexterity of a tightrope walker without a pole, addressed him from time to time:

"Oh, man, just you wait! We're gonna twist out one more number an' then we'll give you a skin."

Baby Dodds, next to his brother Johnny, the clarinetist, towered like a god behind his pagoda of drums. From time to time he would rise, hammer out a few notes on the small drum with his twinkling sticks, and then relaxing into a melancholy smile, scrape the calfskin with his drum brush (a wired peacock tail) and wink broadly at Louis.

"How d'you feel, Satchmo'?"

"I feel like a million."

At the right time Honoré Dutrey moved up to the edge of the platform. Joe Oliver shouted:

"Sock it, Dutrey!"

As Dutrey attacked *Muskrat Ramble,* the dancers panted to the rhythm. Louis scanned the faces smiling at the band. He saw one of the dancers halt near King Oliver and speak to him in the friendliest fashion; Louis could not believe his eyes and his ears.

"A second, oh, man! A second!" screamed Joe, holding his cornet with the fervor of a preacher holding the Bible.

And the rapturous crowd began to beat on the tables. The dancing couples, half-crazed with delight, added their cries to the pandemonium.

"A second, a second!"

Honoré Dutrey plunged into a second chorus, drawing raucous and sensual sounds from his instrument. Louis realized that only this evening was he learning the true meaning of jazz. In a few hours he had passed from the land of crude rhythm to the capital of a more civilized form of music. He wondered if he would ever be able to acquire enough polish to play in this band, the best he had ever heard.

Suddenly Joe Oliver drew himself up to his full height and took Dutrey's place. Dancers were stopping or moving slowly before the orchestra, their eyes dreamy with pleasure. Lovers forgot their partners, abandoning themselves to the concentrated power of this newly organized form of noise. Now and again, Joe Oliver stopped playing, and Bobby, with outspread arms, underlined the measured ritual of a break in which the pianist broke in to recall the triumphant notes of the cornet.

The dying notes of the music were drowned out in a tumult of applause. Putting down their instruments, the musicians hurried over to Louis's table.

"Hello, Pop!"

"Hello, Gate!"

"I wasn't lookin' for you today," said King Joe, shaking hands with Louis. "You know everybody?"

"Yes—I mean—well, jus' about everybody."

"How's good ol' New Orleans?" Johnny Dodds asked eagerly.

So Louis launched into the latest gossip from the Crescent City. Eddie Vinson's father was dead . . . Picou was still a zinc worker and played at night . . . Bob Lyons seldom missed a day at his stand in Rampart Street . . . Papa Celestine sent his best regards to Joe and all the boys . . . Funky Butt Hall was shut tight.

"An' your ol' lady?" inquired Dutrey. "She's here with you?"

"Oh, no! We broke up a good while ago."

"I'll never forget the time she wanted to give you a lick with her razor just before the Zulu parade."

This sally provoked a train of reminiscences amid general laughter. A white waiter brought steins of beer. From the piano, the strains of a waltz accompanied a white singer's slightly naughty song.

Weaving his way between tables, the manager stopped before King Oliver. "Everything ready for the last half-hour?"

"I'd like you to meet my second cornetist," Oliver told him. "Louis Armstrong. He's from New Orleans."

Louis jumped quickly to his feet and mumbled something polite, and the manager went off with a smile.

"Louis," said Joe, "I'm dyin' to hear you play. I've heard a million about you. I know you can twist them tunes. But, you see, our style of music has changed plenty since Pete Lala's time. Listen close to us tonight, and tomorrow come

[158]

:o the rehearsal at three. . . . Get it, fellows! Tomorrow at
:hree, rehearsal!"

So the miracle was actually happening! Yesterday a mule
driver, today a player greeted as peer by the members of a famous orchestra. What magic powers did the music possess
which slept in the souls of the blacks and raised them from their
helpless state, yes, even as high as the esteem of the white man?
Never as tonight had the will to surpass himself been stronger
in the man. Not only must he equal these musicians; he must
strive to excel his master, the great King Oliver. His thoughts
turned to the royal line of Perdido: King Bolden, followed
by Keppard; from Keppard, the crown had descended to Emmanuel Perez; after Perez, King Oliver had mounted the
hrone—and beyond that, he knew only that his own heart
overflowed with fervent resolves. Now he stood before this
orchestra like the forlorn boy of the Waifs' Home looking
longingly at Peter Davis's cornet. There, in a few days, he
had become better than all the rest! A wave of pride swept
over him as he remembered his success. But it was no longer
the pointless and stupid pride which led to a fall. Indeed not.
This was a keener and purer emotion. And Louis was suddenly
struck by the memory of the dynamic force which had impressed him in his early youth on those nights long ago when
Buddy Bolden played at Funky Butt. The crowds shifting
from one emotion to another, but always dominated by the
music's spell; the men stricken dumb by that supernatural
power, the women hypnotized to the point of giving themselves up, body and soul, to the musician who interpreted the
black man's soul to the blacks. And then Louis was startled by
the idea that perhaps there was a way to interpret the black
man's soul to the whites and win them over, bind them under
the spell of the genius native to the race whose tribulations

began on the shores of Africa and did not end in the civilized jungle of the New World.

The band resumed its playing—passionate, earthy, violent—mingling the melody of the blues with the wrench of the dance-steps. Louis felt he had already won the friendship of the musicians. They had all heard about the trumpeter who played with Pete Lala and the Tuxedo Band, and Joe Oliver, who had won his laurels through unquestioned ability, was eager to cross swords with this young upstart who used to play at Matranga's and of whom it was said sometimes that he played as well as the King. All this Louis felt, and more—that Johnson was kindly disposed toward him and that Bobby Dodds was quite friendly.

Suddenly *Panama* exploded like a bombshell. Following this, Joe Oliver played the prelude of a new tune that bore some resemblance to the *Barnyard Blues*. What was it? Louis whispered the question, and the bass fiddler leaned forward and enlightened him:

"*Wang Wang Blues!*"

Louis was intoxicated to the point of forgetting his fatigue. Abruptly the players slowed the tempo, and a few bars in a minor key played on the piano induced a melancholy mood in the dancers. The new melody filled Louis with happiness. He promised himself he would teach his own compositions to the orchestra, as he listened to the new air, which was the *Choo-choo Blues*.

> *Choo-choo Blues, they're with me night and day,*
> *And they won't go away—*
> *Those Blues, I cannot lose—*
> *I've tried 'most ev'ry town,*
> *But I just can't settle down!*

The singer took up the poignant chorus which enraptured the women and yet wrenched the men's hearts. Louis closed his eyes, seeing again the prairies, the fields, the towns large and small that he had passed on the way from New Orleans, hearing again the steady chug of the train. . . .

Surely this was the greatest night of his life! If he could have played, the walls of Lincoln Garden would have crumbled like Jericho under the sound of his trumpet.

Joe Oliver announced the final number. From the very first notes Louis knew what was coming. It was *Tiger Rag.* Couples hopped about madly; the sitters pounded their glasses on the tables; excited women imitated the roar of the tiger. Louis kept his eyes shut fast, striving to fill his cup of happiness to the brim. In his pocket his right hand pressed imaginary pistons and when Joe Oliver broke off a solo, Louis continued to improvise, climbing very high, way up to the top of the scale. He held that note for a long time, and—in his dream imagining its effect on the crowd—he stood up himself, eyes closed, swaying blissfully, oblivious of time and space.

When he opened his eyes, the lights were being turned off and the patrons were leaving. Some were saying good-bye to Joe Oliver. The Dodds brothers, leaving together, reminded him about the next day's rehearsal. Joe Oliver took Louis under his wing, having decided that Louis should stay with him.

Once more Louis climbed the stairs of the Elevated. Gradually the great white city of stone and tall buildings faded from sight. Smaller homes could now be seen. Presently he and Joe got off and walked several blocks. The houses were more and more shabby in appearance, and they saw an increasing number of blackfaces. They climbed a staircase. Joe pushed open a door, and a familiar New Orleans odor assailed Joe's nostrils: pork and beans!

Suddenly he awoke to the fact that he was ravenous. Joe's wife, Mama Joe, was stirring something on the stove. After brief introductions, she silently set another place at the table. Joe sank into one chair, Louis quickly took the other, and Mama Joe put before them the pot filled with red beans. The whole place was spotlessly clean, and never in his life had Louis sat at such a table. Mama Joe filled their plates and they dispatched with proper gusto this favorite dish of the children of the South.

When they had finished, the two men pushed their chairs back and started to talk.

"Tell me, Dipper, what pieces do you know?"

"Oh, Papa Joe, them beans and rice was delicious! I play *Tiger Rag, Panama* an' *High Society.*"

"Can you read?"

"Jus' a little, Papa Joe."

"How's about some more red beans, Dipper?" interrupted Mama Joe.

"Gee, thanks, Mama Joe!"

"Red beans is a wonderful dish. An' Mama Joe sure knows how to cook 'em."

That night, whether from too much excitement or too many red beans, Louis Armstrong did not sleep a wink.

17

FOR THE first few weeks things were not easy for Louis in King Oliver's orchestra. The role of second trumpeter proved rather dull, especially since it seemed to consist chiefly in playing courtier to the King and acknowledging his superiority in all matters. In one field, however, Joe Oliver gave the new member a free rein—singing; and here Louis was to attain immediate success.

He had brought with him from New Orleans a tune that, though old, was extremely catchy, and he delighted in singing it, with his lips trembling and his chin in the air. *Sister Kate* had marked the heyday of his popularity during the period he had spent with Pete Lala.

I wish I could shimmy like my sister Kate—
She dances like a jelly on a plate. . . .

When he sang this song at Lincoln Garden everybody laughed and exclaimed in pleasure, and each night the patrons clamored for it. The original version popular in New Orleans had used another word than *shimmy*, but Louis did not dare follow the unexpurgated form in his new and more "refined" environment. In any case, the substituted word was timely, for this was the era of the shimmy, that jerky, epileptic dance which was the rage all over the country.

Horn of Plenty:

Never had a dance hall enjoyed such popularity as did the Lincoln Garden this season. Only early comers could be sure of getting seats. The tables near the band were usually reserved for regular customers, who demonstrated their admiration of the music by making themselves familiar with all the numbers, following the orchestra's rhythm, and generally going wild with enthusiasm.

From time to time Louis managed to escape from the week's routine. Toward the shank of the evening, when Joe's exertions had fatigued him, he would signal to Louis—whereupon the latter would plunge into a dizzy solo with such tonal power and such assurance in the upper register as to make Joe envious.

One evening—it was his night off—Louis sauntered over to the "Dreamland" to kill time. A young woman in evening dress was sitting at the piano, and once or twice Louis caught her eye, but she always averted his glance. Never had Louis seen a colored girl dressed in such good taste. Her gown was long and very décolleté, and her arms were bare. The curve of her lips was emphasized by a touch of orange lipstick, and her straight black hair was pulled tight behind her ears. But Louis was fascinated by her eyes, light-colored eyes sparkling with intelligence. Irresistibly attracted, he wondered how he could meet this girl.

Louis did not have long to wait, for a few days later the girl joined King Oliver's orchestra as pianist. Louis, delighted when he saw her at rehearsal, found out that she was an accomplished pianist, a college graduate, and able to read music without effort.

A little awestruck upon discovering such an array of talent in one person, Louis nevertheless persisted in his design and asked Joe to introduce him.

"Louis, this is Lil Hardin, the best pianist in the world.

Lil, meet Louis Armstrong from down yonder in New Orleans."

As Lil held out her hand, Joe noticed how pink it was against the darker shade of his own palm. He managed to stammer a few words of greeting; but Lil quickly put him at his ease and soon they were talking like two old friends. Thereafter, they were often in each other's company and Louis was often twitted by the other players for having succumbed so quickly to Lil's charms. A slow grin would spread over his features whenever they teased him; he did not mind—he was biding his time, for he wanted to be sure of his footing.

One day a hot discussion broke out at a rehearsal. Lil Hardin openly came out as Joe's champion, supported by the Dodds brothers.

"Papa Joe, you ought to give Satchmo' a break."

"What do you mean?"

"You don't give Louis a chance to blow like you know he can. The customers think you're afraid."

"Afraid o' what?" Joe was shaking with anger, and his bad eye fluttered. "You can tell 'em that the King ain't scared of no livin' trumpet. I'm the King, ain't I?"

Louis, pretending not to listen, was humming a little tune to himself, his eyes turned away.

Lil was persistent.

"The only way the orchestra can really hit its stride is if Louis gets a few solos."

"I never turned Satchmo' down on a solo," Joe retorted hotly. "I know he can blow like hell. He can blow himself out as long as he stays with me. But I'm still the King!"

Here Louis interrupted pleadingly.

"Papa Joe, you know doggone well I ain't never gonna leave you!"

This ended the discussion, and the rehearsal went on. But

that evening Louis went home in a thoughtful mood. He could not stop thinking about Lil Hardin's heated arguments on his behalf.

When he returned to the Garden, he found her already seated at the piano. Wishing to express his thanks, he laid his hand lightly on her shoulder and thrilled at the touch of her. What attracted him so strongly, however, was not her physical charms, but the unattainable prestige that surrounded her person—she seemed so far above an ex-mule-driver. Now she turned her head and gave him a winning smile. But he dared not raise his hopes too high. He knew that she was the belle of the orchestra. The men vied in paying her compliments and tried to win her favor. But Lil was indifferent, moving among them like a good pal who knew how to make them keep their distance. Louis knew also that he was incapable of finding the precise words that would go straight to Lil's heart. However, he faltered through a phrase or two, relieved when he heard Joe's call to the orchestra.

"Let's go, boys!"

They swang into *Muskrat Ramble*, Johnny Dodds doing the solo. The two trumpets groped for the theme of a dazzling break; suddenly the musical chasm yawned. The cataract of noise was followed by an identical inspiration—Joe and Louis playing the same passage in thirds and evoking from the audience a tremendous burst of applause.

At the end of the piece, enthusiastic couples milled around the orchestra. At the tables, people were striking their glasses with spoons and knives. All chanted in unison:

"The same thing! The same thing!"

There was nothing to do but repeat *Muskrat Ramble*. With an engaging smile, Lil began the overture. Suddenly Louis turned to face her; she looked deep into his eyes and her eyelids fluttered once. The idea came to him that some indefinable bond existed between them. . . .

Toward the end of the piece Joe broke into his solo, Louis playing a routine accompaniment. In the midst of it, there was a cry from the floor: "Come on, Armstrong! Come on, Louis! Go to town!"

Lil Hardin joined in the applause and seemed to plead with Louis. He hesitated, and cast a sidelong glance at Joe, who wound up with a flourish and pointed his trumpet at Louis. In a flash the young musician was blowing out his soul through the mouth of his trumpet. He blew so hard that the skin on his nape was stretched hard; he had closed his eyes, and seemed in a trance, out of the living world, completely possessed by unalloyed musical exaltation. Vaguely he knew that Lil was stamping her foot close by. The crowd howled; even Joe was irresistibly swept into the current, clapping his hands to urge on Louis as he concluded the number.

"Come on, Pop, a second!"

And Louis soared to greater heights, louder than before, filling the room with an orgy of rhythm. The manager leaned against the rear door as if bracing himself against this hurricane of sound. Musicians and patrons alike, as Louis paused, applauded madly to persuade him to continue. Thus chorus followed chorus until the moment when Louis held a note with one breath through ten whole beats, broke off abruptly, looked at the petrified audience, then resumed the rhythm, climbing to unbelievable heights with the joy of a mountain climber scaling a peak that others can reach only in their dreams.

It was over. Then pandemonium! Women started throwing their handbags at the orchestra. A slender white girl with deeply circled eyes held out both her hands toward Louis, who was incredulous in the face of this fantastic reality. Joe himself congratulated Satchmo', though there was an undertone of uneasiness that Louis alone detected. Dodds and the others expressed their admiration in the familiar slang of Perdido. Honoré Dutrey was laughing and making signs to Bill Johnson.

"What you say, Honoré!"

"Oh, nothing! Oh, man! I only wish Buddy Bolden was here!"

Louis bowed his head, overcome with emotion. Grinning widely, teeth clenched with delight, he babbled a plea for a tribute to the man whose crown was toppling:

"Oh, yeah, Gates! Sure—oh, yeah! Come on, King Joe! That's the man!"

Through all this, Lil Hardin remained silent. But Louis repeatedly threw a glance her way and each time caught a distant, mysterious, impassioned look. He felt her close to him in spirit—close in a tie that was entirely different from the friendship that bound them all together.

When the evening ended, Louis was jubilant. Joe Oliver was waiting for him at the door, his manner rather cool.

"Come on, Satchmo'," he said to Louis. "There's red beans and rice waitin' for us!"

But Louis had heard a voice behind him—a voice he recognized at once. So he made no reply to the King, but waited for what Lil had to say.

"No, Papa Joe!" Lil told Oliver teasingly. "Tonight Louis and I are going out together. We have to discuss a new arrangement for *Smiles*."

"All right!" grumbled Joe. "I'll tell the ol' lady to leave your share on the stove."

Everybody was leaving, and the doorman was preparing to lock up. The two walked off together, Louis taking the girl's arm. How he wished that May Ann or Mama Lucy might see him now! To think that he was walking out into the night with a university graduate!

"Where we goin'?" he asked.

"Let's find a little honky-tonk where we can relax."

"Yeah, I jus' want to look in yo' eyes, a long, long time."

"Oh, Louis, you were marvelous this evening! You turned me inside out like a glove. Nobody else can thrill me the way you do."

Louis repressed a sudden urge to take her in his arms and hold her close. But the thought of her education damped his ardor, and he hesitated. Yet she was natural and gay, her eyes brimming with happiness.

In the black belt they found a quiet spot where a nasal phonograph was playing Paul Whiteman's latest tunes. They sat down alone in a small booth and ordered spare ribs and barbecue. Of course they talked music.

"Louis, you must learn solfeggio. There's a lot more to music than just jazz. The white folks have their own music. You ought to learn some operatic numbers. I'll play *Carmen* for you, and you'll just love *Il Trovatore.* Tomorrow night, after work, come over to my house. You'll see!"

"Suits me fine, sweet Lil. You know, I'd like to tell you——"

"Never mind . . . I understand!"

Louis's hand grasped hers and held it tight. The walk home in Lil's company was sheer delight. Already the first struggling rays of dawn were dispelling the shadows. They reached a street of small houses. He lingered long at her door. Perhaps he told her that he would very much like to hear *Carmen.* She was laughing and happy, but unyielding.

"No, Louis. We'll keep that for tomorrow."

"Never put off till tomorrow what you can do today!" He tried to kiss her.

Quickly she slipped out of his embrace, ran up the stairs, turned the key in the lock, opened the door and, turning to face Louis blew him a kiss and disappeared.

Next day King Joe made fun of Louis for turning down his supper of red beans and rice. Everybody was in gay spirits. Louis's secret happiness was shining in his eyes and Lil shyly avoided his glances. During the rest period the King, bubbling with good humor, began to spin a fanciful yarn to the assembled musicians, who listened with open mouths. He declared that Willy Armstrong was not really Louis's father. If the young fellow could blow the trumpet like nobody's business, well, boys, he got it all from the King. Yes, indeed, Joe was going to tell them the big secret of his life. He had never wanted to talk about it before, but tonight—well, he just had to confess. Louis Armstrong was his own true son! Yes, sir, blood was thicker than water and he had been remorseful for a long time. He had been shamefully lax in his duties as a father, but now everything would be straightened out. He was ashamed of his men, that they had not guessed the relationship! But they must button their lips; not a word of all this must ever reach Mama Joe's ears. No, sir, it wouldn't do if she ever found out that the King had strayed from the conjugal path. Just think, she might even refuse to cook any more red beans! And another thing, Lil Hardin had better do the right thing. If her intentions were serious, she must not forget to talk to Louis's "father"!

The merciless chaffing went on for weeks. Joe's tale became a classic joke, which never failed to send the musicians into gales of laughter.

Louis now saw Lil every night. Joe perforce resigned himself to accept the new situation and told Mama Joe that their boarder was busy elsewhere. Much of Louis's and Lil's time was spent at the piano, Louis listening for hours to Lil's wizardry—an artistic skill to be acquired only in schools. He was competely happy, now that he had learned that Lil loved him. Each night they went off together like a pair of turtledoves, flitting from one night club to another, where under the spell of jazz, hand in hand, they shared their dreams of the future.

One morning Louis got up at the crack of dawn, to spend the day conferring with various lawyers. For a definite plan was forming in his mind. He felt that life was about to begin anew for him; the past must be forgotten, buried forever—he must divorce his wife so as to marry Lil. . . .

On Sundays, when the warm beaches of Lake Michigan were particularly inviting, Louis would dress hurriedly and run off to meet Lil. The two shared a love of the outdoors, the sight and smell of trees and flowers and grass. In his memory Louis preserved the fragrant recollection of azaleas, magnolias, camphor-trees, Spanish moss, Japanese medlar trees, and the sweet-smelling catalpas. Somewhere along the road to the North, all these wonders of Nature had vanished. Up here, everything was strangely different. But the blue and purple waters of the lake held their own charm when twilight came.

In the late hours, surrounded by other amorous couples seeking a solitude they could not find, Louis and Lil wove the fabric of their romance. From a distant phonograph came the muted strains of *Alexander's Ragtime Band*. Sometimes Lil, interrupting Louis's kisses, would show him a sheet of music paper with the notes of a break which he had played the night before with Papa Joe. Invariably Louis wondered at her skill.

"Read that chorus for me, Louis!"

"Aw, shucks! What's the good of readin'? The main thing is what comes out of the bell!"

"That's true. But you'll never amount to anything until

[171]

you can read at sight as well as the white folks who study music."

Painstakingly, Lil would go over the lesson with him a dozen times, and always the motion of his fingers followed the music on imaginary pistons.

One evening, as King Oliver joined the orchestra, he was all smiles. He had been complaining that Louis never came home to supper any more, but now he said: "Tomorrow, Satchmo', you're comin' up with Lil. My wife says you're shunnin' her!"

Armstrong grinned back and accepted. As he took his instrument out of its case he handed Lil a piece of paper. She thought it must be some new tune, and gasped when it turned out to be a certificate attesting that Louis Armstrong was divorced from Daisy Parker!

On the following day, when Lil and Louis arrived at Joe's house, they were welcomed with fried chicken and red beans. Louis's contribution to the meal was two bottles of wine, which he set down carefully before throwing his arms around Mama Joe.

"It's sho' nice of you to celebrate our engagement!" he told her.

Joe looked at them in astonishment. "What you mean?"

"We want to get married—and we will, as soon as Lil gets her divorce!"

Little by little Louis had become the oustanding personality of the orchestra. Two or three times each night King Joe would retire from the spotlight and yield his place to Satchmo', who would blow a veritable storm of rhythm through Lincoln Garden. Occasionally, white musicians stole in to listen to this new power in the music world.

One night, Louis had shut his eyes and was giving an ecstatic rendition of his customary solo, the *St. Louis Blues*. He started off by singing, with Lil accompanying as usual; and his warm, husky, captivating voice vibrated with all the tragic melancholy that smolders in the heart of the Negro.

As soon as he finished his song, he seized his trumpet. Lil noticed—though Louis did not—that some sort of commotion had started at the far end of the room. The waiters were laughing. The dancing couples had stopped. All were eyeing the shabbily dressed Negress who had just appeared in the doorway. The poor woman, overwhelmed by the rhythmic bedlam, could only gesture helplessly in the general direction of the band. Then, guided by friendly hands, she made her way through the maze of tables, awkwardly and timidly, stumbling against the patrons.

Meanwhile, Louis was reaching for the sky. He forced the notes, tearing them out or swelling them, only to let them die abruptly. The tune ended under a deluge of drum beats. When Louis opened his eyes, he saw his mother! She was seated at the table reserved for the orchestra, and she was crying. He stared briefly, unwilling to believe his eyes. In one bound he leaped from the platform and was at the table. Throwing his arms around her, he too broke into tears. Everybody looked on in astonishment. Who *was* this woman?

Louis's words came tumbling out as he held May Ann's hands tight:

"Somethin's happened! Mamma Lucy's dead?"

"No, no," his mother hastened to reply. "But somebody tol' me you was sick—was goin' to kill yo'self. Oh, Louis!"

By now Joe and Lil had approached the table. Louis exclaimed indignantly:

"I'd like to know what crazy fool told you that! Why, I'm the happiest man alive! Wait a minute, here she is. Mama—here's my gal!"

Louis drew Lil forward to kiss her future mother-in-law, who was utterly dazed by this sudden transition from nightmare to fairy tale.

"Of course, you know *this* guy," Louis went on, pointing to Joe. "You sho' oughta know him, 'cause he's all the time braggin' he's my Pa!"

Louis had hit on precisely the right device for turning May Ann's worry into gaiety. As the others guffawed at the old jest, she dried her tears and looked hard at her boy. How much taller and heavier he had grown! As he went back to the orchestra and played on his trumpet like a dusky Gabriel, May Ann marveled that he should be her son.

18

WHEN SOMEONE in New Orleans told May Ann that Louis was very ill and was thinking of committing suicide, she had instantly scraped together the price of a ticket to Chicago, at that time expecting to return to Perdido within a few days. But Louis, abetted by Lil's attentive affection, was able to persuade his mother to stay on with them, and he found an apartment for her at St. Lawrence and 45th Streets.

One morning, Louis rose at daybreak (in the middle of the night, he called it) and went to fetch his mother to the hotel in order to show her the new quarters. Everything was clean, neat, and shiny.

"Here it is, May Ann, all for you!"

She began to sob, overcome by joy. Characteristically, she crossed herself and thanked the Lord for having wrought this miracle in her behalf.

Not long afterward, Louis and Lil were married and set up housekeeping. Armstrong's popularity was increasing every day. At night a mob would jam every inch of space in the Garden, and the owner promptly raised his prices. In the orchestra's corner, the wildest fans stood up and beat time with the music. Louis was showered with attention and compliments.

"Let's have the *St. Louis Blues!*"

And Joe Oliver would smile benignly, no longer caring that his own solos were not in demand. One evening, the band was playing softly: Joe and Louis, seated side by side, were following each other in third, when they saw a messenger approaching the orchestra.

"Louis Armstrong!" the boy sang out.

"That's me!" cried Louis, putting down his trumpet.

He unfolded the yellow slip and read that his cousin Flora Miles had just died, leaving her little Clarence alone in the world. Memories of the boy flooded back as Louis resumed his playing of fox trots. Clarence Hatfield had been born under an unlucky star in 1915; for three or four years later he had fallen from a second-story window and injured himself so badly that his mental development was arrested. And now the boy was left an orphan. Where would he go? How would he live? . . .

At the end of the night's entertainment a throng of youthful admirers were waiting for Louis at the exit.

"We want your autograph!" they clamored.

"You-all like music?" Louis asked them.

"Sure—we play, too."

"Where at?"

"The Three Deuces—with Mezz Mezzrow and Bud Freeman and Teschmaker. We could have a lot of fun if we came over some day to listen to you. Then we could have a few drinks and talk about jazz!"

"Sure," Louis agreed. "But not today, fellows. Sorry!"

It was plain that they did not believe him, thought he was just getting rid of them. Louis therefore produced the telegram so that they might understand his refusal.

When he reached the house he found his mother sitting up with Lil. Both saw at once that something was troubling him.

"What's the matter, Louis?" his mother asked.

He handed her the telegram, and the two women read it. May Ann began to cry silently, and Louis explained to Lil who Flora and Clarence were. Then he voiced the natural question:

"What's the poor boy goin' to do?" He paused for a moment, thinking. Then he went on abruptly: "I know what!" The women looked at him inquiringly.

"If you both think it's all right, I'll adopt Clarence."

Lil hugged her husband, and May Ann's tears of relief showed that she too approved the idea. It would involve no real sacrifice for any of them, since Louis was now earning a good deal of money and his own requirements had not changed much from the old Perdido days. He did not drink, he did not smoke, and he seldom went out. Being a generous man, he therefore shared his money whenever he could do good with it—as when, for instance, he bought a typewriter for Lil's mother.

Lil had been shopping most of the day and, instead of going home, she decided to meet Louis at Lincoln Garden. She found her husband in great form. People were being turned away and a group of white musicians, playing in a nearby theater, had come over between two shows to listen to Louis. They gave him a rousing ovation. In a few months, his style had greatly improved, owing largely to Joe's presence and to the silent rivalry that existed between the two trumpeters. Each evening he arrived on the scene with new ideas. For instance, in a solo rendition of Margie, he suddenly introduced a passage from *O Sole Mio*, to the joy of the audience. By this time many were calling him the best trumpet-player in the country.

When they returned home on this evening, Lil entered the apartment first. On reaching the dining-room she uttered a cry of delighted surprise.

"No, Louis—I can't believe it! A baby grand!"

She turned to her broadly smiling husband and threw her arms around his neck. Then she ran over and opened the piano, took some music from a shelf, and sat down to play some Chopin for Louis.

At the kitchen door appeared May Ann's happy face. "Come on an' eat, you-all! Them beans been waitin' for an hour!"

But Louis could not tear himself away from the romantic music that filled the room, coaxed from the instrument by Lil's magic fingers. He was leaning on the piano.

"Lil—play somethin' just for me. You know . . ."

Her fingers swept the keys, and Louis began *sotto voce*:

"Everything is peaches down in Georgia!
What a peach of a clime
For a peach of a time—
Believe me, Paradise is now awaiting there for you!"

And he bent down to kiss his wife and to whisper huskily: "Yes, this is Paradise!"

Two or three days later, Louis and his mother went to the station to meet Clarence, who was coming to them from New Orleans, carefully tagged like a parcel.

The train puffed in, filling the station with its clanging roar. For several minutes Louis and his mother scanned the passing faces before they spied the boy. The sight of him brought a flood of Perdido memories to May Ann's heart. Having removed the identification tag from Clarence's buttonhole, the three headed homeward. It had been decided that the boy would live with Louis and Lil.

May Ann was worrying Louis—she seemed sad so much oftener than she seemed happy.

"What's wrong, Mama?" he asked.

"Nothin', Louis—I'm all right!"

But the truth was that she was homesick, and one day she could not hold it in any longer.

"My son, it's awful! I know I never had all I've got here. But you can't teach an old dog new tricks. I miss Perdido. Down there I was poor, didn't have much clothes. But I was happy. What's the good of havin' fine dresses like you buys me, if I can't show 'em off to my friends in Reverend Cozy's church?"

Though Louis tried to argue her into a better frame of mind, he realized that he was fighting a bad case of homesickness; and finally it was decided that May Ann would leave the following week—and she was serene once more.

"I'd rather be the poorest person in Perdido than the finest lady in Chicago!" she assured Louis and Lil happily.

They arranged to sublet her apartment, and made all the other necessary preparations for her return home. On the eve of her departure Louis came for his mother—they were going out together, alone, for one last look at the town and one grand fling. Louis had asked for this brief holiday from his work in order to devote all his time to his mother. Never had May Ann looked so well and so gay. They visited the Elite, the Nest, and the Dreamland, ending the evening in Lincoln Garden, where Joe Oliver dedicated a piece to her who was going back to the South.

"Way down yonder in New Orleans
Is the land of the dreamy scenes!"

After the orchestra-men finished playing, they gathered to drink a toast to Louis and his mother. Then Louis and May Ann went off together, just the two of them, and drifted from one dive to another; all boasted at least one screechy music-box blaring forth the melodies of the day. In the small hours of the morning, a policeman guided them back to Forty-third Street.

That afternoon, as the train was leaving, May Ann leaned out of the window for a last farewell.

"'Bye, my boy. God bless you. You been a wonderful son!"

Several days later Louis got a letter from his mother describing her pleasure in returning to the Reverend Cozy's services. Also she had news about all their old acquaintances at Liberty and Perdido. More houses had been knocked down. Funky Butt and Matranga's were gone; on the very spot where Buddy Bolden and Bunk Johnson first played jazz, they were going to build a church. A long postscript told how stunned Daisy Parker had been at sight of the dress May Ann had brought back from Chicago, and reported that Daisy had spoken of going to find her husband whom she had never stopped loving. What May Ann did not tell was that she herself had been afraid to mention Louis's divorce and subsequent remarriage. Louis did not show this letter to Lil, who knew very little about his first wife.

One night when the musicians arrived at Lincoln Garden they saw a young fellow in a sport suit who was seated near the orchestra. Throughout the evening he did not take his eyes off Louis Armstrong and continually begged him to play his favorite tunes. At last, after listening to Louis improvise marvelously as he did every night on such pieces as *Some of These Days*, *St. Louis Blues*, *Stumbling*, *Margie*, and *Basin Street*, the young man started a conversation.

Louis asked him: "How old are you?"

"Sixteen."

"How come you out so late?"

"I ran away from Lake Forest Academy. I'm one of the boarders there."

"That ain't right," admonished Louis.

"I wanted to hear you. You're the best trumpeter I ever listened to!"

"What's your name?"

"Bix Beiderbecke."

After this, Louis often saw the youthful enthusiast. Sometimes at intermission Bix fondled Louis's trumpet as if it were some precious relic. As a rule, he would leave rather early in order to get back to the Academy on time. One night he stayed till the end and left with Louis and Lil.

"Why did you stay so late? Ain't you goin' back to Lake Forest?"

"No, I was expelled."

"Why?"

"Because I like jazz too well, I guess."

When Louis shook the youngster's hand at the end of the evening, he had no idea that his admirer was one day to become his rival—a rival who would not be given the time to fulfill the burning ambition already rising in him. To Louis, Bix was merely one of the numberless boys who were passionately devoted to the new form of music, and he soon forgot the meeting.

One evening while he was playing he noticed a mob forming at the entrance. People were shouting and pushing. Losing no time, Joe Oliver called out:

"Guys—play Number Two!"

This was the number specially dedicated to fights: *Tiger Rag*, which they played fast and furious so as to drown out the noise of battle. A young fellow told the bass fiddler:

"It's a crazy Negress who wants to sit down. Says she's Louis Armstrong's wife. We tried to calm her down by telling her that his wife was at the piano. Then she got wild and wants to fight with everybody!"

Louis had caught a few words and now let his trumpet fall. He left the stand, and soon reached the mob. Beyond a doubt it was Daisy! What a scene!

Without waiting to pick up his hat, he went out through another door, pushed his way to Daisy, and took her off to a night-club in the colored section. He knew that it would be no easy task to appease her, as he sat next to her he noted the outline of the razor hidden under her garter. When he showed her the divorce decree she began to scream and threaten him: "Who's that piano-playin' woman they say's your wife?"

So Louis showed her his marriage certificate, too. Daisy seized it and tore it into shreds. Finally, he managed to pacify her to some extent and even extracted her promise to return to New Orleans at the end of the week.

Two days later Louis was summoned to the hospital. In one of the colored dives, Daisy had gotten into an argument with a foolhardy black who would not agree that Louis Armstrong was the best trumpeter in the world. Seeking to convince him, Daisy had produced her razor, and in the ensuing duel the two participants carved each other cruelly, and it was not until two weeks later that Daisy was sufficiently recovered to leave for Perdido and Louis was able to resume his interrupted honeymoon with Lil.

19

FOR THE first time in his life Louis was tasting the joys of family life in a relatively calm atmosphere. His salary had increased considerably and—even after helping his mother back in Perdido, his sister Mama Lucy, his grandmother Joséphine, Daisy Parker (whom he had pacified with a small sum of money), and Lil's mother—he still managed to be the best-dressed man in the orchestra.

At first, he clung to his old-fashioned notions: a black suit set off by the wing collar and the derby hat; and he sometimes gasped at the conspicuous raiment of other young Negroes he encountered, with their tight trousers and fancy jackets. But by now he had acquired a dozen suits or more from a good tailor, and every day he donned one of "those ol' shiny new white shirts."

One morning Louis went off quite early. An idea had been running through his mind for several days, and in the afternoon he went to get Lil to take her to look at a house in 44th Street that he was thinking of buying. Lil was pleased with the place, and two days later the deal was concluded. Now Louis and Lil were home-owners.

They moved in shortly afterward, and to them it was heaven on earth. Lil's piano, in its special nook, was displayed with great pride. Even little Clarence had his own room. The boy's development was very slow, and Louis was especially kind to him, telling himself that one's love should go out not to the well and the strong only, but above all to unfortunates like Clarence. Louis sent him to a training school, where he was soon nicknamed "Little Louis Armstrong."

While Louis was boarding with Joe Oliver, he had marveled at Joe's infinite capacity to absorb food. Joe would consume whole dishes of red beans, and dozens of hamburgers; and, as for doughnuts, whenever he was asked how many he could eat at one sitting, he would answer: "No limit!"

Louis was not long in imitating Joe, and his appetite soon reached the same Gargantuan proportions. By the time he married Lil, he had gained a great deal of weight. The thin, frail youth of Perdido had become a muscular fellow whose steel lips never failed to astonish jazz fans by their stamina.

Lil's influence over Louis was tremendous. Until the time that he entered King Oliver's orchestra, he was but a diamond in the rough. His wife worked hard to cultivate his mind, to smooth the rough edges, though without submerging under an indispensable technique the gift of improvisation that she had discovered and admired.

Of an evening, just after supper, and during the lull that preceded the nightly departure for Lincoln Garden, Louis and Clarence would lounge comfortably in the rocking-chairs on the porch, the quiet street contrasting strikingly with the seething agitation of Perdido that both remembered.

Often Lil would sit at the piano, playing finer music than Louis had ever heard—or dreamed existed—and he would try to acquire a taste that was not his birthright. He felt the conflicting yet persistent power of these two forms of music, one based on melody and harmony, the other on rhythm alone. One had been conceived in the minds of Europe's geniuses, the other in the simple hearts of lowly African tribes. By what curious process had the tomtom of the Congo nights created a new way of feeling and thinking? Once he raised this question when he was talking with his wife about music. She kissed him and replied:

"Jazz is great because it is the only artistic and moral heritage that our race has kept. God put jazz in our hearts, a spark sufficient to kindle the fires of love. Have you ever noticed how some white folks fall under the orchestra's spell?"

So it *was* possible, Louis reflected, for the blacks to shake off the ignoble chains of servitude. But what in Heaven's name could one man do so that all the race might find its place in the sun of liberty?

"Lil, how about playin' one of them classics for me? You know . . . the pieces I like best."

And Lil opened her fine piano, Clarence coming in to sit quietly at her side. Alone, Louis listened to the noblest tonal fabrics of the great musical geniuses. He shut his eyes. It was now quite dark. In the distance the rumble of the Elevated could be heard. Lil had begun with *Carmen*, the "Toreador Song"; then Verdi's *La donna è mobile*; and a romantic love song from a French opera.

Finally Louis roused himself from his reverie; it was time to leave for Lincoln Garden. There at least, he felt better and safer the moment he broke into his improvisation of the *St. Louis Blues*; it gave him a feeling of security. By now he saw Chicago as the answer to all his problems, believed that he could continue to lead forever this effortless life of a musician at Lil's side, thought that every month would bring closer his ownership of their home—and thus he would one day be firmly rooted in the Windy City.

One evening after work, Joe Oliver asked his musicians to

return the next day at three for a particularly important announcement. Then he disappeared, and Bobby Dodds and Louis began to speculate on the meaning of this summons.

That evening Lil and Louis went to the "Nest" to listen to an outlaw band, and while there they discussed the future. A white group from New Orleans was playing at "Friar's Inn," and Louis had several times met Leon Rappollo and George Brunies, who were in that group. Toward the end of the evening the white band arrived. Among them was Paul Mares, cornetist of the New Orleans Rhythm Kings. When Brunies struck up the *Tin Roof Blues*, Lil was called to the piano. Paul Mares played the trumpet, and Louis was delighted to hear the man who, with Nick La Rocca, was reputed to be the best white instrumentalist. The patrons were soon going wild over the new band. Mezz Mezzrow, a young Chicago musician, was tearing at the saxophone. For the first time, Louis was witnessing a sort of brotherhood in which racial differences were ignored. . . .

After each piece, a thunder of applause rewarded the soloist Louis had seen for himself that Paul Mares's playing, though very true in tone and having a fine explosive quality, could not compete with his own. The orchestra was improvising in a jam session; indeed, it was perhaps on this night that the phrase "jam session" was used for the first time. By the time Mares had rendered *Nobody's Sweetheart*, *Margie*, *Some of These Days*, *Indiana*, and *Shimmy-Sha-Wabble*, the people were jumping to their feet to applaud more easily. Lil, triumphant, beat out a ringing rhythm with frequent winks at her husband, who was listening raptly and clapping wildly.

Presently a delegation approached Louis with an invitation In spite of his shyness he went up to the orchestra, congratulated Paul Mares, and took his stance between Mezz and Rappolo. Handkerchief in hand, eyes closed, concentrating at his faculties as if his whole being were focused on his mouth-piece, he struck up *Basin Street*. Never had he felt in such fine fettle or more inspired; he climbed into the upper register with the ease of a well-greased elevator. And he communicated his inspiration to his colleagues. In *St. Louis Blues* he repeated the chorus a dozen times, each time surpassing the previous rendition. The dancers had stopped and were listening in ecstasy. Women were swaying tipsily, drunk with rhythm.

"Go on, Dipper! One more. Sock it out!"

By now, however, Louis could do no more; his neck was swollen to the size of a football, his eyes were popping out of their sockets, sweat was pouring down his shirt front. But he struck up the final chorus, dipped into a break which sent a shiver of emotion over the whole audience; then climbed, climbed in skyscraper style, and held a note for ten beats! When he finally broke off abruptly, a deluge of howls broke over him. With a grin that displayed all his teeth, he mumbled joyfully:

"Yeah, men! Oh, sure, why not! Thank you, Gates! Thank you for Satchmo'!"

All the musicians were standing up on the platform, their hands outstretched.

"Louis, you're the best of all. Atta boy!"

Tears were rolling down Mezz Mezzrow's cheeks, while Lil was laughing almost hysterically.

At three o'clock sharp that afternoon, Louis and Lil arrived to hear what King Oliver had to say. Joe was already there, talking with the drummer. When all had finally gathered around him, the leader produced a letter from his inside pocket.

"Boys," he said, "I called you all for a big decision. I just got a sensational offer. A certain manager wants us to tour the country. He'll pay us twice the dough we gets here at the Lincoln. How about it?"

The musicians looked at one another. The Dodds brothers were whispering together. Most of them had come to look upon Chicago as their real and final home. The prospect of one-night stands across the country was none too inviting. Louis and Lil were thinking about the house they had just bought and which they would now have to give up. Honoré Dutrey was the first to voice objection.

"I knows one thing—a rollin' stone don't gather no moss!"

"But remember, boys, you gets double pay," Joe repeated. "In fact, it looked so good to me I signed up. I can't back out now."

But Dutrey shook his head and declared that he would not leave Chicago, come what might. His refusal was supported by the Dodds brothers. Bill Johnson chimed in timidly, stating that he too prefered to stay.

Old man Joe was unnerved. He was lost. What could he do without an orchestra?

"What *you* say, Louis?"

Louis hesitated.

"Well, Papa Joe, I sure felt like stayin' here in Chicago. We just bought us a house. Everythin' is okay by us as is. Fack is, Lil and me just decided we was gonna stay. But we can't let you down. You can count us in. Right, Lil?"

Lil approved with a nod of the head.

That night, after work, Joe was crying. He begged Louis and Lil to go home with him. Silently they walked off together in the dark.

"What we gonna do, Louis?" asked Joe as they entered his apartment.

A steaming dish of red beans and rice was waiting for them. The King did not let his worries affect his appetite, and it was only after he had put away several platefuls that he returned to the main topic:

"What's to do, Louis?"

Louis came forth with a suggestion.

"I just got word from New Orleans about a new bunch of fellows that plays real good jazz. I got their names. How about writin' to 'em? Maybe we can make up a band, an' you won't need the quitters. Let's see—there's a clarinet called Picou, an' Barney Bigard, an' Buster Bailey . . ."

A few days later all the places were filled. Buster Bailey, clarinetist, Johnny Lindsay, bass fiddler, Rudy Jackson, saxophonist, and Buddy Christian, banjoist, replaced the timid souls who preferred the security of Lincoln Garden to the adventures of the road.

Louis was a very busy man these days. His initiative had won him considerable importance in the orchestra and he had many new duties; indeed, Papa Joe felt overwhelmed by young Louis's dynamic energy. Among the newcomers was a youngster whose slightly oriental cast of countenance had nothing to do with the Creole conception of style he brought to his clarinet. This was Buster Bailey. He did not use the winding breaks that characterized Dodds's playing; his notes were more closely knit, more mellow, in the traditional manner of the Downtown clarinetist.

Joe Oliver's new orchestra proved to be a huge success as they traveled from town to town to satisfy the enthusiastic curiosity of thousands. In the spring of 1924 they stopped at the Gennett Studios in Richmond, Indiana, for a recording of *Chimes Blues.* This was indeed the supreme reward of Joe's efforts. The sound engineer had placed Louis next to Papa Joe, and after the test it was discovered that only Armstrong's trumpet could be heard, against an indistinct background. So the record was made over, with Louis playing ten feet behind the others. Another tribute to his power! Throughout the United States, every jazz fan now knew that the country's best trumpet-player was a young Negro in King Oliver's orchestra.

After several months of travel, the orchestra returned to Chicago. There was talk of reopening at the Lincoln Garden in sensational fashion in order to eclipse the Dreamland. But bad luck was dogging the Old Man's footsteps. One night the Lincoln Garden went up in flames like a pile of straw, and Joe was obliged to dismiss his orchestra.

After this misfortune, King found a place as soloist in Dave Payton's band at the Plantation Café—at Calumet Avenue and 39th Street. Louis Armstrong had gone back to his house and was taking things easy. Whereas Papa Joe had had to resume the role of a mere musician, Louis was receiving propositions from all sides. Now and then Joe and Louis would meet over a plate of red beans. The Old Man would sigh:

"What you gonna do? When the fruit's ripe, it falls from the tree. I knowed doggone well I couldn't keep you forever. But I'm fed up with Dave Payton. I got a new scheme for the Plantation . . ."

But Joe was too late—Louis showed him a telegram from Fletcher Henderson, asking him to come to New York.

Joe said nothing, only held out a hand that was trembling with emotion.

Thus it was that Joe Oliver started at the Plantation with Luis Russel (piano), Albert Nicholas (clarinet), and Paul Barbarin (drums); while Louis Armstrong left with his wife for the city he had dreamed about since childhood: New York, capital of the world. He was the best in Chicago. What would he achieve in New York?

20

LONG AGO, New York had loomed in Joe's mind as an impregnable bastion whose walls he could never hope to scale. In his mind, Chicago represented the culmination of his career. What was the use of buying a home, if one did not live in it for good? Louis was resolved to spend the rest of his life on the shores of Lake Michigan.

At that time, Fletcher Henderson led the best jazz band in America. About 1922 he developed a new style, which was to become "swing" music. During this period Paul Whiteman was seeking to bridge the gap between improvised jazz and real orchestral music, and Ferdie Grofé had tried to orchestrate for him the improvisations of the small bands, white or colored. But Fletcher Henderson had a gift that Whiteman's arrangers lacked, giving his compositions a special significance that contrasted sharply with the somewhat savage conceptions of King Oliver. In two years Fletcher had reached the peak of his reputation. At one of his music stands he had a young clarinetist, Buster Bailey, who had formerly played with King Oliver's orchestra. Bailey often praised the extraordinary quality of Louis Armstrong's work, saying: "You never heard nothin' till you hear that guy blow. Hell breaks loose when he uses them steel lips of his."

Fletcher's thoughts often turned to Louis. When—it was

about 1924—he was at the Roseland Ballroom on Broadway, he decided to increase the size of his orchestra. On learning that there was some discord in King's orchestra, he sent immediately for Louis. At this time he had three brass instruments and three saxophones. Though it seemed odd to add a fourth brass player since—between the two trumpets, Howard Scott and Elmer Chambers—he had Charlie Green at the trombone, he nevertheless assumed the new responsibility with a light heart.

So it came about that Louis Armstrong left Chicago with his wife to take his place among the following aggregation, which had already scored some notable triumphs in New York: Elmer Chambers and Howard Scott (trumpets), Charlie Green (trombone), Buster Bailey (clarinet), Don Redman (alto), Coleman Hawkins (tenor), Fletcher Henderson (piano), Charlie Dixon (guitar), Escudero (bass), and Kaiser Marshall (drums).

On their trip eastward, Louis had discussed with his wife the prospects of this new venture. He was now entering a really big-time orchestra, and he had to admit to himself that he was far from being a polished professional. Both of them wondered whether he was doing the wise thing. . . .

On the winter morning when Armstrong and Lil arrived in New York, he telephoned to Fletcher Henderson, who told him that rehearsal would be at the Roseland at about five. They decided to wait till after this before looking for a room. The question meanwhile was how to kill time until then. Lil stayed at the station to watch their luggage, and Louis went out for a walk. On reaching Times Square he discovered Broadway, and stood for a long time at the Astor Hotel corner, filling his eyes with the bustle and the excitement of the famous crossroads of the world. He looked at the buildings, the signs, the shop windows. He mingled freely with the unconcerned white crowd. He went up Broadway as far as the Roseland. Everything was shut tight. He retraced his steps, decided he was hungry but dared not venture into one of the places where he saw only white people. He was afraid of this first contact with the mysterious and awe-inspiring city. Separating New Orleans and Chicago there had been a deep social chasm that was to be bridged only in the imagination. Would New York offer a different experience? . . .

He asked a Negro the way to Harlem. The man pointed to the north, said "Uptown," and showed Louis the subway entrance.

Once in the subway train, Louis discovered that it was the wrong train! He must go back to the 96th Street station and transfer. By this time he was so bewildered that he feared he would never arrive at his destination. But a train marked "Lenox" carried him there safely. On reaching Harlem he found himself surrounded by a throng of Negroes of all shades, most of them better dressed than even the richest blacks had been in New Orleans. A feeling of warmth stole over him, and for the moment he forgot his hunger. Truly, he was content only in the midst of his own.

On 125th Street he stood for a long time at the corner of Lenox Avenue. The houses here were small—but how fine they were, compared with the hovels of New Orleans! He walked along the Avenue, came back, followed 125th Street, entranced by the scene. Here was the black capital of the world. Women were laughing and calling gaily to one another. Men were looking at displays of haberdashery and clothing. An icy wind was blowing from the east. On the left the Theresa Hotel reared its structure above the surrounding roofs. Seventh Avenue buses went rushing by. A newsboy was screaming the headlines. Louis noticed a lunchroom patronized by Negroes. He went in, ordered a sandwich and a soft drink. His neighbor engaged him in conversation and he was regaled with the latest Harlem gossip.

He still had two hours to wait before meeting Lil. He decided to take the Fifth Avenue bus down town. Climbing to the top of the bus, he walked to the front. Silently he gazed on the strange city sights. Everywhere he saw Negroes: at every street corner, going into the stores, coming out of the houses. Black urchins were dancing a jig on the sidewalk while another beat on a soapbox—and suddenly Louis saw himself as he had played years ago in front of Maylie's Restaurant. What had become of Little Mack, of Georgie Gray, of Redhead Happy? Fourteen years in the past, those friendships were. Inevitably his playmates must have followed the destiny prescribed for Perdido folk: they were laborers, or dancers, or pimps. How surprised they would be if they could see him now atop a Fifth Avenue bus!

Little by little the black faces disappeared and white predominated. The bus was now traveling on Fifth Avenue, and within a few blocks a transformation had taken place. The houses he looked at now were tall, handsome buildings that reached for the sky. In Central Park on his right he saw a fine-looking Negress on horseback—riding among white ladies; this struck him with the force of a revelation. Passing the Metropolitan Museum, he took in the Park's impressive background of concrete buildings aglow in the rays of the setting sun.

On getting off at 50th Street, Louis felt almost dizzied by the sights he had seen. Walking westward he reached Broadway once more, and found Lil waiting for him at the corner. It was almost five. Already dusk was creeping over the city and softening the geometric outlines of the buildings. Near the Hudson the rosy sky was rapidly losing its fire. Lights were coming on. In Times Square a myriad of dazzling signs began to write their nightly hyperbole. Louis and Lil thought this the most glorious night of their lives.

When they reached the Roseland they walked in, their footsteps muffled by the thick carpets. A trumpet was practicing the scale. They went upstairs, where they met a black fellow.

"Where's Fletcher Henderson?" Louis asked him.

"You mean Smack? He ain't here yet. Who's you?"

"Louis Armstrong."

"Oh, you're the new trumpet. Sit down."

Louis took off his overcoat and his derby and laid his trumpet down carefully before continuing the conversation with his new acquaintance, Kaiser Marshall. Lil had meanwhile found a seat in the ballroom and was waiting quietly. Soon Buster Bailey arrived, wild with joy at finding Louis there. The interchange of greetings was rapid, almost hysterical.

"Watcha say, oh, man!" Buster exclaimed.

"Feel all right!"

"What about Papa Oliver back in Chicago?"

"Still eatin' his fill of red beans."

"You gettin' stout, Louis."

"Oh, man, don't I know it?"

The two stood there with hands clasped, laughing and stamping their feet. Louis was introduced to each new arrival. Don Redman offered him a cigarette. Hawkins did not have much to say. The two trumpet players looked at the newcomer from the corner of their eyes. Presently Fletcher Henderson arrived and shook hands.

"So you're Louis Armstrong! Glad to see you!"

That was all. Louis, taken aback by this rather offhand reception, suddenly felt panicky. But Fletcher was talking to the others already.

"Let's get going. Today we're trying out some new arrangements. Louis, you'll play the third trumpet. You'll find the scores on your stands."

Buster Bailey had fallen silent; Coleman Hawkins was fondling his tenor horn; Dixon adjusted a string carefully. None of them were looking at Louis, but he realized nevertheless that he was the center of attention.

Fletcher sat down at the piano and shuffled some papers. Louis got ready. He sensed the burning curiosity of his colleagues: all were waiting to hear how he played! More noticeably than the other, the two trumpets remained aloof, secretly smiling at the newcomer's nervousness.

"Let's tackle *By the Waters of Minnetonka!*" cried Fletcher. Then Louis saw that the arrangements were written by hand, and a cold sweat broke over him. He recalled the torturous hours of drill beneath Lil's stern tutelage. Cautiously, he stole a glance at the score; it did not look terribly difficult. Fletcher played the melody several times and then the saxophone section took over. Louis, fingering the pistons of his trumpet, played soundlessly. Then it was the turn of the brass instruments. Once, twice, three times they went over the accompaniment, then the brass and the saxophones played together. Only now was the music beginning to reveal its true meaning, like a jigsaw picture puzzle.

This was a far cry from King Oliver's rehearsals, when only the inspiration of the moment had counted! Everything here depended on Smack's inspiration, and, from time to time, the flight of fancy of this or that soloist. For several days, Louis was content to follow the orchestra's routine. Piece by piece, he learned to decipher the few "licks" that were reserved for him. Buster Bailey or Coleman Hawkins would occasionally cut loose on their instruments, but only for eight or sixteen bars—then everything fell back into the masterly rhythmic order prepared in advance by Fletcher. Like all the others, Louis was limited, and he could not express his real personality under these conditions.

Very late one Saturday night Louis escaped from the prudent bounds he had set for himself. Twirling couples were massed before the orchestra. Louis, sitting in the same row as his two friends, was unleashing a cascade of syncopation, carefully arranged beforehand. God only knows where the wild tempest came from that swept over the Roseland that night. Suddenly Smack himself, at the piano, lost the control that rarely left him. Hawkins had begun a resounding solo. Louis was singing in low tones:

"Everybody loves my baby—
But my baby don't love nobody but me!
Nobody but me!"

A loud burst of applause marked the solo's finish. Smack, elated, cried to Hawkins: "One more, Coleman!"

And Coleman continued thunderously for several choruses. Smack hammered out the rhythm, urging on the tenor. Dixon and Escudero, seconded by Kaiser, were strumming a feverish beat in support of the soloist as he soared to the sky and came down to earth again. The audience applauded wildly. Louis's eyes were on the hundreds of transfigured dancers, wreathed in smiles, blowing kisses, shouting with joy. For the first time in his life, he grasped what this music, emerged from its primitive tribal obscurity, had given to the world. He perceived clearly the unbreakable strength of the bridge it threw between the two races. He felt stronger and better, felt that at last he had climbed to equality with those who, their eyes shining, were intent on every movement and note of the orchestra. And so his thoughts were led gradually to a resolution: he would raise himself to the tenor's level, would send shivers through the whites he was facing, would prove that his race was the bearer of a message that could reconcile their differences. . . .

They played *Copenhagen*, bristling with syncopation and crisp, spasmodic rhythm. Now it was no longer inspired improvisation that shaped the modulations of the novel music; it was, rather, perfectly organized noise—orchestral power harnessed by the talent of a gifted arranger. Now the fire that burned in the audience kindled the orchestra men: they played as if inspired, and the salvos of applause rang to the roof. Presently they went into *Alabamy Bound* and *I'll See You in My Dreams*.

During the piano solo, Louis thought about Lil and the porch of their pretty home in Chicago. Suddenly he felt Smack looking at him. He understood. Though the audience did not suspect the telepathy that controls every jazz orchestra, all were aware that some signal had been sent to Louis. Until that moment, the laurels of Scottie and Elmer had been secure, and Louis was but a humble third trumpeter. But there came a sudden break in the time. People felt shivers run down their spines; they stopped talking and stayed frozen in their places. Then three notes were torn out in an incredible register! Louis was erect, his features shrunken, his eyes closed, and as in a trance he delivered the age-old song of his race. He had lived every note of that refrain, and now he was rendering it with all the feeling that he alone possessed.

Now he owed nothing to Freddie Keppard, nothing to Bunk Johnson, nothing to King Oliver, nothing to Scottie or to Elmer, nothing even to Fletcher Henderson! At first impressed by the orchestra's greatness, he had escaped being swallowed up by it, and now he had risen above it. In Smack's eyes he read boundless admiration. Those who were not play-

ing could hardly believe their ears. Here was rhythm tamed
and made human. Louis climbed into the upper register with
incredibly rapid glissandos, then stopped, subdued the rhythm,
dominated the drums. He was no longer playing for the orchestra—the orchestra was playing for him. Scottie and Elmer,
who once had quietly mocked, were now looking at him with
silent respect.

Five times, six times, always stronger, always purer, ever
renewing his ecstasy, Louis made hearts pound faster and
faster. Nothing could stop him now. He towered above all.
Smack himself bowed before this inexhaustible feat of breathing. By degrees, the spectators regained their critical faculties, and after the seventh chorus they applauded until they
were exhausted. Women screamed at the top of their voices.
The musicians stared in wonder at the man who had done the
impossible.

When the moment came for them to start playing a new
piece, they struck up Louis's own number. The first bars of
Dippermouth Blues stirred a long train of memories in his
mind: The Waifs' Home; the enthusiastic glances of Peter
Davis; Kid Rena's jokes; the fights with the other boys. . . .
Now the rough poetry of those childhood days had been
civilized; for the white man's consumption, the power of the
"big lips" had been transformed into the music that walked
in the *Sugar-Foot Stomp.* Here was Louis's own piece! Every
note was hot with the breath of a day spent in Perdido or a
torrid night in the Tenderloin. That jerky melody reminded
him of the motions of the railway laborers who moaned as
they swung their pickaxes.

And that break yawning wide like a chasm brought to his
mind the gap of silence that Buddy Bolden inserted in his tunes
at Funky Butt and——Louis stopped suddenly. The silence
was fearful, and hearts beat faster under the shock. Possessed

by the association of old ideas, Louis threw his head back and
opened his eyes and shouted: *"Oh! Play that thing!"*

It touched off a prolonged howl of joy. The people in the
Roseland that night went crazy! The orchestra's half-hour
now being up, men jumped on the platform and tried to carry
Louis on their shoulders. Drenched with perspiration, panting, lips open, teeth clenched, he muttered words without
meaning, drunk with triumph. Women and men alike pressed
forward to the orchestra's platform to congratulate him.
Smack got up and came over to shake his hand—a thing
he had never done before, though Louis did not know it. But
the other musicians were not slow to grasp how important the
newcomer was destined to become, and—such was Louis's
demonstrated superiority—not one of them said a word in dis-
paragement.

That night, beside himself with happiness, he returned to
Harlem with Lil, Smack, and Buster Bailey. From now on he
was to call Henderson by his nickname and was tacitly granted
to be on an equal footing with him.

"So now," Buster told him as they walked toward the subway, "King Oliver's no longer the King."

"What you mean?"

"Man, you gives Joe Oliver cards and spades!"

Times Square was still bright; it was hard to tell whether
dawn was breaking in the clear sky or whether it was the perpetual daylight of this hub of the world that bathed the great
white buildings. In the subway a youth approached the group.

"You're Louis Armstrong?"

"Yassuh!"

"I've just left the Roseland. You're great!" And he shook
Louis's hand.

In Harlem they walked past the Y.M.C.A., where some

blacks were chatting. Small's Paradise was festooned with lights. It was too late for them to try to visit any speakeasies, so they went to a basement place, one of the spots where musicians gathered for friendly musical bouts. The instant they opened the door they were hit by a hellish din rising from the murk beyond. They found a table and ordered whisky, but they could not hear themselves talk. In an alcove, five trumpeters were wildly blowing their lungs out, accompanied by a piano and a drum. Dancers bobbed up and down epileptically on the brassy tide.

Smack shouted, cupping his hands for a megaphone:

"What came over you, Satchmo'? What made you sing during the break? That was really something!"

Louis screamed back, trying to be heard above the din:

"Don't know, Smack. It was a break like I used to hear at Funky Butt when I was a kid. An' I don't know why I cut loose with that old Perdido cry—the one the folks used to holler at Buddy Bolden: '*Oh, Buddy, play that thing!*'"

A few weeks later, when Lil had gone back to Chicago, Fletcher Henderson's orchestra made a recording of *Sugar Foot Stomp*, and it was thus that the primitive cry of the New Orleans blacks reached a vast audience of whites—the cry uttered by Louis Armstrong, Fletcher's third trumpet. Already he burned with the desire to become the new King of Jazz. He may have recalled that the original King—Buddy Bolden, the man who had been the soul of that stammering music, the old King of Perdido—was insane within the walls of the Louisiana state asylum at Jackson. Indeed, if Buddy Bolden could have been brought back to the realities of 1925, could have heard that kid of Funky Butt utter the call, he might have echoed:

"*Oh, play that thing, Satchmo'—play that thing again!*"

21

LOUIS SPENT the winter in New York. This was the gaudy era when Paul Whiteman, appearing every night at the Palais-Royal in a blaze of glory and spotlights, was crowned King of Jazz. Very quickly the reputation of Fletcher Henderson's trumpeter had become established. Many white musicians came to wind up their evening at the Roseland; indeed, those who happened to be in the neighborhood would hasten out during the dinner hour to get a thrill by listening to one or two choruses played by Louis, now the kingpin of the orchestra.

For hours on end, jazz fans remained standing near the stage while Smack at his piano conducted by means of slight but meaningful signs. One look and Coleman Hawkins would strike up a piece on his tenor horn, possibly the only one in use at that time. Or else the leader half-shut one eye and Big Green took the break as if it had been foreordained by a decree of Providence.

Louis was acquainted with all the trumpeters of his day, from Charlie Margulis to Red Nichols, including those who had built up a reputation in New York. Every one of them admitted that Satchmo' stood head and shoulders above them all. Often they came to listen and draw inspiration from his playing.

One evening when the band was playing, Scottie whispered to Louis, taking advantage of the fact that the trumpet section was resting:

"Watch out, Louis. There goes the Wolverines' trumpet!"

"Who that?"

"A kid from the Middle West. Name's Bix. You know him?"

"No."

Louis's searching eyes soon spotted the Chicago college boy who was beginning to make a name for himself. Bix was sitting silent, his eyes shut in order to enjoy the music better.

Another evening, Ted Lewis strolled in (minus his top hat), and settled down comfortably to watch the show. When the band left for its private quarters upstairs, he followed a group of white musicians who wanted to talk shop with the boys— a radical innovation; usually Louis was the first one they sought because he was really the only musician whose superiority they acknowledged. Of course, had Louis been white or if Paul Whiteman had been as bold as Benny Goodman, the King of Jazz would have paid a goodly sum to get Louis into his band.

That Louis was not destined to cross the dividing line was no source of anxiety or resentment to him. He had become a privileged character among a privileged class. At night when he reached Harlem and beheld the widespread evidences of neglect and poverty, he would wonder if he were really the person who had lived through the terrible days of Perdido. He saw coal venders passing slowly along Lenox or, very late, milkmen going on their rounds at ungodly hours—and he watched them with indifference, having decided that it was useless to rack his brains over the distribution of the prizes in life's incomprehensible lottery.

Whenever he entered the Savoy's ballroom—that inferno

of milling blacks electrified by the impact of the new music—
he was conscious that something was changed in the world.
When he looked at the white sitting in boxes and admiring
the unrestrained and exhausting dances, he realized all that
separated New York from New Orleans. And he dreamed
of healing the breach. He remembered one night when he returned from the Tenderloin very low in spirits, but resigned
and murmuring to himself, as if to plunge himself deeper into
his misery: "Go on, mule."

Now and again Lil would come east to New York and
spend a few days with her husband. Though she knew that
he had become the best player in the city, it was not possible
for her to hear him, since colored people were barred from
the Roseland. As a meager consolation, she attended rehearsals to judge what progress he was making.

But this kind of life was hardly worth while. She was lonesome, terribly lonesome in the little house in Chicago. Louis
had several times told her that Fletcher's orchestra was booked
to play in Chicago, but nothing ever came of it. Several times,
too, she herself had come to New York on an engagement to
accompany some vocalist, and always seized the opportunity
to stay with Louis. On these rare visits, they would go out
together late at night and listen to Harlem's bands, dreaming
and making plans to be reunited very soon. Then Lil would
return to Chicago, hoping that next month Fletcher Henderson would surely come west for a long engagement. Louis
himself wanted to get back to their cozy home. But the months
dragged on, and Lil became fretful and worried.

It was at about this time that Louis, one evening at the
Cotton Club, caught a glimpse of a little chorus girl who
quickened his pulse. His love for Lil was still both genuine
and paramount; but musicians have a greater opportunity—if

not a greater excuse—for straying from the narrow path than ordinary mortals. The girl was pretty and witty, and a marvelous dancer, and she sang as well as she danced. Her name was Fanny. On many an evening Louis waited for her at the Cotton Club's stage-door and they would dart off to some speakeasy on 123rd Street where the tough characters and insomniacs of Harlem kept late hours. In this spot, night merged into broad daylight. And when all was quiet, the patrons made their exit through a trapdoor opening into a back alley, and emerged on the sidewalk only after getting the doorman's cautious signal that no policeman was in sight.

Soon springtime brought buds to the trees in the Park. But Louis, who had never forgotten the luxuriant springs of New Orleans, had long been craving the sight of green and growing things. He was weary of living in a city of stone and concrete whence man has banished the wonders of Nature.

One evening Fletcher announced to his musicians that the promise of a Chicago billing had fallen flat and that they would soon leave on an extended tour of New England. Louis hardly knew how to break the bad news to Lil—or to Fanny either. When finally he did so, he immediately got a peremptory summons from his wife demanding that he come back to Chicago. But what was there for him in Chicago? King Oliver was in a rut, and—from all reports—a pall of gloom hung over the night clubs of the Middle West.

Fletcher Henderson and his orchestra settled down in a Massachusetts town: Lawrence. It was cold in this thriving and sprawling center. Early in May, when the azaleas, the catalpas and the magnolias of the Crescent City were already scorched by the burning sun, New England showed few signs of vegetation. Then suddenly spring arrived in a rush, and within a few days the trees were green. Then, almost before they knew it, summer was on them, and the orchestra was busy every night. The manager had chosen this particular town because it was a railroad hub. In an hour or so, a score of neighboring communities could be reached—seaside resorts or big industrial towns in Connecticut, New Hampshire, or Maine. Catholic Youth Clubs heard Fletcher in Nashua; from Manchester, French Canadian organizations extended an invitation; the new rhythm brought thrills to the Smith College girls at Northampton. It was a wonderful life!

The musicians were a clannish group. Some of the married men had brought their wives along; others, married or single, had bachelor quarters in boarding-houses. During July the countryside was drenched with sunshine, and every afternoon the men would go for a swim in the Merrimack River.

Fletcher played in Boston several times, and there Louis met Fanny again. She was obliged to return to New York on the next day, though Louis had rashly promised marriage if she would stay with him.

Toward the end of their New England tour, they played one evening in Woonsocket at a big dance attended by French Canadians and college students from surrounding towns. The audience was responsive and enthusiastic, which is always a stimulating influence, since an orchestra performs well only when the listeners' warmth reacts on the players. There were a few new faces in the orchestra, some of the old players having left during the summer. That evening Jimmy Harrison sat in the second row and the brass section was in particularly fine fettle.

Sugar-Foot Stomp brought down the house as usual. Coleman Hawkins cut loose. Jimmy Harrison sang the *Sheik of Araby*, providing Valentino fans with nostalgic thrills. When a more melancholy tune such as *After the Storm* was played, the listeners showed themselves to be in no mood for sad music. They craved real jazz and kept calling for their favorite pieces. In the front rank stood two colored boys, beating time and nodding approval. Excitement mounted in the hall with each successive tune, and every solo evoked a thunder of applause. Fletcher Henderson, grinning from ear to ear, winked at Louis in mute understanding. The orchestra began to play *Hard-Hearted Hannah*. As Louis twisted out two or three choruses, a lovely white girl with flashing eyes called out:

"Come on, Louis, I love you. Give us another!"

He blew out another chorus, hit a succession of high notes, held them, then tumbled down in a cascade of crystal-clear sounds. Finally he opened his eyes, and was back to earth in Woonsocket, thinking of Lil's latest ultimatum and his darling Fanny's trip to St. Louis. He poured out his heart in a song:

> "*Hard-hearted Hannah,*
> *Vamp of Savannah,*
> *The meanest gal in town.*
> *Leather's rough, but Hannah's heart is rougher—*
> *She's a gal who likes to see men suffer!*"

At the end of the piece a crowd of youngsters almost mobbed Louis as they tried to shake his hand. When he came down from the stand, the two colored boys were waiting for him.

"Satchmo', you was marvelous!"

"Yeah, Pops! You-all like jazz?" Louis asked them.

"We plays in a band. We was goin' to Providence, but we finds out Fletcher's here, so we comes in to listen for a while. An' now the last train's good an' gone—but it sho' was worth it!"

Horn of Plenty:

"What's your name?"

"Roy Eldridge, an' this here's Benny Carter."

Louis went back to join his pals. Two days later they were on their way to New York. Until the very last moment he hoped against hope that the band would be booked for Chicago—which would put everything right with Lil. Louis had made up his mind: come what might, he was going back to Chicago.

In New York, Fletcher announced to the men that they would start playing at the Roseland on the next day. Louis was undecided once more. It was damp and warm that day, and he spent most of it on a wild-goose chase in Harlem, looking for Fanny. But no luck: she was in Pittsburgh. What should he do? New York was unbearable. Louis went off to drown his blues at a honky-tonk run by Big Jones on 131st Street. Sooner or later, one met all the musicians in the passing parade before John Reda's bar. Harlem's wantons were in evidence here, but they lacked the local color and the razors of their scarlet sisters down Perdido way.

That night Louis had a letter from Lil. "Take it or leave it," she wrote. "You must choose between Fletcher Henderson and me."

Later, during intermission, Louis drew Smack aside and showed him Lil's letter.

"Well, Satchmo'?"

"I gotta get back to Chi."

"You're right. I get you, boy. Louis, I'm gonna miss you. Any time you say, you come back an' play with us. When you figure on leavin'?"

"Next Sunday. You can find somebody in a week."

"Man, I could spend the rest of my days tryin' to find somebody to fill your shoes, an' I wouldn't have no luck. I got somebody in mind, though."

"Yeah? Who's that?"
"Tommy Ladnier."

The last few days found Louis feeling dreary. By now his popularity among other musicians was assured. Hardly a night went by that some of them did not troop in to listen to his playing, and his style was beginning to influence such players as Jack Purvis, Muggsy Spanier, Jimmy McPartland, and even young Roy Eldridge whom he had just met in New England.

On the final Saturday Louis was his own natural self. Already Tommy Ladnier had participated in rehearsals and was doing his level best; he took Louis's place in several numbers. At the end of the show Fletcher announced that all the musicians were invited to a farewell banquet in honor of Louis Armstrong at Small's Paradise, where a large table had been reserved for them. This was a famous cellar where soft music was a specialty.

That night, as usual, bootleg whisky and gin flowed freely. Louis, in the seat of honor, was introduced by the master of ceremonies. Whites and blacks filed past to shake his hand. Fletcher Henderson himself rose and paid a moving tribute to the departing musician. At last it was Louis's turn to speak.

"Dippers and Gates," he said, "Satchmo's thick lips knows only one kind o' talk. I'm ready for a long speech, if I can make it with my trumpet."

The crowd roared: "Strike up the band! Hurray for Fletcher! Hurray for Armstrong!"

And Henderson's orchestra started to play, the house band having yielded its rights for the occasion. Everybody had been drinking a good deal, and by this hour many a tipsy couple, fast asleep at their table, were roused by a sudden rhythmic break that rattled the doors. Fletcher was loose, and Armstrong was living up to the epithet that was beginning to stick to him: the skyscraper trumpeter! Drunk with liquor and rhythm, he sent out such powerful trumpet blasts that his audience reeled.

When the music had ended, a final tribute was paid to Louis Armstrong: a pretty mulatto, delegated by the audience, stepped forward and kissed him on both cheeks. Then Fletcher addressed the crowd:

"New York's losin' its finest trumpet, 'cause Louis 'Satchmo' Armstrong is goin' back to Chicago. He's a right guy. We're all pullin' for him!"

The next day at noon, still groggy from the night's carousal, Louis Armstrong boarded the train.

22

CHICAGO WAS in Louis's blood. To him the city represented the miracle of escape, the measure of his liberation. Once more he could walk along Michigan Avenue with its rows of light-standards, and sniff again the odors wafted inland when the wind blows from the lake. What real fun it was to be with Lil and Clarence! Both had been looking forward to his coming as though he were a Messiah; his wife especially regarded his return as a miracle that would bring fresh happiness into their lives after the dreary interval of separation.

It was good to sit again in the big easy chair whose covering bore green sprays that contrasted with the pink lampshade hanging above. It was good to be part of a happy household once more. Clarence was overjoyed by Louis's return and particularly by his decision to stay on in Chicago permanently.

It soon became evident, however, that there was not to be any second honeymoon for Louis and Lil. The past could not be recaptured. A year and a half of separation had cloven a chasm between the two. Minor irritations such as had once been overlooked or brushed aside now rose to the surface with exacerbating frequency. The ardor that two years ago had swept them off their feet was replaced by mutually critical coolness.

Nor did it make things any better that Louis was having

trouble finding work. Artlessly, he had imagined that on his arrival he would be swamped with offers—would shortly be holding a better job than he had had with Henderson. What had actually happened was that he had dropped the substance for the shadow. He recalled with regret the wonderful evenings in New York when the crowd at the Roseland had jumped to its feet and clamored wildly for encores, the lazy afternoons when he would visit friends' studios. Now it was in vain that he searched for something, for someone, who could bring back that creative ardor which had bound him to his friends Clarence Williams and Sidney Bechet, Buddy Christian and Charley Ems.

Clarence and Sidney had also come from New Orleans, had shared the common joy of the creators of jazz. The old spirit of Funky Butt linked them in a fierce search after new music, an outlet for their rebellion against an oppressive past. All the romantic poignancy of the exiled race found feverish expression in nostalgic airs: *New Orleans Hop-Scop Blues; Coal-cart Blues; Go 'long, Mule; 12th Street Blues; Mississippi River Blues; Railroad Blues; Cake-walking Babies Back Home.* Such tunes were the breath of life to Louis. He had conceived them, lived them and loved them, modified them time and again with this or that orchestra. They had become the natural mold into which his inspiration flowed.

His thoughts turned often to the friends he had made in Lawrence, and he felt a twinge of regret as he recalled the woman who had appeared one day at the studio. High cheekbones she had, and liquid, deep-set eyes; he had never forgotten those features. Louis did not then know who she was; but when she sang the first time, her voice twisted his heartstrings. Here was emotion personified. In tragic couplets she voiced the lament of a black woman bewailing the tragic destiny of her people, crying in anguish over the shameful fate of lost women crushed under the double burden of drink and wantonness. Such was his first encounter with the great Bessie Smith. He never forgot her, for among the many admirable and sensitive vocalists whom the trumpet had inspired, Bessie Smith had made the strongest impression on him.

Louis still retained the rough simplicity of Perdido, and his manners bore the imprint of his apprenticeship at Segretta's and Matranga's. Lil, on the other hand, was a university graduate, refined and cultured, unable—even if she had been willing—to adopt her husband's colorful and earthy speech. Her love for him had once led her to make an effort toward creating a semblance of congeniality; but by now she did not care to continue the effort. The one thing that had originally thrown them into each other's arms, the passion they still shared, might yet have saved the situation: jazz. Its magic had enthralled them in those days when they were glad to pay scant attention to the outside world in order to find themselves. Now, however, while Louis was idle, they were together too continuously, and their personalities clashed. Louis, for a time unable to find work, grew irritable, heaping reproaches on his wife as if she were to blame. Quarrels arose easily and frequently.

At that time, Lil Armstrong was playing at the old Dreamland cabaret at 35th and State Streets. King Oliver was leading an orchestra at the Plantation, but his fame was already eclipsed by Louis's, and it would have cost Louis his self-respect to go to work under him again. Presently, however, an opening appeared when the Dreamland's cornetist left the orchestra, and Louis took his place.

He felt himself to be entering on a new phase. In New York he had immersed himself in music fashioned by Fletcher. Now it was his turn to put the stamp of *his* personality on the music he played. His technique had improved at the Roseland, and he had plenty of new ideas. It made him supremely happy to realize that he could now express himself as he pleased.

Soon the musicians were flocking to the Dreamland to hail him as the best cornetist in the city. Mezz Mezzrow came every night, with Bud Freeman, Teschmaker, or Jimmy McPartland, all looking like children playing hooky. Their enthusiasm for the orchestra was unflagging and their greatest pleasure was to discuss new arrangements with Louis and the other players.

"Louis, play the *Heebie Jeebies*—or *Muskrat Ramble!*"

"Just a minute, Mezz, I'm gonna twist out an old favorite for you. I'm gonna shake it for you, oh, man!

He laughed, showing all his white teeth, closed his eyes, and played, handkerchief held tight in his left fist. Suddenly he broke off and advanced to the edge of the platform to sing of the chop-suey joints in Chicago's colored section:

"*Chinatown, my Chinatown—*"

Raptly, the others watched as Louis grabbed his trumpet and climbed to dizzy heights where he executed rhythmic evolutions comparable to those of a tightrope artist balancing himself without a stick.

One night as he was leaving the Dreamland, a voice hailed him:

"You Louis Armstrong?"

"Sure, Pops! What's your name?"

"I'm Erskine Tate, and I'd like to have a little talk with you. I conduct the orchestra at the Vendome Theater."

"Yes, I know. My wife'll be here in a minute, if you'll wait."

"I'd rather see you alone."

"All right," Louis agreed. "Be with you in five minutes at the corner cafeteria."

Louis went over to tell Lil, but—save for a pout of displeasure—she seemed not to hear him. Snow was falling, an icy wind blew, and when Louis entered the cafeteria he was glad to find himself in cozy warmth. Erskine Tate was already drinking hot coffee gratefully.

"Dipper," he said, "I've got a proposition for you. How much do you get at the Dreamland?"

"Seventy-five bucks a week."

"How would you like to boost that by fifty?"

Always slow to make up his mind and pledge his word, Louis rolled his eyes and shook his head doubtfully. "Could be," he replied noncommittally.

"How would you like to play solo in my band? Keep your Dreamland job, too, of course."

Louis's heart stopped beating. Impossible! Erskine Tate's orchestra was a symphonic ensemble of some twenty professional musicians. Why, you had to be at least a conservatory graduate before you could hope to play with such an ensemble! Louis asked for further details, wanted to know exactly what would be expected of him, demurred at giving an immediate answer.

"But I've got to know today, Dipper."

"Nothin' shakin', Erskine. Gotta talk it over with Lil."

Louis reached home late that night, and Lil was asleep. When he woke her she sat up startled, and listened to his rush of words. He had a proposition: to double up at the Vendome Theater. Ought he to accept it? Was he good enough to take the job? Wouldn't he make a fool of himself?

"Of course, you've got to take it, Louis. If you don't, I'll skin you alive. Do you realize what it means? They didn't ask King Oliver—they came to *you!*"

Several days later Louis came for Lil shortly after dusk.

"Where are we going?" she asked.

"You'll see."

The snow lay dark and wet in the streets, and the slippery pavements made hard walking. As they reached a corner, Louis stopped short, catching Lil by the arm and pointing with his free hand. In the darkness settling over the city she saw the Vendome Theater's green sign. Below the huge luminous letters marking the theater, Erskine Tate's name was spelled out in red lights, and just below: LOUIS ARMSTRONG. Lil screamed with delight, and even Louis himself could hardly believe it. Arm in arm they walked slowly toward the marquee and stood looking up at the sign for a long while, stamping their feet to keep warm. They wondered why the whole world did not stop and gather here to stare in admiration at the triumph of the black man whose star was rising in the sky of fame—TRUMPET: LOUIS ARMSTRONG. . . .

On beginning his new engagement, Louis—at Erskine's suggestion—discarded the good old cornet and bought a shiny trumpet. When he sat down at the music-stand for the first time, a cowboy picture was unreeling on the screen, hero chasing villain hell-for-leather across wild country. It was a "silent" picture, of course, and the orchestra's soft playing kept pace with the action.

At the end of the film it was the orchestra's turn to appear on the stage to render classical pieces. These ended in a flourish when Louis Armstrong was singled out by a crisscross of colored spotlights playing on him—an experience he had never had before. He sensed that Lil, in her seat in the front row, was watching him, holding him in check; perhaps she was a little envious of glory that she could not share directly.

Louis blinked as he moved toward the footlights. He felt but could not see the countless pairs of eyes turned on him by the faceless crowd, lost in the darkness of the vast theater. Yet by degrees, as his eyes grew accustomed to the lights and shadows, he began to make out some features. He experienced the same poignant emotion that had gripped him three years earlier when he had arrived one night at the Lincoln Garden to play with King Oliver. And now, he was a star in his own right and was climbing higher than all those he cared for.

The melody played by the orchestra—*Spanish Shawl*—was throbbing in Louis's veins. Not that he was fond of this particular piece—it did not allow him to develop the abrupt power of his personality, and there was a vague suggestion of *Carmen* about it that irritated him somewhat. Suddenly he broke the contact and stood alone before the audience, blowing like one possessed. Eyes closed, he felt himself borne to heaven on the wings of inspiration, and came down to earth only when a thunder of applause brought him back to reality.

All the lights were on, and he felt hopelessly trapped in the projectors' beams. Lil, due at the Dreamland before him, had left after waving to him in triumph. The spectators were wild with joy. Never had Louis received such an ovation and his heart pounded within him. He stood there, swaying, uncertain, moved to the core. Erskine Tate made a sign to him, and the orchestra struck up the theme song. Then time stood still once more. Louis shed all restraint and played. He was a pure musical spirit freed of all earthly ties. When he had taken repeated bows, he noticed in the first row, in the same seat that Lil had occupied, a young Negress who stood up and clapped madly. Twice she stirred up a new burst as the applause was dying out. Louis felt her eyes burning into his soul. He gave two more encores of *Spanish Shawl*. Each time his triumph was greater than before. Erskine Tate was jubilant.

"You see, Louis—I was right to make you change instruments."

By now Louis had not a moment to waste. He mopped his brow, tidied up as best he could, and left hurriedly for the Dreamland, the musicians congratulating him as he went out. Dashing through the door into the street, he turned up his overcoat collar and started to walk fast along the wet pavement. Excited groups were leaving the theater. As he passed some girls he heard one of them cry: "There he goes—Louis Armstrong!" Then he felt a tug on his sleeve, and turned to see the young Negress who had been feasting her eyes on him inside.

"Louis, you were wonderful! Let me kiss you."

Throwing her arms around his neck, she kissed him twice, in quick succession.

"I'm in a hurry," gasped Louis. "They're waitin' for me at the Dreamland."

"Never mind. I'll be back Friday when the show changes."

"What's your name?"

"Alpha."

And Louis hurried on his way. He was overflowing with joy. "That's funny," he mused. "That gal Alpha sat down right where Lil was sittin'. If I was superstitious I'd think that mean somethin'. Oh, well—I'll never see her again."

He entered the Dreamland as the orchestra was starting to play. Louis quickly snapped his case open and raised his trumpet. When he had finished his piece, he leaned over to Lil.

"Well?" he queried.

"It was marvelous, Louis . . . but . . ."

"But what?"

"Who's the other woman?"

And she pointed to the traces of lipstick on his cheek.

Louis laughed mockingly and did not reply. Already the orchestra was tuning up.

"Come on, Dipper!" cried the frantic youngsters.

Louis came out in front of the orchestra. He sang, laying heavy stress on the rhythm and letting the words come out with explosive force:

"*No gal made has got a shade*
On sweet Georgia Brown."

The cheers that broke out were deafening. Louis wiped off the lipstick with his handkerchief, and shut his eyes for an encore. Alpha's image was bright in his mind, but it would soon become blurred and fade away. On he played, repeating the haunting words: "*I'll tell her just why, you know I don't lie.*"

23

THERE WAS a change of program at the Vendome twice a week. Every time a new film was shown, Alpha sat in the first row, watching Louis who, highly flattered, played for her alone. He had a habit of strutting to the edge of the stage and, in his throaty voice, he would growl:

"An' now, I'm gonna shake out a good ol' favorite for you all, includin' the little lady in the first row."

From all sections of the house conflicting cries would ring out:

"*Swanee! Ya Do! Sweet Georgia Brown! Heebe Jeebies!*"

Louis would swing the trumpet to his lips with a flourish, look straight at Alpha, smile, and drop his instrument to his side with a low bow as the audience roared with laughter. Then a shout from Alpha:

"*My Buddy!*"

And Louis would respond:

"*Nights are long since you went away—
I think about you all through the day.*"

He meant every word of it. Night and day he thought about her. Things were about over between him and Lil. The pretty home was now merely a major item in their community property which must some time be liquidated. Louis always came home late—and every night brought new quarrels and scenes, often with poor little Clarence looking on in terror. Louis and Lil had drifted miles apart. Nothing remained but to make the separation legal.

Alpha, who was only fifteen or sixteen, worked as nursemaid for a white family, the Taylors, who thought highly of her. A new love had come into Louis's life. Fully conscious of the inequality between himself and Lil, he felt the need to return to the simple ways of his own kind. It was wonderful to meet Alpha every day and blurt out, in his own inimitable and colorful words, that she was the whole meaning of his life.

One hot morning in July the sun beat down fiercely on the city. Louis knew that Alpha would be alone in the house of her employers, who had gone away for the day to Winnetka, and he started out early to spend the day with his darling. Spirited colored girls idled by, exchanging quips and jokes, and flirting with the men. At the corner, as he waited for the streetcar, a "high yellow" looked hard at him and winked invitingly. The car was jammed with colored folks. As they rode on, however, more and more white people boarded the car. Servant girls and laborers were alighting along the route. By the time the car entered the town's well-to-do section, Louis was the only Negro aboard. He got off at a stop in the park near the Zoo. An attractive white girl passed on a cantering horse, holding a cigarette and humming a jazzy piece that Louis had helped to make popular just a few weeks ago. Soon he was ringing the Taylors' bell. Alpha opened the door.

"Oh, my! Sure 'nuf it's you! Ain't it wonderful, oh man! Come in—make yourself at home. I got the best food in the house all ready for you, honey. This afternoon, dig me if you ain't Mister Taylor!"

Horn of Plenty:

Louis took off his coat, selected a choice Havana from the box on Mr. Taylor's desk, and followed Alpha out to the terrace where a rocking-chair stood invitingly in the shade. He tried a mint julep, and decided it would bear repeating. Alpha was doing things in grand style—she had found the best bottle of Scotch in the house. Louis lolled contentedly in Mr. Taylor's chair and decided that not even its owner could be any happier than he.

Alpha returned to announce that the steaks were done and everything was ready in the kitchen, but that they would eat in the dining-room. Louis, by now a little tipsy, sat down heavily. He frowned, wondering what Mr. Taylor would have done next, then nodded gravely to himself, and got up and fetched his coat, into which he struggled with some difficulty. Now he felt more like Mr. Taylor.

"Lordy! This steak is some juicy. Alpha, baby, I can't tell what's best—your lovin' or your cookin'!"

"Louis, I got an idea. Mr. Taylor always drinks some wine with his dinner. How's about a drink out that ol' French bottle over there? Just to celebrate. If he could hear you play, I bet he'd pour it out hisself!"

As he sipped the fine Burgundy, Louis thought how wonderful life was after all. He removed his coat once more, loosened his tie and collar, and heaved a sigh of deep satisfaction as he fondled the bottle of imported French wine.

At this ecstatic juncture, a key turned in the front door lock and a moment later Mr. and Mrs. Taylor appeared in the dining-room doorway. Louis, abandoning a hasty impulse to dive under the table, sat petrified, staring stupidly at the strawberry shortcake before him. And in the space of a few seconds, Louis was on the outside and moving fast.

An oppressive summer weighed down the city. Every day

now, as soon as he was free, Louis called at Alpha's mother's house at Cottage Grove and 33rd Streets, in the poorest section of Chicago. These visits were like a pilgrimage into the past. In order to reach the house, Louis gradually descended the scale of human habitation: after he had left the better homes behind, he passed tenements—from tenements he came to the shanties—after the shanties he found the hovels—until finally he knocked at the door of the miserable hut that housed Alpha and her mother. Yet he preferred the warmth and affection of these simple people to the comfort of his own home.

One day he took Clarence along, and for supper they feasted on fried chicken and red beans. They ate quickly, for it was almost time to go to the Vendome. The abundance of food on the table contrasted strangely with the general air of poverty. Through the open door, one could see the wretched bedroom, with its wooden wash basin so like those of Perdido.

"You likes chicken, eh, Louis?" Alpha's mother cackled. "I done read it in the lines o' your hand."

"Yeah, I'm crazy 'bout chicken. How 'bout you, Clarence?"

The boy opened his eyes wide and held his fork poised in midair to reply:

"Pop, you know I love chicken. It's swell here. I'd like to leave Lil and live here. I belong here!"

Louis was astonished to hear such words from the lad, and tears came to his eyes.

Several weeks went by. Louis was torn between a remnant of loyalty to Lil and his new love for Alpha. In truth, he had already seen his lawyer and had asked him to obtain a divorce. Apparently Lil and her mother sought an outlet for their resentment by venting their ill humor on Clarence. One of them once spoke very sharply to the little fellow, who burst into tears. Immediately Louis took up the cudgels, and a terrific row ensued. Louis was boiling with impotent rage. He had still two long hours to wait before it would be time to go to the Vendome. Suddenly a great decision formed in his mind. He opened his trunk, packed his clothes, and told Clarence to get his own valise ready. In a short while he was ready to leave all the possessions he had acquired with his first earnings, and was on his way to Cottage Grove. Until the last moment, insults flew thick and fast. Lil's parting words were a threat:

"You'll hear from me pretty soon. I'll surprise you when you least expect it!"

Louis now gave scant thought to the lamp with the pink shade and the easy-chair upholstered in green sprays. All of that now belonged to the past and melted away into the still remoter past of Jane Alley, of Perdido. At any rate, he had severed all connection with the things that irked his very soul and now, back in the slums, in the squalid hovel, the dingy room, Louis Armstrong—guest star of the Vendome Theater, who appeared nightly in the blaze of spotlights before sighing admirers—could revert to his old care-free existence, once more free and independent.

Everything went along very smoothly. Clarence was happy and Alpha's mother took wonderfully good care of him. Louis and Alpha spent long, blissful hours together. The mild days of September were cool and pleasant on the lakeshore. Louis bought a present for Alpha, a coat with caracul collar. The first time her mother saw her wearing it, she raised her arms and exclaimed:

"Lordy, Alpha, what you doin' here in Cottage Grove? Child, you looks like the Queen o' Sheba! Me, oh my! You can't never wash in that ol' basin no more."

A few days later Louis made a sensational appearance in

Cottage Grove. The tooting of an automobile horn sounded outside the house. Alpha's mother opened the window. A Model T with dazzling yellow wheels was parked in front of the door. The blowing continued. A woman's head popped out of the car window. All the neighborhood was agog by now and there was a general peeking and whispering from all corners. Suddenly Alpha stepped from the Ford, wearing a new powder-blue dress, while Louis Armstrong followed close behind in a dark coat, wing collar, and a huge derby as crowning glory. Clarence, utterly fascinated by all these goings-on, came running out of the house and jumped on the running-board. By this time all the darkies were congregating in little groups and discussing this unusual event from the sidewalk:

"Hey, Pop, look over yonder . . . the man with the football on his head. Oh, yea, man! That guy's a sure 'nuf ace. He packs 'em in at the Vendome. He's gettin' hitched to Mis' Smith's gal. You know, she was just a kid in school last year with my gal Muriel."

"Lucky break for her. Take a peep at them yaller wheels. Boy, that's some chariot!"

"He's sure ridin' high. He used to be at the Vendome, an' now he's doublin' up at the Sunset an' makin' twice as much as the other guys."

"Shut up! Youse talkin' foolish. Louis Armstrong's a big shot. They ain't no colored man ever dragged down so much dough 'ceptin' Jack Johnson, the prize fighter. He's coinin' money with them records, rolls o' hundreds an' thousands . . ."

This is what had really happened.

Louis usually finished playing at the Vendome about eleven. One evening, a man who was destined to play an important part in his life was waiting for him at the theater exit.

"You're Louis Armstrong."

"Yeah. An' who's you, Pops?"

"Joe Glaser. I'm the owner of the Sunset. I've got a spot for you and Earl Hines in Carroll Dickerson's orchestra."

Shortly afterward, Louis and Earl were playing at the Sunset and the establishment, which had been doing poorly on account of the competition furnished by the famous King Oliver at the Plantation, soon found its receipts soaring and the customers flocking to hear the new attractions.

Very early one Sunday morning, while it was still dark, Louis woke up with a start. Someone was moving at the window. He listened intently, trying to locate the noise; then a weird thought struck him—Lil was putting her threat into execution! She knew that the window would be flung wide open on this summer night, and she had come to frighten him. What would happen next? He did not relish the idea of facing the .38 revolver she had often shown him. . . . The eerie creaking continued at the window. Louis lay as if frozen. Now a shape detached itself from the shadows and something dropped inside the room. In a panic, he jumped from the bed, shouting for Lil to come out of hiding. Soon the whole household was awake—running in to find out the cause of the uproar. When lights were turned on they revealed nothing unusual. Louis began to wonder if he had been the victim of a nightmare, and Alpha's mother jeered at him.

"All right—let me alone! I *wasn't* seein' things!" he protested heatedly.

But the mystery was cleared up when Clarence crawled under the bed and dragged Sit out by the scruff. Sit was the family's coal-black tomcat, who had been locked out and had chosen the easiest means of entry to find his bed after a late prowl.

So great was Louis's relief that he decided to take a trip

into the country. An hour later they left in the flivver, stopping near by to rout out Tubby Hall, the ace drummer from New Orleans, and his wife. Tubby came to the door, sleepily rubbing his eyes.

"Hello, Satchmo'," he yawned. "Alpha, you look like a million! Where do we go in your brand-new yellow 'pneumonia special'?"

"Let's go to Bill Bottom's at Blue Island."

They skirted the lake as far as Washington Park, where they turned and followed Vincennes Avenue in a stream of outbound traffic. Their destination was a small restaurant set in a grove; it was run by Joe Louis's doctor. After they had picnicked on the banks of Stony Creek in the cool of the evening, Louis took out his portable phonograph and played the *Stomp Off Let's Go,* a disc he had made with Erskine Tate, and *Georgia Hobo,* made with Lil's Hot Shots. He sprawled on the grass looking up at the clouds and caressing Alpha's hand while Tubby Hall beat time with his foot against the nearest tree.

They changed records; this time it was *Gut Bucket Blues,* a recording by Louis Armstrong's Hot Five. And he described to his friends that first session at the Okeh Studio, when Lil sat at the piano, Kid Ory played the trombone, Johnny St. Cyr strummed the banjo, and Johnny Dodds fingered the clarinet. The art of making records was still in its infancy, the electrical process being as yet unknown, and in order to give the soloists a breathing-spell after each solo, one of the musicians would speak a few words. For *Gut Bucket Blues,* Johnny Dodds was called on to pronounce the conventional phrase: "*Oh, play it! Papa Dipp, play it—huh!*" He drew up to his full height at the microphone and took a deep breath. Now he was all set to speak his piece—but not a sound came from his lips, he merely gasped like a trout out of water. And this same thing happened several times. Mr. Fern, Okeh's president, who was present at the rehearsal, had to laugh at the overgrown boy who could not overcome his bashfulness.

Not long thereafter Louis sought out more suitable living quarters. He rented a room at Susie's Apartments and from time to time Alpha, who now worked downtown in a department store, would drop in to see him on her way home.

One day Louis, in his dressing-gown, was waving good-bye to Alpha as she left the house after bringing some clothes she had pressed for him. Suddenly Lil Armstrong stood before her, barring the way. Standing at the window, Louis watched a fierce struggle between the two women. They rolled on the ground together, pulled each other's hair with all their might, and tore each other's blouses. Out he dashed in his dressing-gown, but by the time he reached the sidewalk both women's skirts were in tatters and Lil, now ignoring Alpha, turned on Louis and furiously brandished her .38 under his nose. Only the arrival of the police served to separate the brawlers and disperse the crowd that had gathered.

A few hours later Louis was at the Sunset. Though his nerves were somewhat upset by the day's exciting events, he was as successful as ever in an old hit, whose melody was expertly carried by Earl Hines:

"Oh, you beautiful doll—
You great big beautiful doll!
Let me put my arms around you—
I could never live without you!"

24

THIS WAS the era when Calumet and 35th Streets resounded nightly with the jazziest of rhythms. Carroll Dickerson held forth at the Sunset; at the Plantation, just opposite, King Oliver blew a mighty trumpet; and, a little farther on, at the Nest, there was Jimmie Noone. The whole night was filled with vibrant arpeggios and solos.

One evening, after dark, Louis left Susie's Apartments accompanied by Alpha. They stopped first at the Vendome, then continued toward the Sunset. All along the way, they walked very close together, hand in hand, now and then stopping for a kiss.

"That's enough!" cried Louis after one of these embraces. "I been fined a dozen times on account o' you, Alpha."

"Louis, honey, you don't know how scared an' lonely I get. I hate to go back to Cottage Grove—that awful, stinky hole. Stay with me a little while, sugar."

And Louis, yielding to these loving entreaties, lingered a little longer, holding his trumpet case in one hand and caressing Alpha with the other.

"Shucks! I'm ten minutes late again. Mr. Glaser gonna give me hell."

They had arrived in front of the Sunset. No sooner had they turned the corner of the block than they hugged each other once more. Alpha's eyes, half-closed in pleasure, looked at the Sunset's glittering façade and a surge of pride rose in her heart as she read Louis Armstrong's name emblazoned there—the star of the show.

Louis entered the night club in great haste—Earl Hines was already at the piano running over the keys. The piece tapered off into a soft finish. The bandleader pointed an accusing finger at Louis:

"That'll be twenty dollars for the kitty!"

The very next day, Louis resigned from the Vendome's show. He felt he could enjoy life without owning the world. Between his work at the Sunset and his recordings, he was earning a great deal of money and the future seemed secure.

This was the great period when Louis, drawing solely on his own inspiration, produced the Hot Five's most noted selections: *Yes, I'm in the Barrel*, *Gut Bucket Blues*, *Cornet Chop Suey*, *Heebie Jeebies*, *The King of the Zulus*, *Sunset Café Stomp*, some of which were his own compositions.

Louis saw his wife only when he made records at the Okeh Studios, where Mr. Fern had become a fast friend of his. At the outset he had insisted that Louis play "commercial" songs. Louis had refused point-blank.

"Why don't you play like Paul Whiteman?"

"Because my kind of jazz ain't his kind o' jazz."

"We could sell thousands of records."

"Mr. Fern, I'd rather play good jazz than make good money. Anyhow, I think that ain't a bad way to make money."

Fern, impressed by Louis's earnestness, realized that it was best not to attempt to dilute or tone down the enormous power of this particular musician. On the contrary, he sensibly gave him full freedom to express himself completely and totally.

The Hot Five was succeeded by the Hot Seven. Finally, the entire personnel that Louis had been using at the studio was replaced. Lil was forgotten and an extraordinary group of recruits came together. They were members of Carroll Dickerson's orchestra at the Sunset. All were his buddies, all were wild about jazz, and, for the first time, Louis had with him a drummer who beat out music with the frenzy which is the very soul of jazz. Zutty Singleton was Louis's rhythmic shadow, the lengthening and pulsation of his musicianship. But there was another who had rapidly scaled the same heights of musical genius as his friend: Earl Hines. With Louis at his side acting as a sort of solvent, he cut loose from himself, his huge hands imposed the rhythm on the keyboard, he shaped melody and syncopation, ended with a break, and suddenly took a fresh start with an effortless ease rare in the annals of jazz music.

One day at the studio on Washington Street they were all sitting around, chatting about the previous night's doings. Louis was trying to conceal the anxiety he had been feeling since news had come from the Crescent City that his mother was ailing.

"What's the record for today, Earl?" he asked.

"Let's beat out a real jazzy number."

"Don't feel like it!"

"Well, how's about a good old blues, like the one you played the other night."

"Oh!" cried Louis, "that's an old piece. First time I heard it was in Gretna, over the river."

"How do it go again?" asked the trombonist.

Louis hummed the tune, his lips quivering. The theme penetrated them like alcohol flowing through their veins. It intoxicated them as they tried to harmonize. Earl writhed and squirmed on his piano-stool, pausing now and then to shake the ashes from his cigar. Then the operator gave the signal. A red light flashed the "go" sign.

Seldom before in his life had Louis felt so downcast. Perhaps he was thinking of Gretna, of that night long ago on the banks of the Mississippi, of the dim lights of New Orleans blinking in the distance, over the river, of May Ann, his mother, ill and suffering in Perdido.

When it was all over they looked at one another.

"I got the feelin' it ain't so hot," whispered Zutty.

Just then the engineer came out from his booth, said the recording was perfect, and announced they were ready to play it back. They listened entranced, unable to understand the miracle that had happened.

In a corner of the room a man gripped his chair and tried to hold back the tears. This was Joe Glaser, manager of the Sunset. He wanted to hug Louis and Earl and Zutty.

"What's the name of that piece?" inquired the engineer.

They scratched their heads—no one had thought of a name. One man proposed *Washington Blues*, another *Calumet Blues* —a title that Mezz Mezzrow was to use at a later date. But they wanted something more "poetic." Someone suggested *West End Blues*, and approval was unanimous.

As they left the studio, Earl Hines and Louis walked side by side.

"You know, Pops," said Louis, "I think nobody never played the piano like you did just now. Every time I think o' that little break . . . you know, when you stop and then go on again quick-like . . ."

"And you, Dipper, when you reached for the sky, I thought you was goin' straight up to the pearly gates!"

In like manner they recorded *Basin Street Blues*, *No One*

Else But You, and *St. James Infirmary*. Sometimes a new alto joined them, a man who prepared arrangements for Carroll Dickerson's tunes, Don Redman. Another time, when Jimmy Strong was sick and Jimmie Noone was routed out to replace him, in less than an hour they had made *I Can't Give You Anything But Love*.

Once Louis was approached by Johnny Dodds. Johnny had a contract with Vocalion, while Louis was bound by an exclusive agreement with Okeh. But Johnny was looking for a vocalist and persuaded Louis to come to his studio and sing for him, arguing that he could disguise his voice. These songs were *Wild Man Blues* and *Melancholy*.

A few weeks later the record went on sale and became a hit. Then Louis was summoned by Okeh's president. Nonchalantly Louis walked into Mr. Fern's office. Fern did not say a word—merely picked up a disc and put it on the phonograph. Louis listened without at first understanding what it all meant. Johnny Dodds's music blared out, with Kid Ory at the trombone, Earl at the piano, and Babe Dodds at the drums. At last Louis grasped the meaning of the ceremony. It might have been possible to mistake Earl Hines for somebody else, but Louis's presence was as palpable as if his name had been shouted through a loud-speaker. As the record ground to a close, the president's grim silence was oppressive.

Louis got up, hung his head and mumbled apologetically: "Please forgive me, Mr. Fern. It won't happen again!"

Every night at the Sunset the steady patrons arrived to absorb rhythm. Among them were Paul Whiteman, Jean Goldkette, Bud Freeman, Jimmie MacPartland, Art Hodes, and invariably Mezz Mezzrow. Joe Glaser had immediately realized the potentialities of Louis Armstrong's amazing personality. Here was a musician who towered above all the others, stood in a class by himself. The incident at the Vocalion confirmed him in his belief that Louis Armstrong was the only one to whom such a thing could happen because he was the most personalized of them all.

Once when Louis fell sick and was in bed for ten days, an extraordinary thing happened. At the end of the first week, a white man was ushered into the patient's room. It was Joe Glaser, bringing Louis his week's pay, although strictly speaking he had not earned it. Since that day, the two have been linked by a very close friendship.

When Louis appeared at the Sunset after his illness he was greeted by an ovation. A new tune was sweeping the world, and in its wake came a new dance: the Charleston. Joe Glaser had the idea of organizing Charleston contests but realized a great amount of showmanship was necessary in order to woo the crowds.

Joe Glaser did not approach the bandmaster, Carroll Dickerson. He confided his plans to Louis Armstrong. It was thus that Louis was given charge of the Charleston part of the program. With Earl Hines, Tubby Hall at the drums, Joe Walker playing the alto, and another trumpeter, Bill Wilson, the show was climaxed by a whirlwind Charleston finale. It was so unexpected and so irresistible that all Chicago flocked to see it. Louis, in a sort of convulsive rage, would get angry at his trumpet and chase it out to the dance-floor, all the while shouting meaningless words that fanned the enthusiasm of a generation of boys and girls caught by this latest craze.

When Carroll Dickerson left the orchestra in a huff, Joe Glaser's unfailing business instinct told him that here was the chance of a lifetime. He called in Louis Armstrong and offered to name the orchestra after him. Here was the road to glory! Louis was jubilant. Barely five years since he had left New Orleans, and now he was Chicago's outstanding musician. On warm nights all the windows were flung open both at the Sunset and at the Plantation and late promenaders passed by under a double barrage of warring trumpets, for the heavy musical artillery of King Oliver and of Louis Armstrong thundered until the small hours of the morning. Long since, however, King had realized he was beaten by his pupil, and he had written to Picou:

"Write a few good blues for me, and don't worry about the top notes. I've got to keep up with Louis—he's slaying me with high notes. He climbs up to heaven like tempo with wings. He can pinch the stratosphere with his big steel lips. Atta boy!"

Louis appointed Earl Hines to direct the orchestra, and the new bandleader's name now appeared in larger letters on the electric signs. From time to time Lil, hopeless yet fascinated, tried to make up with the man who had played such a dynamic rôle in her life. But she knew that only one thing really mattered for Louis: jazz—and there, Earl Hines counted far more than she did. How could she hope to fight successfully?

Back stage, Joe Glaser's voice could be heard, calling down the wrath of heaven on the heads of the musicians or the chorus girls in his rapid-fire Chicago slang:

"Jeez—shake it up, you bums! Ten minutes late again. I'll mow you down with me tommy-gun! I'm ruined . . . where the hell's Earl Hines?"

Everything was ready for the show, but they were still looking for Father Hines. Joe Glaser bit his nails and swore. Suddenly spying Hines, he pointed dramatically at the pianist who, cigar stuck in his mouth, was calmly making a knot in his tie behind the piano whose shiny surface served as a mirror. The audience was standing up, breathlessly shouting, and on stage everybody was waiting impatiently for the first note, down to the last man in the wings. Louis was growling as he manipulated his trumpet. But Earl Hines was not yet satisfied with his knot, and carried on imperturbably. Joe Glaser bellowed:

"Why the hell don't he start the damn'd show, this sharp pianist?"

Earl, stung into action, dropped his tie and his cigar, rushed up to Joe threateningly, then walked off slowly, leaving him gasping against the wall. Stormy rounds of applause swept through the Sunset, crossed the street, and brought grief to the heart of King Oliver.

One night Louis heard a knock at his dressing-room door. "Come in," he invited. It was Fanny—Fanny Cotton, more beautiful, more bewitching than ever, and still in love with the genius of the trumpet. But alas, Alpha was keeping watch not far away and would be waiting for him after the show!

Some time afterward, a telegram came from New Orleans. His mother was failing. He sat for a long time thinking. What could he do? It was out of the question to leave for Louisiana. Clarence, poor little fellow, was unable to travel alone. And his mother did not even know that Alpha existed. He wept in desperation.

When night fell, Louis set out with bowed head. He reached his old house and stopped outside, listening in the warm shadows. Lil was playing classical music, which revived memories of the past and deepened his sorrow. The door was ajar and he entered noiselessly. There was Lil at the piano he had chosen for her, ages ago it seemed. Suddenly aware of his presence, she turned, and gave a little cry of fear when she recognized him.

"What do you want, Louis?"

"Listen, Lil, we don't get along no more, but we can't forget everything. Just because we was married, 'tain't no reason to fight like cats an' dogs."

"What do you mean?" asked Lil, puzzled by this preamble.

"Mama's pretty sick."

"Oh, I'm sorry. But I don't understand . . ."

"Well, it's like this. If you could go to New Orleans an' fetch her for me . . . I'd go myself, but—well, you ain't workin' now an' . . ."

"All right, Louis, I'll go."

A few days later May Ann arrived in Chicago for the second time. Lil had said nothing to her about the divorce; on the contrary, she had pretended that all was as before. May Ann was taken at once to the hospital. The doctors told Louis there was no chance of saving her life. Each day, Lil went to visit the dying woman; and Louis, at the bedside, never disclosed that their honeymoon days belonged to the dead past. May Ann passed away, blessing her son and his wife. But when she had breathed her last, Louis and Lil felt that the last tie of affection was irrevocably broken and they parted forever.

Louis could not decide what to do about the burial. All those of his race—the old slaves and the cotton-pickers and the workers on the levee—had been laid to rest at the river's bend where long ago a slave-ship had unloaded its human cargo. And before she died, May Ann had spoken feelingly of the Reverend Cozy, whose church stood opposite the Fisk School. He wondered whether he ought to send her body back to New Orleans. If he did so, he would never be able to say a prayer at the grave of the mother he had loved so well. . . . But finally his decision was made, and he followed the body along Chicago's streets to Lincoln Cemetery, accompanied by his friends who mourned with him.

Horn of Plenty:

For two days Louis stayed away from work; he wanted to be alone with his thoughts. But the music in his soul would not be stilled. For hours on end, he hummed over and over again the *West End Blues*, with its doleful and warmly human melody. He kept asking himself how he would ever have the heart to climb back on the stage and play the clown for the crowds. Just the same, he had to go back to work. Enthusiastic audiences were impatiently awaiting his return.

When he walked up to the footlights with his trumpet, he was acclaimed joyfully. Then the requests swamped him from all sides. Someone shouted, louder than the rest:

"*St. James Infirmary!*"

The cry was caught up and repeated all over the house. But that particular piece was full of recent sad associations for Louis, and he did not feel like playing it. Earl Hines—who had instantly sensed this—shook his head, and Zutty tried to propose a tune that would have no such associations for Louis. As for Louis himself, however, he conquered almost instantly his original reluctance, and called to Hines: "All right, Father —let's stomp *St. James!*"

He shut his eyes to hold back the tears, mouthed his trumpet, and blew the tragic and funereal notes. One could have heard a pin drop during the pauses in the rhythm. Then Louis, surpassing himself, sang the words that reopened the wounds of his grief:

"*I went down to St. James Infirmary—
Saw my baby there. . . .*"

But he had to leave the stage without taking a single curtain call. Offstage he hid behind a door and wept. Joe Glaser came out to pat him on the shoulder and try to comfort him.

"Louis, your mother died happy. She knew you were the best trumpeter in America!"

[238]

But Louis's fame was already reaching beyond America. His first discs had just arrived in Europe where university students and groups of intellectuals forswore food and drink to absorb the message of beauty and grandeur that America was giving to the world—even though herself not yet quite comprehending its true significance.

25

WHEN LOUIS'S one-year contract at the Sunset expired he had to look for something else. With Zutty Singleton he was engaged by Clarence Jones's orchestra, which was playing for the Metropolitan movie house in Chicago's South Side. At the Sunset Louis had been publicized in neon on the marquee; here the Armstrong name headed the billing. Fame and publicity went hand in hand.

It was a treat to be in the audience when Louis and his old crony Zutty enacted a comic skit built around a tune entitled *I Ain't Gonna Play No Second Fiddle*.

As the scene opened, Ol' Barrel House Louis appeared, drunk and wearing a battered hat. Swaying from side to side, he sang an appealing little ditty, when suddenly an enormously fat washwoman ran up from the audience to mingle with the orchestra—it was Zutty Singleton, his calico dress stuffed with pillows at the right spots. The sight of his heaving bosom and billowing posterior always brought down the house. Once on the stage, Zutty lost no time in belaboring the old sot— Louis Armstrong himself—until they reached the uproarious climax. Louis grabbed his trumpet, blew like mad, climbed up to the sky, and rolled his eyes as big as billiard balls while the frantic washwoman beat the drums for all she (or rather he) was worth.

The Metropolitan contract was a short one, and Louis was soon unemployed again. He had saved a little money, so he stayed on in Chicago in order to be near his beloved Alpha.

One night, as he and Zutty were making the rounds of the honky-tonks in the South Side, they encountered Earl Hines, chewing a cigar as always, and the three were soon discussing prospects. It seemed that these were all bad—there was no work to be found. At last Earl suggested that they open up a place of their own.

"Look, Louis, with you an' this ol' washwoman Zutty, us three could clean up. We got what it takes. Let's open up a dance joint. We'll make hundreds, thousands . . . All them dance-hall guys is filthy with money."

They all agreed that this was a good idea, and Louis having larger savings than the others and a brand new Hupmobile into the bargain, was delegated to find a promising location. After a search that lasted two or three days, he thought he had found it in Warwick Hall—in a building on 47th Street near Forrestville Avenue, two blocks from South Parkway—and he started negotiations with the building manager.

"So you want to rent Warwick Hall? It'll cost you something—it's the best spot in Chicago. It's the only hall in this section, do you realize that?"

In his innocence, Louis swallowed the bait whole, signing a lease for a year at a monthly rental of $375. The manager omitted to mention that at that very moment painters were working fast on a dance hall at 47th Street and South Parkway which was scheduled to open on the exact date when Louis and his friends were planning to open theirs. This was to be the famous Savoy Ballroom, whose façade sported peacocks that preened themselves in the brilliant lights.

Warwick Hall's opening was disastrous. Earl Hines wore himself out at the keyboard, Zutty slammed his drums with all his might, Louis scraped the highest clouds with his trumpet—but all to no avail. Even Alpha had tried her best to advertise the place, spreading the word among her friends. Apparently the Savoy Ballroom's lighted peacocks had a persuasive charm for the blacks that pure jazz lacked, and after a few dismal nights Warwick Hall was closed.

On the final evening, as the trio counted the night's slim receipts, they knew they had lost their gamble. After a brief discussion, they decided it would be foolish to go on. They locked up for the last time, their minds fully made up that this was the end, and walked off to Louis's car, muttering imprecations on the Savoy and all its works.

Suddenly Louis stopped short, a worried look on his face. "Wait a minute, I had the car parked right here . . . Yes—the Hupmobile's gone!"

Frantically they looked on both sides of the street, walked around the block, their despair growing more acute by the minute. The automobile had vanished. Crushed by this fresh misfortune, the three left for the heart of town.

Next day the car was found on the outskirts of town, but when Louis reached the spot he discovered that the thieves had stripped it of every removable part. The Hupmobile was a total wreck! He had the car towed to a garage and got the loan of a Ford that suggested a Smithsonian exhibit: a yellow roadster with the garage's name painted in black on its sides. Louis and Alpha were a chastened pair as they drove about Chicago.

Everybody was laughing in Cottage Grove.

"Say, ol' man, they tells me Louis Armstrong ain't doin' so hot. He went busted in Warwick Hall. Just look at that ol' yellow toilet he's ridin' his sweetie in!"

"Another thing," laughed another; "you don't smell that fried chicken so frequent."

There could be no doubt that things looked badly. Louis's savings were used up, and he was obliged to hire out for "one-night stands," which was almost a disgrace. Gradually it went from bad to worse, all three of them living in the single hope of scraping up enough to eat with.

Just the same, every blessed day, Louis managed to put on that good old white shirt, and—through God knows what financial juggling—Earl still smoked his cigars; though, as Louis used to remark, they were easier on the eyes than on the nose.

What was the next step? They never stopped looking for jobs, but luck ran against them. Though the Hupmobile was by now repaired, Louis did not dare ask for the bill. They had agreed among themselves that whoever found work first must share his earnings with the other two.

One day, having saved a few dollars, they toyed once more with the idea of opening a dance-hall. Someone told them about a vacant place on the West Side, in the heart of Chicago's worst district—the hangout of its tough guys, hoodlums, and gangsters. However, it was decided that they would give the place a try. This time Louis, having learned his lesson, refused to sign a long lease, or even a lease for a month; after endless argument he succeeded in renting the place for one night. Alpha spent an afternoon looking for liquor and managed to get a few cases on credit.

When they arrived that evening the outlook was bleak. First, Earl discovered that the upright piano was minus several keys. Then Louis noticed that the rickety platform threatened to collapse at any moment.

About nine o'clock a few curious couples straggled in, and as more people arrived Zutty's face cleared. This looked better. They would cover their overhead; from now on, the rest would be clear profit. Back of the counter, Alpha was smiling at Louis, a little smile that meant:

"Satchmo', hurry up with that intermission. Give them colored boys a chance to drink so's I can fill up that register."

This was unexpected luck. From time to time, Earl craned his neck above the upright, trying to count the crowd. About half-past nine, confident that the evening would be a success, he sent out for a handful of two-for-nickel cigars.

Between numbers, Zutty spoke with his two buddies.

"It looks like our ship's come home."

"Shut your mouth, man," Earl growled. "Let's keep our fingers crossed till it's all over."

"You got the wrong slant. I ain't down in the dumps no more. We gotta work fast. We ought to rent the place over right this minute. If we waits till tomorrow, the owner's gonna get wise an' he'll soak us."

Earl had not smoked at all that day, and he was waiting for the cigars as the parched ground waits for rain. Alpha said to him:

"Me, I'm lookin' for the intermission."

"Me, I'd like to have my cigars!" sighed Earl.

Just then the side door opened. Father Hines grunted with satisfaction—that must be the boy with his cigars. But the door stayed open and no one entered. Impatiently Earl cried:

"Come on, you, hustle!"

Then they saw the barrel of a gun jutting across the door jamb. The dancers stopped short and cries of terror rose from the crowd. A Negro in ragged clothes closed the door behind him and brandished a vicious-looking .45.

Heebie Jeebies stopped with startling abruptness. The hoodlum, his eyes shifting from one couple to the next, waved his pistol wildly. Women shrieked and fainted. Those nearest the entrance fled in a panic. Then a fight broke out near the door as someone knocked the cash register to the floor.

Louis found enough courage to remain on the scene for a few seconds. Earl Hines, however, dived for the floor so quickly that he seemed to have gone right through his piano. Zutty was hiding behind his drums. Alpha was crouching behind the counter. Suddenly realizing what an excellent target he made, Louis threw himself beside Earl on the platform. At that moment, the bandit turned slightly and pointed his gun at the orchestra. Women were crushed in the ensuing scramble. In a few minutes the hall was practically empty.

The shriek of sirens announced the arrival of the police. Louis ventured to peek out from behind the piano and saw the Negro run toward them and around the bandstand, escaping through the private door with the police in close pursuit.

"Come on, come on!" Zutty was urging. "The cash register!"

They ran to the front door and searched, but the register had disappeared. They rushed outside, where some frightened blacks pointed to the corner of the building, which was raised on concrete piles. Several shots rang out.

"Where's the register?" Zutty wailed.

"To hell with the register! Better not try to catch all that lead flyin' 'round here!" retorted Louis.

The bandit had crawled under the dance-hall, where he was hopelessly trapped. The policemen had recognized him as a dangerous gangster wanted for killing a detective just two days before.

More shots cracked out, followed by yells of pain. In an instant the few remaining spectators were gone. Alpha appeared, her arms upraised in a gesture of despair.

"Oh, Lord, it's awful!"

[245]

"Let's beat it," Hines suggested.

"Hold on. What about the money?"

The gun play was soon over. Several police vans arrived on the scene. In the glare of the headlights Louis and his friends saw the policemen drag out a corpse as full of holes as a sieve—practically every shot had found its mark.

Thus were their hopes for a successful evening dashed to the ground. Going back into the hall, they found it sacked. The cash register had been stolen—that was certain. At that moment the door opened, and they all turned with revived hope.

"Maybe somebody's bringin' back the money!" Louis said.

A black boy shuffled in, and what he carried was—a box of cigars. Earl Hines could only shake his head disconsolately; he was as penniless as the others.

As the quartet went off to climb into the borrowed Ford, Louis intoned in a preacher's sepulchral voice:

"You-all better pray the good Lord that we don't run out o' gas before we get home!"

The gas proved to be sufficient to get them back, and they spent the rest of the night discussing the tragedy.

"It sure is tough luck," lamented Earl. "Them cigars come just five minutes too late—I'd have had me enough smokes for a week!"

For a while Louis cast hopeful eyes in the Savoy's direction, but bad luck was dogging his footsteps. The Savoy engaged the orchestras of Clarence Blank and Charles Elgar, and this ended another hope. He began to lose self-confidence, took to wondering whether he had any real ability. Sometimes a friend proffered a free drink and advice:

"Satchmo', you're a sucker. You was a star in them big

movie places, an' you kept on playin' hot music. Why don't you try some sweet stuff? You know ... give it to them fancy, sort of symphony style."

"Me, I ain't lookin' for business—I want to play jazz straight," Louis would reply.

Louis had given up his ambition to be the King. All he wanted was a chance to work for a living. He was going through a period of terrible mental depression. Then Alpha found some work and earned a little money. One evening Earl Hines came in wearing a worried look. Louis looked up at him.

"Well, Father?"

"Satchmo', I got somethin' to tell you. You know I promised not to take no job without you—but ..." He bowed his head. "We been in the dog-house for weeks now. A man's gotta live—and—well, I've promised Jimmie Noone I'd play for him at the Apex. I'll split with you, don't worry!"

"That's perfect, Father," Louis returned. "You done the right thing. All I'm mad about is that them guys ain't got 'nuf sense to see we'd knock 'em dead together!"

"Ain't it the truth! You remember the *West End Blues?*"

Two days later Carroll Dickerson called on Louis.

"Satchmo', I've got something for you-all."

"Who's 'you-all,' Pops?"

"Earl and Zutty, and you!"

"Too late, Carroll. Earl's startin' tonight with Jimmie Noone at the Apex."

"That's too bad!"

"Yeah, it's worse 'n that," replied Louis. "Ivory-ticklers like Earl don't grow on trees in Chicago."

"Well, we'll just have to do without him."

"What's the job?"

"At the Savoy."

The Savoy! Louis reflected grimly that this was the place that had ruined Warwick Hall. He told Carroll he would join the group, but he vowed to himself that he would have his revenge.

26

LOUIS'S FAME had now spread far and wide through the recordings he had made. Dame Fortune had been fickle, however. There had been times when he thought he had become America's idol—and others when he fell back into the old rut, dismal periods of enforced idleness.

Carroll Dickerson, unable to get Earl Hines, had succeeded in procuring the services of Jean Anderson, who was about the best pianist to be found after Earl. Besides Louis, the orchestra was composed of Homer Hobson (trumpet), Fred Robinson (trombone), Jimmy Strong (clarinet), Bert Curry and Crawford Wethington (saxophones), Peck Carr (banjo), Pete Briggs (bass fiddle), and Zutty (drums), with Carroll as the violinist.

From the very first rehearsals the orchestra revealed exceptional qualities. New pieces had been prepared with great care, enabling Louis to give full scope to his personality: *Ain't Misbehavin'*, *Black and Blue*, *That Rhythm Man*, *Sweet Savannah Sue*, *When You're Smiling*, and the tried and true favorites with their expressive rhythmic beat: *After You've Gone* and *Some of These Days*. These tunes constitute Armstrong's contribution to recorded music during this period when his reputation was becoming more and more solid among the connoisseurs who loved straight jazz.

Horn of Plenty:

At the first rehearsal Carroll gave his musicians a little talk:
"Boys, it's gonna be a tough fight. You-all know Clarence Blanck's orchestra's gonna play across the way, an' it's a damn powerful bunch. They been goin' strong now for months here at the Savoy, an' they've knocked all the other bands dead. So what?"

Jimmy Strong stood up to reply.

"That's no lie! Clarence is plenty good. But after all he's only got one piece an' he repeats it all the time to hook the suckers: *I Left My Sugar Standing in the Rain!*"

Peck Carr interrupted:

"We can take him on, we'll cook him down to a low gravy."

"We can't miss. They ain't got Louis or Zutty!" said Carroll. "Let's go, boys. Let's hit the finale of *Some of These Days*, the part where Satchmo' climbs up an' up."

The Savoy Ballroom had concocted a marvelous publicity stunt. Throughout the Midwest, the superiority of its orchestras was advertised by a basketball team carrying the gospel of jazz to all sport-loving Negroes. Dickerson's manager had now conceived the brilliant idea of improving on this promotion by going one step farther.

"Look, Carroll—Clarence Blanck's orchestra is being ballyhooed by a basketball team. We'll get up a team with your own orchestra. That'll clinch it for you!"

On the first night when the members of Dickerson's orchestra arrived on the platform, Clarence Blanck's musicians, already settled in their seats, smiled disparagingly at the upstarts whom they were going to crush as they had the previous band.

As soon as the large hall was opened, the crowd began a violent demonstration in favor of Clarence. Cries of encouragement rang out:

"Go to it, Clarence! Don't hurt 'em too much. Just give 'em your cannon ball: *I Lef' My Sugar!*"

Clarence's orchestra played a few anonymous pieces. The jazzmen were sparring like cautious boxers in the ring. Carroll's first number was *I Can't Give You Anything But Love.* Louis jumped to his feet and blew his skyscraper notes. The audience hesitated, it was so abrupt and so breath-taking that they could not easily make the transition from Clarence's sugary melodies to Carroll's pure rhythm. Suddenly Louis sang—with unseeing eyes, quivering lips, and swaying head:

"I can't give you anything but love, baby!"

He wrenched out the word *baby* as if torn from the depths of his being. A shiver ran through his listeners. Everybody had stopped dancing. Louis finished the stanza and broke out at once into a toothy grin, wrapped his lips around the trumpet, shut his eyes, and climbed up and up. The spectators were frozen into silence at the sight of this giant with the bulging neck, his nose flattened by the force of vibrancy, his left hand clutching a spotless handkerchief, who could stir up a whirlwind of strange music. For half an hour there was veritable pandemonium among the throng as enthusiasm was fanned to white heat, and the shouting became more insistent after every encore. *St. James Infirmary* moved them to tears, *Some of These Days* was given a poignant rendition.

During the subsequent period, Clarence Blanck held back, played sweet music appealing particularly to the feminine element. He knew he was beaten already in the field of rhythm and sensibly confined himself to his own easier specialty of slow and romantic music. The audience, who at first had experienced some difficulty in leaving the peaks for the valleys, now succumbed to the charm of the type of music that had enchanted them just a few days before. This was no mere personal contest between Clarence and Carroll—it was a battle between two kinds of jazz.

Finally, in order to bring the half-hour to a fitting climax, the lights were dimmed, the piano gave the key, and in a sweeping overture that had been skillfully prepared Clarence attacked *I Left My Sugar*. It threw the crowd into a delirium. Girls closed their eyes in order to let the melancholy and tender theme seep into their hearts. Continuous applause broke in on the solos. When the piece came to an end, a howl of triumph was loosed by the entire throng.

Now it was Dickerson's turn again. His banjoist, Carr, suggested that they play a blues in order to get the audience back into the right mood. But Dickerson, on consulting Louis with his eyes, said:

"No, we're gonna knock 'em down with the big guns. Let's go with *Tiger Rag!*"

And the old tune—born at the quadroon balls, the hit that had made a fortune for the original Dixieland Band—was now triumphantly resurrected. The trombone barked sharply, pursuing the tiger. Zutty, from time to time, fired a heavy barrage against the wild beast. Then, pointing his extended drumstick at the spectators, he pressed an imaginary trigger and extracted a soul-stirring explosion from the bass drum. Jimmy Strong leaped into the fray. The onlookers were packed tight around the platform, no one caring to dance. Leaning against the piano, Clarence Blanck smiled wryly. But Louis was just getting warmed up. They were saving him for the grand finale. At last he joined the chase, soared, plummeted down to earth, blew like a demon. Ten times, a dozen times, he took up the chorus, each time his fertile imagination weaving a novel pattern. Now he stroked the melody gently; again he climbed into the stratosphere on a wild chase, slid crazily down melodic slopes, rebounded gracefully, stopped abruptly

—only to dash on again and blow a complete chorus exultantly played on a single note.

Clarence Blanck was still on the stand but his musicians, acknowledging defeat, had come down to egg on this dauntless giant. Deeply moved by this exhibition of real jazz, they screamed madly:

"A thirteenth!"

And the public, driven insane by it all, fell in with their game and yelled:

"A fifteenth, Louis, come on!" *Play that thing!*"

When the half-hour was entirely used up in a succession of passionate *Tiger Rags,* Clarence Blanck descended slowly from the stand and approached Louis, who was pouring sweat like a boxer at the end of a hard fight.

"I give up, Pops! Nobody can whip you. You're the Napoleon of the trumpet!"

While he was playing, Louis had felt a pair of burning eyes boring through him. Under the spell of his ecstasy he had played on; but now, coming back to reality, he recognized Fanny Cotton's lovely face. He wanted to go over to her, but wild-eyed women were kissing, pushing, questioning, admiring him as though he were some adored god.

Eventually Louis escaped to join Fanny. "What you doin' here, Fanny?" he asked her.

"I'm working out in the West Side for the last night. You look great, Louis. Remember our last time together? Are you still in love?"

"I'm in love, Fanny—but not with you!"

"Did you forget me?"

"I could never forget them bright eyes o' yours!"

"Well?"

But he could not talk further, for Alpha was not far away;

and when Louis saw Fanny again two days later, she told him that she had signed a contract to tour the Continent.

"The air of Paris is just what I need. And you'll forget me all over again."

"I'll never forget, Fanny! I'll come get you soon. The day you hear Louis Armstrong's bound for Europe, it'll be to get you, Sweet Eyes!"

A few days afterward the famous basketball game took place. The players on the opposing team were all young and fast and they were equipped like professionals. From Carroll Dickerson's band a team of sorts was chosen. Louis, who now weighed two hundred and thirty pounds and ate like a wolf, spent two afternoons looking for a basketball outfit for himself; his search was fruitless. On the day of the game Louis and Zutty had not any suits at all. At the last moment, under pressure from the manager, Louis and Zutty decided to wear their bathing suits. When they appeared on the court, the crowd roared with laughter. The opening whistle blew, and then began the greatest burlesque exhibition of basketball that has ever been seen. Louis, mincing up and down the court like a bathing beauty, drew the undivided attention of the spectators. Zutty was at his side, scurring about like a jackrabbit. By some chance, Louis got hold of the ball, and instead of dribbling, pressed it against his heart and dashed through the swarm of players in a zigzag run, knocking down some of the players, stiff-arming others, or merely dodging those who tried to halt him. A salvo of applause mingled with wholehearted laughter rewarded the skyscraping trumpeter's unorthodox performance. At the start of the second period, he was worn out. Zutty could hardly move, able only to drag one leg after the other.

"Say, Pops, ain't it almost over?" he called to the umpire.

"Twelve more minutes!"

"Gawd! Them minutes last like hours. Can't you pull me out? Ah'm so tired."

Ham Watson, the captain, was enjoying Zutty's plight. He barked a sharp command:

"Let's go, Zutty—chin up!"

"Oh boy," wailed Zutty. "Ah'm tired like a million."

Blanck's team won the game, 2 to 0.

That night Louis dragged himself painfully to the Savoy. Every muscle in his body pulled and ached. Never had he felt so bruised. As for Zutty, he had aged ten years.

When Louis arrived in front of the Savoy, the crowd howled with joy on recognizing the trumpeter. A sort of idolatrous frenzy possessed them. Some boys, urged on by their girls, picked Louis up bodily, making him scream with pain. Heedless of his cries, they lifted him to their shoulders, carried him around, pulled him, pushed him, battered him to a pulp. This agonizing march finally took him to the platform, bobbing up and down over the heads of the mob like a cork tossed about by the waves.

Art Hodes, who related this incident to me, avers that never before had he seen such a wild exhibition of mass exaltation. Louis was tossed up the stairs like a puppet passed from one hand to the next. When he reached the orchestra, almost fainting from the ordeal, he crumpled into a chair.

Then a backward push of the crowd created a terrific jam at the door. Women were crushed, and it took Art Hodes more than half an hour to cross the floor. He spoke to a group of Negroes.

"I'm glad you gave Louis such a grand reception. He's a great man!"

"Louis," replied one of them, "is mor'n a great man; he's the idol of our race. He gave us a soul and the right to express it to the white folks."

"Yes," said another. "Louis is great because he never sold out to anybody."

That night Louis did not sleep a minute; he could not move his right leg. When morning came, he stayed in bed and did not get up for a week.

Little by little, as the months passed, the fortunes of Carroll Dickerson's band declined. The Savoy's manager, Fagan, found a different excuse every Saturday night to cut their pay; on some Saturdays, indeed, he found excuses for not paying them at all. Then, one fine day the band were told that a new contract had been signed with Tommy Rockwell's combination in New York.

Hard times began for Dickerson's musicians; but they were linked by a solid friendship which they had sworn never to break. Then came a day when Louis Armstrong got a telegram from Rockwell telling him that he—Louis—was engaged to star in a forthcoming production of Vincent Youmans's *Great Day*.

Louis called a meeting of the orchestra men. Already Carroll had heard the news and could hardly conceal his resentment at the prospect of Louis's leaving by himself. But Louis began:

"Boys, I ain't the kind of guy to drop you in the dirt. A friend ain't like a broom handle. So I got a proposition."

"Let's hear it," demanded Zutty.

"I just received two hundred dollars. I'll give every one of you guys twenty bucks. We'll get our cars fixed up, an' we'll all leave together for New York!"

The offer was so generous and so tempting that after two

hours of discussion everybody agreed that it was a wonderful idea. They decided that they would leave in four days. The last few hours in Chicago were spent carousing with Muggsy Spanier, Mezz Mezzrow, and others. On the eve of departure they renewed their protestations of undying friendship over a stupendous pot of steaming Creole gumbo. On the following day, as the four automobiles were ready to start, their white friends arrived punctually at the rendezvous—all, that is, except Art Hodes.

"Where's Art?" asked Louis.

"He's sick!"

"What's wrong with him?"

"Last night at the gumbo party he ate and drank so much his belly's pokin' way out!"

Louis's ancient Hupmobile was parked next to a Marmon that Carroll had bought at second hand. Gene Anderson was crouched behind the wheel of a tiny Essex, and Fred Robinson was driving a Chevrolet. It was a balmy afternoon with a slight breeze coming from the lake. Everybody felt pretty sad, and hands were wrung repeatedly. Finally the signal to leave was given and the four cars pulled out while their passengers waved farewell to good old Chicago.

The caravan passed through Toledo, Cleveland, Detroit, and Buffalo, stopping at all the Negro centers to play dance music. In Buffalo they held a council of war.

"We can't leave without seein' Niagara Falls."

"Oh, man, they say it's the greatest wonder in the world!"

They rolled on for forty miles and stopped before the falls to gaze respectfully at the awesome spectacle. Zutty wanted to ride down in the elevator. Peck Carr, more thrifty, warned that it would be throwing money away, since they had only a few cents left among them all.

In the course of the trip they learned that youthful jazz addicts listened regularly to the broadcast from the Savoy Ballroom, and it was highly significant that Louis Armstrong's name was the one that stirred up the greatest enthusiasm.

The Hupmobile was being driven by Zutty and Louis—though actually Louis spent most of the time asleep on the rear seat. At one point the Hup was supposed to meet the Marmon some thirty miles farther on, but when they got there—no Marmon. They waited on the outskirts of the town for one hour; then for two. "Something musta happened," Louis guessed. And Zutty growled that he supposed they would have to go back.

They went back the whole way. As they reached the edge of a small country town they spied Carroll Dickerson arguing hotly with another man near the Marmon, which was badly smashed up. There was nothing to do but leave the car in a repair shop, and the Marmon's passengers were distributed among the three remaining cars. They were very anxious to reach New York before their funds ran out completely. Finally they discerned the outline of the skyscrapers in the distance. By now their caravan presented a ludicrous appearance. The cars were caked with dust and covered with bundles and valises perched precariously at all angles. People turned to stare and laugh.

Just as they reached Times Square, in the middle of traffic, the Hupmobile's radiator cap exploded and the steam hissed out as if from a locomotive boiler. Instantly a curious mob gathered to gape curiously at the travel-stained blacks. A traffic cop walked up and read the Illinois license plate.

Chicago gangsters were in their heyday at this period, and the New York police kept a sharp lookout for undesirable migrants from the Windy City.

"All right, darkies—let's keep moving."

"Yessirree!"

"What's in all those bundles?"

"Just clothes, Mister."

"And in the last car over there—what's that? A coffin?"

"That's a bass fiddle!"

"Hum . . . you're sure you don't have a tommy-gun hidden in the bass drum?"

Going uptown through Central Park, they arrived in Harlem at last. Louis lost no time in washing up and left by subway for Tommy Rockwell's.

"So you're here at last!" Rockwell exclaimed.

"Yessir, Mr. Rockwell, we come by automobile."

"*We?*—Lil's with you?

"I don't mean Lil—I mean the orchestra."

Rockwell leaped to his feet as if stung by a bee. "What do you mean?"

"Exactly what I'm sayin'. All the band come with me."

"But I sent only for you."

"I know, Mr. Rockwell, but it's such a grand orchestra."

"Why, that's the craziest thing I ever heard! What can I do with a whole orchestra?"

"That's easy for a big man like you, Mr. Rockwell."

"Well, I'll see what I can do. But it's a dirty trick."

"The main thing now, sir, is to give me a little advance, 'cause we-all sure is hungry."

And Louis returned to Harlem, fortified with a hundred-dollar bill. They were rich! Then he began to rehearse for the hit show of the next day. Two days later he was practicing on *Ain't Misbehavin'*, newly written by Fats Waller for the *Hot Chocolates* revue.

Now for the first time Louis saw his name in electric lights on Broadway. And a few days afterward the orchestra members learned that Louis had just landed them a job at the celebrated Connie's Inn. So great had his reputation grown that his name was a fortune in itself, and Carroll Dickerson's orchestra was accepted only on condition that it be known as Armstrong's band. And so it came about that Louis became a renowned bandleader and all Manhattan flocked to hear him.

On his very first night at Connie's Inn, he was greeted by a smiling face. It was Fanny Cotton. He beamed happily. Louis had become a great favorite. He sang a ballad that melted their hearts:

> " 'Cause my hair is curly,
> 'Cause my teeth are pearly,
> Just because I always wear a smile,
> Just to get you in the latest style!"

He had sung the words while looking straight at Fanny, and he had stressed the "you" forcibly. After the show, they left together.

"Hurry up, Louis, you're almost too late. Tomorrow I'm leaving for Paris!"

27

IT WAS hard to say how it had all come about. Louis was basking in fame and fortune. Once Zutty told him jokingly:

"You know somethin', Louis? Life's a funny business. Yestiddy we was starvin', folks out in Niagara Falls took you for a shoeshine boy, an' now just look at you—you're the talk o' the town."

"I'll tell you somethin' else," replied Louis. "Besides Connie's Inn I got me an offer to solo for Connie's *Hot Chocolate* downtown."

All the members of the orchestra had recovered their good spirits now that the money was rolling in steadily. Harlem was on a spree, riding the crest of a wonderful boom. Langston Hughes was writing his first verses, Claude McKay had just returned from Marseilles with a new novel, Carl Van Vechten had recently launched the Negroes' Paradise. But death had come to the great Florence Mills. . . .

Here was truly the world's Negro capital. Every train from the South disgorged its quota of blacks who swarmed to Harlem like moths attracted by the flame.

Louis made such a hit at Connie's Inn that it was not long before the management of the Lafayette Theater across the street offered a complete show to the greatest exponent of jazz. That was the supreme accolade!

Louis would sleep into the later afternoon and then join the band at rehearsals with Carroll Dickerson who actually conducted. Toward dusk the musicians met again in some barbecue joint or other, and someone was always there with a funny story that would send Louis into gales of laughter.

As night fell, every corner was packed with black-faced crowds waiting expectantly.

"Let's go," Louis would cry. "It's eight o'clock."

"Lemme swallow one more spare rib," Zutty would plead.

The double-decked Fifth Avenue buses lumbered northward and soon all the players were swallowed up in Connie's entrance. Louise Cook, the dancer, was there already with a kerchief wrapped around her head, her face shiny with cold cream.

"How's tricks, Louis?"

"Better than the best! I got my steel lips with me."

"Pops, you sure can blow them high notes. How many last night?"

"Forty-two without a stop."

"I thought the whole show was comin' down."

"An' you, ol' Louise, God only knows you can shake that thing."

"You know how it is, Louis," she replied. "When I hear Zutty beat the tom-tom, I get drunk, so drunk I just gotta hop."

Already Zutty Singleton was laying out his paraphernalia like a barman arranging his bottles. Backstage, the manager wandered about in a dither of preparation.

"Two minutes to go. Are you all set, Carroll?"

"Yes."

"Let's go! Louis, play some sweet melodies—that's what they like."

"Trouble is, Pops, if I played like that I'd be through in a month."

"You're smart enough to beat Lombardo at his own game."

"Anybody can play that kind o' jazz. Some folks like my kind! Play it loud and straight!"

The orchestra opened up the show. The audience was entranced, but the feature spot was reserved for Louise Cook, strikingly handsome under the spotlight, her skin the color of bronze. In her Shake Dance, she appeared to be shivering; one would have sworn that Louis was blowing her into the dance, so vehement was his playing. Already Zutty had swung into action. Who would have dared predict a century ago that the throbbing beat of the tom-tom born in the African jungle and carried on the slave-ships would survive and captivate the capital of the world? Who could have foretold that the same swaying motion of a distant ancestress in the Congo would be reincarnated in Louise Cook's sinuous hips? The crowd was carried away and applauded thunderously for five or six encores. As the curtain came down Louise breathed a sigh of relief:

"That' ol' Zutty slays me the way he beats them tom-toms!"

Immediately after the show there was general dancing. The audience had been shaken by the wildest exhibition of jazz in the world. Now it was time to play sweet and low.

Standing on the stage Louis slowly dropped his lids. The very first notes threw a flutter into Manhattan's glamour girls, who had deserted their penthouses to dance and order theirs straight, and who now cooed delightedly:

"Oh, my dear, do listen to that plaintive melody. What is it?"

Louis was playing *Indian Cradle Song*.

One Sunday evening the attendance was huge. After the

first show, the orchestra was playing dance numbers. Berna-
dine Curry and Jimmy Strong almost interrupted one of
Louis Armstrong's solos.

"Go on, Louis, sock it—Broadway is there!"

Louis had not opened his eyes. Zutty understood, and be-
labored his drums while the bass fiddler hopped up and down.

"Go on, Louis. Send them!"

A compact group had drawn close to the orchestra. All
the notables of Broadway were there, men and women who
earned money hand over fist. What were they doing here?
Listening? Louis finished *Indian Cradle Song* and suddenly a
white man leaped to the stage. It was Ben Pollack. Everybody
clapped heartily. Louis felt shy and awkward. What was he
supposed to do? He hurried forward with his trumpet, repeating senseless words in his grunting style:

"Oh you, oh man, sure, we'll sock it—yea, man. . . ."

Ben Pollack addressed the audience:

"Ladies and gentlemen! The musicians of Tin Pan Alley
on Broadway sent us here as a delegation to express our esteem
for a great trumpeter, Louis Armstrong."

Salvos of applause drowned out the speaker's voice. Louis
had slowly backed away from the glare of the spotlight. Ben
Pollack drew a box from his pocket and gestured for silence.

"And as a token of the bond which links all jazzmen, we
take great pleasure in presenting a wrist-watch to the man
who revolutionized jazz music."

He handed the watch to Louis, who read this inscription on
the back:

Good luck always
To Louis Armstrong
    From
The Musicians on Broadway

Louis furtively brushed his left sleeve across wet eyes. He did not know what to say. Gently propelled to the edge of the stage, he stood there grinning with all his flashing teeth.

"Thank you, folks!"

Never before had a like emotion swept through Louis. The thing that was happening to him was absolutely without precedent. Now white musicians had hailed him officially and publicly. At the end of *After You've Gone*, he backed away from the lights. The applause was deafening. Zutty had stopped hammering the drum. He darted a quick look at Louis.

"What's the matter, Satchmo'? You're cryin'?"

"It's nothin', Pops."

"Is you crazy, man?"

"No, Zutty, I was just thinkin' Mama died a little too soon. She ought to be here with all the Perdido gang—they'd eat this up!"

Uninterrupted success filled Connie's hall for six straight months. But gradually some of the players, thinking they were indispensable, fell into slipshod ways. One would come late, another would smoke on the stage, a third played without his tuxedo. Fights broke out continuously between the waiters and the musicians who overdrank. One fine day Connie called in Louis and gave him two weeks' notice.

When Louis broke the news, his men were stunned.

"I told you so," Armstrong flung at them. "You took advantage of a good thing."

Louis despaired once again. Was he throughout his life to be thwarted thus at the peak of success? For two or three days he hoped against hope that Connie would keep him, but one night he learned that the irrevocable had happened: posters were up announcing the new orchestra—Ally Ross.

Horn of Plenty:

And on their last evening Zutty waited until the end of the performance to break some further bad news.

"I know it ain't right, Pops, but a man's gotta live, an' I'm gonna play with Ross."

"I don't hold nothin' against you, Zutty. Ally Ross got him a good drummer!"

"Satchmo', you done plenty for us," Zutty stammered, "but—"

"Oh, don't worry about it. I'm getting used to it. . . . First time, though, when Earl Hines quit, it sort of hurt. . . ."

"Listen, Louis—I'll stay with you!"

"But I ain't got no work for you, Zutty. You stay right here in Connie's Inn."

And so ended the rosy dream. Across Louis's mind there flashed the picture of the four cars, of the money he had so freely given out, of his pleading with Rockwell . . . and now he was left in the lurch. Carroll and Gene joined the *Mills Blue Rhythm Band*, Zutty remained in Harlem.

And everything was going wrong, too. Lil Armstrong wrote threatening letters; Alpha sent despairing ones; Fanny Cotton was in Paris. That night, the musicians were meeting at a bar on 126th Street. Louis could not muster courage to join them. He went home immediately, thinking about the beautiful thing that might have gone on forever. A wonderful orchestra had died a-borning. As he walked wearily along Seventh Avenue, heartsick and lonely, he whistled softly *After You've Gone.*

A few days later Louis took a train for California, riding in a Pullman for the first time. In a short while every porter and conductor on the train was greeting him admiringly and begging for his autograph. He whirled through cities that had long fired his imagination, and finally, one radiant morning, he caught his first glimpse of the Pacific and Hollywood, sprawling drowsily among trees and flowers. He paused for a few moments to enjoy the view. So this was Hollywood, capital of Movieland. Then he went on to Los Angeles where he intended to live.

On the next night, he landed at "Frank Sebastian's Cotton Club" in Culver City, a half-hour drive from Los Angeles. Louis was happy to work as soloist for Sebastian, whose orchestra at the Cotton Club was Elkins' Band. They were all strangers to him. There were some young musicians like Lawrence Brown (trombonist), Les Hite (saxophonist), Jimmie Prince (pianist), and Lionel Hampton (drummer)— players who were unknown to him but who greeted him warmly. They had long since been impressed by Louis's spreading reputation. They spoke expertly and with fine appreciation of his latest recordings: *St. Louis Blues, Rockin' Chair Blues, Bessie Couldn't Help It.*

From the very outset Louis was made to feel at home. He had all but forgotten the unhappy termination of his period with Carroll Dickerson's band. On the train he had often regretted his good old Zutty, but the present drummer was just as fine as the one he had lost. Louis was also indebted to the imaginative and creative qualities of Lionel and Lawrence.

A few days later, the giant of the trumpet was calling Lionel the 'swingin'est drummer in the world." The young fellow, who had innovated a different style calling for free use of the bells, was so captivated by Louis's prowess that he could not restrain his enthusiasm.

"Oh, Louis, you sockened me wet . . . wa-wa! Pops, it's grand! One mo', Pops! One mo' chorus!"

Louis tore out again with renewed passion and fury, giving a frenzied rendition of *I'm a Ding-dong Daddy* and *I'm in the Market for You.*

Lionel, Lawrence, and Louis constituted a heart-warming threesome. The first two had the gift of exciting Louis—of making him repeat one chorus after another, each time in a different version. Radio had contributed enormously to Armstrong's prestige, and he was now idolized by the fans everywhere.

"Play one more, Pops!"

And this would last all through the night. Once they kept actual count. Louis was in a trance. Women threw their hats on the stage. The sweat was pouring from Louis. He had to change handkerchiefs six times. He stopped, utterly worn out, and leaned against the rail. Lionel was laughing, his mouth wide open.

"How many was that?" asked Louis.

"Forty-one, Pops. That's pretty good!"

Louis stayed almost a year with the Cotton Club. Lawrence Brown left shortly after making a recording of *Confessin'*, a tune that twisted the heartstrings.

Louis was at his peak. Never had he felt so powerful. *Body and Soul, Memories of You, You're Driving Me Crazy, Shine* —all these songs and many more carried his message throughout the world. For the multitude, Paul Whiteman was still King of Jazz, but for those who really knew something about it, Louis Armstrong was without a peer, in a class by himself.

Lil had caught up with him in Culver City, and they tried again to make a go of it. But Louis was continually quarreling with her on account of a masseur whom she visited far too frequently for his peace of mind. Fanny Cotton urged him in every cable to meet her in Paris, Alpha wrote heartbreaking letters declaring that she was dying a slow death without him. Since Louis was gone, Alpha had climbed up the ladder; she was now chorus girl in a burlesque show at Al Capone's night club in Cicero where Lucky Millinder was the producer.

One evening, after playing the *Peanut Vendor* at least ten times, Louis returned to his dressing-room and found the door open. Alpha was sobbing on the couch. Without raising her head she cried:

"Louis!"

"Alpha! What's happened?"

"I missed you so much. I saved up the money I made in Cicero an' I came all the way in a day coach."

"You crazy gal! You know Lil's here!"

"Yes, I know . . . but I couldn't live without you. Mama's dump in Cottage Grove give me the blues."

"Get out of here quick an' wait for me at the corner cafeteria. Lil might come in any minute, an' if she does—Lord help us!"

None the less, Louis was happy to have his beloved Alpha near him. This was exactly the encouragement he needed to stay in Los Angeles. He found a quiet little place for her to live. And shortly afterward Lil left for Chicago with her masseur.

Then it was time for Louis to leave the West, for his latest manager, Johnny Collins, had signed up for a week's engagement at the Regal Theater in Chicago. It was a triumph! People fought for seats. Youngsters formed an endless queue at the box-office early in the morning. After the week was up, Louis took a short vacation, finding pleasure in revisiting the good old haunts of the Windy City.

One morning, Johnny Collins came to announce that they were going to have a sensational opening.

"Where?" Louis wanted to know.

"At a spot they used to call 'My Cellar.' It's going to re-open in a few days. You'll have tough going, because a young trumpeter by the name of Wingy Mannone has built up a big rep there."

"What they call the night club now?"

" 'Show Boat.' And believe me, Pops, you'll have to rock the joint."

Louis handpicked the group that accompanied him at the Showboat: Charlie Alexander (pianist), Zelmer Randolph (trumpeter), Preston Jackson (trombonist), George James, Al Washington, and Lester Boone (saxophonists), Johnny Lindsay (bass fiddler), Tubby Hall (drummer), and Mike McKendrick (guitarist).

The first exhibition surpassed anything they might have expected. The orchestra did not go off the air at all that night. Louis was in dazzling form and every half-hour a noted white jazzman stepped up to the microphone and read a special tribute dedicated to Louis. Among those present were members of Paul Whiteman's and Ted Lewis's bands; the Chicago aggregation with Eddie Condon; Jean Goldkette, Bing Crosby, and Louis Panico—all come to pay tribute to the greatest of the trumpeters.

Wonderful tunes, now full of syncopation, now sweet and sad, were broadcast from coast to coast, carrying the new musical faith to a listening America. The popular tune of the day was *Sleepy Time Down South*, a song that threw all of Chicago into a mood of romance and reverie. Louis would open softly. All of a sudden he would break off the thrilling words, mouth his trumpet, climb up into the high register, then introduce his orchestra to the audience, calling on Charlie Alexander at the piano to testify in his behalf, since he too came from the South.

There followed a rapid succession of noteworthy tunes, a brilliant train of great musical moments that will never die:

Little Joe, Them There Eyes, and *You Rascal You.* And the entire hall called Louis back, never tired of hearing:

"*I'll be glad when you're dead—you rascal you!*"

After this rhythmic madness followed the tender strains of *Georgia on My Mind,* during which Louis chanted over and over again, for an entire chorus, but one word—*Georgia, Georgia, Georgia*—with such heartfelt expression that women wept openly. And then there were *Chinatown* and *Shine,* in which for the first time Louis substituted unintelligible sounds for the lyrics. A new word was coined to express the surrealism that drove youths wild: to yoodle or scat.

Near the end of the evening Alpha slipped into a corner seat and listened to the flood of harmony and rhythm unloosed by her beloved Louis. Suddenly, Lil entered and took a seat five tables away from her rival who, having sensed the danger, hid her face in her handkerchief. The public was clamoring for *Tiger Rag.* Louis drew a quick breath and wondered what new dramatic page was about to be written in his life.

"*Tiger Rag, Tiger Rag!*"

He approached the edge of the platform, looked at Lillian who sat entranced, at Alpha still hiding behind the handkerchief. He shut his eyes and intoned:

"*Love, you funny thing,*
Look what you did to me!"

Many a feminine head was bowed under awakened memories, and Louis did not breathe easy until he noticed that Alpha had managed to make a quiet exit.

He closed his eyes once more and played with renewed fervor. He leaned against the rail; his fist, draped in a white handkerchief, trembled visibly. Suddenly someone touched his shoulder.

[271]

"Louis, somebody wants to see you in your room!"

Louis did not even glance up but merely nodded assent. When he reached his dressing-room, he found a man with a light beard waiting for him, gun in hand.

"Do you know who I am?"

"Why—er—no."

"I'm Frankie Foster!"

"Dunno Frankie Foster!"

"We'll get acquainted!" The man smiled grimly as he thrust the barrel into Louis's ribs. "I've got a one-way ticket saying as how you're leaving right quick for New York. Mr. Rockwell's got a job for you at Connie's Inn."

"Oh—Mr. Collins didn't tell me nothin' 'bout that!"

"Never mind Johnny Collins—Rockwell's your boss now. Either you promise to leave this morning, or you and me'll take a little stroll. O.K.?"

"No—I mean yes. Oh, sure!"

"That's better. Now march straight out to that 'phone. One false move and you're a dead pigeon."

Louis did not have to be told twice. He entered the booth, squirming under the uncomfortable pressure in the small of his back. He promised everything demanded by the suave voice speaking from New York, and was thanked cordially for his acquiescence.

An hour later Johnny Collins appeared with the police, but the man with the false whiskers had vanished.

"Louis, you're not going to New York!" flatly declared the manager. "I should have told you I was having a little trouble with Rockwell."

"O.K. I ain't goin' to New York. But get this straight—I ain't stayin' in Chicago neither!"

"That's too bad, Louis. I've got a wonderful offer for two months in Chicago's finest theater."

"Nothin' doin'! I'd rather take a walk through the cemetery at midnight."

Johnny Collins sighed, pulled a flask from his pocket to bolster up his courage, and concluded:

"If that's the way it is, I'm going to sign a contract with the 'Suburban' down in New Orleans."

It was nine years since Louis had been in the South. And suddenly he saw Perdido and was overpowered by the odor of spring when the magnolias break into bloom. . . .

28

THE ORCHESTRA set out immediately for the South, interrupting its journey with "one-night stands" in several midwestern towns. They crossed Indiana into Ohio, and made a longer stop in Cincinnati; then they visited the larger towns in Kentucky and Tennessee. Louis now had his own personal secretary, one Professor Cook, who was entrusted with the arrangements for their stay in New Orleans. Forever bursting with ideas, one morning he arrived in a taxicab. Louis opened eyes as big as saucers.

"What goes on? You crazy, man?"

"I'm crazy like a fox. I'm cookin' you up a reception like Jesus Hisself couldn't get in New Orleans!"

"What you talkin' about, man?"

"Look, I'm gonna make the whole trip down to Louisiana in a taxi—and believe you me, that'll make 'em stop, look, and listen. Every time I hit a town, I'll send a hot wire down there, just to pep 'em up!"

How would the South regard its wandering boy who was coming back surrounded by the aura of success? Louis refused to believe that the white people of New Orleans would ever acclaim a Negro. Johnny Collins was worried, and Alpha—brought up above the Mason and Dixon Line—could

[274]

not understand the subservient attitude she was expected to adopt in Tennessee and Mississippi. She had been allowed to join the party at the last moment on the lawyer's guarantee that the divorce was but a matter of days. While they were in Louisville, however, Louis had a telegram saying that the trial was postponed to a much later date.

What should he do? His plan to marry Alpha was wrecked. Still, it was not possible to send her back. That evening a raving audience called for old tunes. Though Louis was feeling blue, he hid his worry behind a cheerful mask. Cheers and calls all but overwhelmed him as he raised his hand for silence:

"All right, all right, folks! I'm gonna play an ol' favorite in honor of one of the local gals!"

"They call the lady Louisville Lou!
Ho, what a vamping baby can do!
She is the most heartbreakin'est,
Shimmy-shakin'est,
That the world ever knew!"

Finally, after an endless round of towns and villages, they arrived in Louisiana. Louis could not mistake the familiar dank smell as he stood on the observation platform. They were crossing the lonely swamps, dark and fascinating with their dense growth and moonlit clearings surrounded by majestic moss-hung oaks. From time to time, a Negro cabin, all but windowless and doorless, was revealed in its nakedness by the pale rays shimmering on the sluggish bayous that meandered through the forest.

In the morning, Louis saw the rows of bungalows on the outskirts of the city, buried in shrubbery and flowers. His heart beat very fast. Professor Cook had telegraphed that everything was going along smoothly, but uncertainty persisted in the party's mind. . . .

When they alighted from the train they could barely move through the crowd! Hundreds of necks craned to see them. Arms were raised. Blacks and whites were mingled in one vast sea of faces. When Louis appeared on the platform, an overwhelming roar greeted him. A brass band blared out—the Zulu Club with all its members in full regalia was parading.

"Hurray for Louis Armstrong! Hurray for Louis! Hurray for the King of Jazz!"

A delegation of twenty policeman was on hand to maintain order. Their captain introduced himself, shook hands with Louis.

"Do you remember the times we used to play soldiers in the empty lots on Perdido?"

"Naturally. I was always an Indian."

"Congratulations! This is some turn-out—more than ten thousand people here to greet you."

Already his sister, Mama Lucy, was embracing him tearfully, while Professor Cook, at the head of a brilliant reception committee from Perdido, hovered solicitously near by.

Louis marched past the brass band, which was playing *Twelfth Street Rag*. Hundreds of handkerchiefs fluttered wildly. The orchestra followed their leader quietly while the Professor appointed some of the men to take charge of the instruments.

Summer's cruel heat was bearing down on the city. All the Negroes had made it a point to dress up in their Sunday best in order to pay homage to their hero. From an obscure corner Johnny Collins moved forward, holding Alpha by the arm, and the spectators gasped in amazement. For the first time in centuries the ancient taboo was broken!

Louis climbed into an open car and the parade moved very

slowly along Canal Street, the enchanted way. He had need to close his eyes in order to assimilate more thoroughly the incredible fact that he was part of a parade in which whites and blacks jostled one another in his honor. What no other member of his race had ever achieved was his to enjoy.

Slowly they went by the buildings and the stores he knew so well. Ten brass bands were going full blast, and at least twenty thousand Negroes lined the curbs and made the welkin ring. A piercing scream reached his ears: *"Louis!"* He recognized the inflection and turned quickly as they came abreast of Royal Street. It was Red Vanzan! Now the St. Charles Hotel loomed to the left. Women were blowing kisses at him. One of them waved a bouquet before tossing it into the passing vehicle.

"Louis, Louis!"

This time it was Irene—little Irene whom he used to visit over the grocery store in Perdido. Was she not the one who had stabbed him in a fit of jealousy? Louis was so moved that he scarcely gave it a thought.

"Louis! Louis!"

Why, there were Bob Lyons and Mrs. Martin!

"Louis, Louis!"

The procession had halted for a few moments and Louis stood up straight and stiff. He was looking at Director Jones flanked by the entire staff of the Waifs' Home.

"Howdy, Mr. Jones!" cried Louis.

"Welcome, Louis! You've come a long way, my boy. We're all very proud of you!"

"Thanks, Mr. Jones. Oh—I see Professor Davis!"

Davis approached, deeply touched and rather shy. He shook hands with his former pupil and gestured silently toward a group of his charges wearing uniforms.

"They're all walking in your footsteps, Louis!"

[277]

Louis read the familiar sign:

WAIFS' HOME
COLORED BAND

The shouts rang out again as the parade began to move once more.

"Hurry, hurry, Joe!" cried Director Jones.

A youngster ran up, carrying a trumpet.

"Do you recognize it?" asked Peter Davis.

Then Louis saw the notches he had filed into the mouthpiece, and he hugged the boy, who was in tears. His automobile had started to roll. Director Jones followed close behind.

"Won't you come to see us, Louis?"

"Sure will, Mr. Jones!"

Louis was still standing at attention just as he had seventeen years before when speaking to the Director.

"When, Louis?"

"Tomorrow."

One of the bands began to play a fast march. One group held up a banner inscribed: "To Louis Armstrong, his friends from Jane Alley." The automobile and its occupants were pelted with flowers.

"*Louis, Louis!*"

A white man had pushed his way through the throng and was hanging on to the moving automobile. Louis remembered him.

"Morris! Oh, Mr. Konowsky!"

Even he had wanted to be there—the coal dealer for whom little Louis had slaved such long hours on the mule-drawn cart. Never in living memory had so many black faces been seen on Canal Street. A white-haired old lady looked grimly at the incredible spectacle, shook her head in despair, and muttered to herself that times had surely changed, and that nothing good would come of a day and age when black rascals were allowed to roam the streets and terrorize law-abiding citizens with such a tumult.

At every intersection, Louis could see the screaming billboards: "Louis Armstrong, King of the Trumpet, at the Suburban."

At the corner of Canal and Rampart the parade came to a halt. Louis, standing in the tonneau, noticed that the crowds were still milling densely far back, near the ferry landing. The parade turned to the left.

Louis leaned against the seat but remained standing. A streamer was hung out across the street that led to the Negro section, his section! On the right stood the Parish Prison; there was Fisk School; and he saw some unfamiliar vacant lots. A church reared its steeple on the very spot that Funky Butt had occupied. As they turned a corner, Louis spied the chinaball tree under which he used to play at cowboys and Indians. Another streamer waved a welcome: "To Our Home-Town Boy, Louis." He saw the place where Clark Wade had been fatally stabbed. A little farther on, Black Benny's blood had flowed. Up in a near-by window a fat Mammy puffed contentedly on her pipe. Little seemed to have changed. . . .

Now they were passing before the Astoria Hotel, where the orchestra had reservations. The brass bands were lined up on the sidewalks, blowing like mad. Scores of outstretched arms gave him no rest—he had been pumping hands for the last half-hour. Suddenly a familiar face smiled up at him:

"*Louis, Louis!*"

She held out her arms in a tender gesture.

"Louis! Is it really you?"

Louis opened wide his arms and clasped his first wife, Daisy —the girl he had met in Gretna when he was singing the blues.

He recalled that first night on the levee, when the Crescent City's lights blinked at them through the darkness.

"You ain't mad at me no more, Louis?" she cried. "I was a foolish kid!"

"No, o' course I ain't mad!"

But his ardent admirers had already seized Louis and were carrying him bodily into the lobby. Professor Cook came to tell him that Alpha had found a room in the hotel across the street. Crowds were blocking the street and the police were having a hard time trying to keep the tracks clear for the streetcars. A policeman advanced to shake hands with Louis. His sister was near, immobile and silent, her eyes scalded by tears as she thought of her brother's return as a hero while their mother slept her last sleep in a Chicago graveyard.

That night he made the rounds of the night spots. A little beyond Bob Lyons's house, a calico banner was stretched from post to post, clear across the street:

WELCOME TO LOUIS ARMSTRONG
THE KING OF PERDIDO

Many a glass was emptied in his honor that evening. The bands still played on the street corners. Dance halls were opening their doors. By now all the urchins of Perdido were tagging behind Louis and his party. Near the Masonic Hall a woman struggled fiercely to reach his side.

"You know who this is, Louis?"

"I sure do!"

"You ain't kiddin'? What's my name?"

"Alberta."

"'Member them blues you used to play at Matranga's?"

"And how! I'll never forget the night you had that big fight with Mary Jack the Bear."

Someone else was grasping his hand. It was Sweet Child, who had hobbled up on his crutches.

"You remember Black Benny?"

"And how!"

"Right there," said Sweet Child, pointing dramatically with one crutch, "one of his women stabbed him to death. Mary Jack the Bear herself got a bleeding here."

"It's been a long time," mused Louis aloud. "I think I was a milkman in them days. Every mornin' I'd go to the hospital to see him. He sang the blues day an' night for a solid week."

"Yeah. He sang the same blues Buddy Bolden used to sing at Funky Butt. Reverend Cozy's church is there now."

"You remember Buddy Bolden's blues?" queried a little man who was wearing an apron.

"Oh, if it ain't Bob Lyons! How goes it, oh, man! I remember listenin' to him under the window, down yonder in the empty lot.

"Love, O careless love,
You flow in my head like a wine!"

"And when the women from the district came down——"

"Yes!" Louis exclaimed.

"I thought I heard Buddy Bolden say:
'Funky Butt, Funky Butt, take it away!'"

Soon a circle formed around Bob Lyons, the veteran, and Louis, the new king.

"I'd like to hear you, Louis," Bob went on. "They say you got Buddy Bolden beat. He was the first King of Perdido. I never heard nobody blow like him. From my stoop there I could hear him on Sunday—yeah, I done heard him plenty times, when everything was still, callin' his brood to Lincoln Park."

Horn of Plenty:

"Listen, Bob, I ain't gonna miss playin' for my pals. To-morrow night at the Suburban it's all for the white folks. But I ain't forgettin' you-all."

More people pushed forward. It was Kid Rena with some friends from the Waifs' Home. They reminisced to their hearts' content. It had been such a long time!

"You know so-and-so's a shoemaker."

"What happened to Jack?"

"Oh, he was a bad egg. He done lef' town."

"An' Peter?"

"He was killed dead."

"And Jack, you know the lil' guy with the sweet voice?"

"He swung at the Parish Prison."

Louis loved it all!

On the next morning he set out to visit the reformatory. It was exactly seventeen years to the day since he had left the Waifs' Home. He was dressed in a light suit, red necktie, and shiny, stiff straw hat. Director Jones had prepared an elaborate program in order to give fitting welcome to his most famous pupil. But Louis was not partial to formality and ceremony. While he was paying his respects to the staff, he caught sight of Louis Duplan, the handy man, returning from the fields. Duplan had been an inmate during Louis' time. They fell on each other's necks and shook hands warmly.

"How's tricks, Satchmo'?"

"Not bad, Gate! Where you goin'?"

"Goin' to eat my dinner. I been in the fields!" replied Duplan.

"Where's yo' dinner at?"

"In the kitchen!"

Louis Armstrong made a bee line for the kitchen, where he quickly dispatched the gumbo and the red beans and the rice

[282]

—in fact, every morsel of food that had been set aside for hard-working Louis Duplan.

"Oh, boy!" he exclaimed contentedly to the admiring circle of boys who were staring at him wide-eyed. "I been waitin' seventeen long years to taste that cookin' again. I'm tellin' you, Mis' Jones beats 'em all when it comes to red beans!"

Thus Louis fell under the spell of the old familiar things, became little Louis Armstrong once again. He ran off, climbed the stairs to the dormitory, quickly found the third bed in the second row—his bed! But Gus Vanzan and Isaac Smooth were no longer there. No matter! Louis pulled down the sheet and, fully clothed, threw himself on the bed and shut his eyes. A few minutes later an awestruck gathering of boys stood at the foot of the bed, gazing in silence at their sleeping hero. Already the sun's rays were slanting in the distance, but they merely stood and looked, feasting their eyes on the King of Jazz who slept on undisturbed.

And, on the following day, Louis sent a large phonograph to the forlorn waifs, who, ever since that time, never fail to listen raptly, whenever they have the chance, to the one who made jazz great and derives his greatness from jazz.

29

ON OPENING night the moon shone bright and clear. It was as if the Crescent City wished to outdo itself for the benefit of its native son. The Suburban was located on the levee guarding the Mississippi. The night carried a trail of perfumed odors. In the distance there was a blinking of lights from the opposite banks. One could hear the sound of lapping water, as the Father of Waters rolled on irresistibly.

When Louis arrived, his heart was beating abnormally. During the long drive out to the Gardens in his new automobile, he could hardly believe that so many people were going out of their way just to hear him. At the Suburban's entrance he was greeted by his secretary.

"Louis, it's terrific. I never seen so many colored folks. Look out there."

Thousands of Negroes, barred from the Suburban proper, were massed near the fence in the hope of hearing their hero play the music that was almost the national anthem of their race.

"How many's there?" inquired Louis.

"They say more 'n ten thousand and plenty more on the way," replied the Professor, pointing to the constantly growing throng.

"I'm afraid they'll scare the white folks away!" said Armstrong.

"Don't be silly. They got more 'n five thousand white people inside."

They went in and settled themselves backstage where Johnny Collins walked about nervously, feverishly rehearsing the introduction with the radio announcer. Everything was going smoothly. Who would have dreamt that thousands of New Orleanians, flouting for the nonce the ancient law of segregation, would gather willingly in one place to listen to a black man's music? The old aristocrats deplored the painful situation. Certain elements had even sought to break up the gathering, by fair means or foul. By and large, however, things had gone smoothly. Nevertheless, Johnny Collins sensed that the least untoward incident could spoil everything and he cursed himself for having accepted an engagement that was giving him so much concern.

It was time for the show to begin. Louis and his orchestra were drawn up on the stage, behind the curtain, ready to open the program with *Sleepy Time Down South*, just as soon as the announcer finished his introduction.

Tingling with anticipation, the management waited with bated breath. Johnny Collins was squirming because it was past the hour and the audience was growing impatient. At last the announcer took his place at the microphone; his appearance was the signal for loud cheers and claps. He began with the usual words:

"Are you listening? This is Suburban Gardens!"

And then—yielding to God knows what hidden impulse of revulsion or, more probably, recalling that he had been bribed by some group or other—he cried:

"I haven't got the heart to announce that nigger!"

[285]

And he bowed out quickly, while the management buried its collective head before the expected storm and Johnny Collins, arms upraised, could only stammer excitedly. The show was sunk! Mocking cries were mounting from the assembly. The manager made a desperate attempt to induce the announcer to go back and retract. Professor Cook was weeping alone in a corner.

Suddenly Louis was on his feet, very straight and steady.

"Hold everything! I'll handle this myself!"

Then he turned to the orchestra:

"Give me a loud one in B flat—and hold it!"

The orchestra obeyed. Louis parted the curtain and, trumpet in hand, expected to be booed, walked up to the microphone. A veritable bedlam greeted his appearance. The spotlights blinded him. Endless seconds went by before he realized that this was an ovation! He had been so frightened that he almost fainted with relief. The applause rolled on unchecked for several minutes.

At last, standing at the microphone, Louis began to speak. The manager and his staff were perspiring freely, and Professor Cook had lost several pounds. Louis held out his trumpet and all at once, everything he had planned to say was forgotten; his mind a total blank. He could only cry in a broken voice:

"Thank you, folks! Thank you!"

A new burst of tremendous applause followed his words. People were calling him by name. In the forefront, some white people he knew were shouting:

"Louis, Louis!"

Then the curtain went up, and he signaled to his orchestra to start—mouthed his trumpet—closed his eyes—and the black angels soared above the heads of the white multitude.

The performance was successful beyond their fondest

hopes. Professor Cook danced gleefully. Johnny Collins was drunk with joy:

"I told you so, I told you so!"

The announcer was sulking in a corner. One of the managers, relieved and cocky, advanced belligerently and shook his fist at him:

"You're a dirty rat! I'll give you two seconds to get out of here before I throw you out."

Never had Louis been so happy. He was delirious with happiness. Alpha was waiting for him in the car and she saw the glowing pride reflected in his face. As they drove off, the crowds cheered themselves hoarse.

Two days later, on the strength of their opening night, Johnny Collins signed for a four-month run. And every day the enthusiasm of whites and blacks alike reached new heights.

One night the crowd went insane when Al Washington held a note without interruption for thirteen minutes on the clarinet. The audience was spellbound. Hats, gloves, purses, all sorts of objects rained at his feet. Louis, feeling in honor bound to exert himself to the limit, unleashed a series of fifty skyscraping notes. As they left they had to shake hundreds of eager hands. That was the supreme triumph!

However, when they went back to town and arrived at the Astoria Hotel some friends warned Louis that his wife, Lil, had just arrived, accompanied by her Chicago masseur. They had tried to put up at the Astoria but had been politely turned away, and finally they registered at the same hotel as Alpha. Louis suspected that a storm was brewing. Within a couple of days gossip was rife. Some old chums from Perdido, led by Johnny Lindsay with whom Louis had once played, came to offer their services, promising to rid him of the masseur in short order. But Louis refused.

[287]

Horn of Plenty:

Toward noon one morning, while Louis was still asleep, Lil contrived to gain admittance to his room. Their painful quarrel dragged on for hours. Finally Lil left, seemingly appeased.

Louis prepared to leave the hotel. At the desk he learned to his astonishment that someone had left in his car. He was told that Lil had claimed the keys, stuffed all her luggage into the rear trunk, and fled to Chicago in the new automobile, duly escorted by her latest conquest, one of the bell-boys.

During four straight months, they were rewarded by unflagging acclaim. Every night after the show, Louis would return to the old haunts in Perdido to join his friends. Everywhere he was fêted. His name was on every tongue. Lil was definitely out of the way, but Alpha remained and Louis was head over heels in love.

Louis's meeting with Johnny Lindsay took place in a café at the corner of Rampart and Perdido. They fell into each other's arms.

"Louis, you still know me!"

"Sure thing, Joe. What's the matter? What you cryin' about?"

"I'm in a mess. Everything's over for me."

"What do you mean, Joe?"

"Well, you was gone nine years, and you got good. Me, I had my fling three-four years ago. I had me a new car, four big diamonds, I was the Sheik of Perdido . . . an' now, just look at me!"

He gazed sadly at his patched coat, his twisted shoes.

"What happened?"

"The drum catches everything the flute can pitch! I had to sell the car an' take my shiners to the pawnshop. Louis, how about givin' a guy a hand?"

They were sipping "rum 'n cokes" at the counter. A phonograph was playing Louis's latest recordings. Now and again some children would peek in at the door and point at Louis. On the following afternoon Joe Lindsay had a new wardrobe and his old friend's promise of a trip to Chicago.

Finally, the last night came. Louis had held numerous conferences with local delegations which wanted him to give a mammoth concert for the city's Negro population. This he accepted, though he would not take any money for that appearance. The generous gesture touched off an explosion of gratitude and wild joy. The huge hall at the Army Base was rented and, in a fever of expectancy, practically every Negro in the city and surrounding territory made plans to attend and pay tribute to the Negroes' hero.

Unfortunately, since he was to play without remuneration, Louis was obliged to do business with a promoter. This made some people angry and, as always in such cases, continuous bickering marred the preparations.

The concert was scheduled to be held on the night following their last appearance at Suburban Gardens. The whole day was marked by a veritable black invasion. By train, by automobile, on foot, a motley throng swooped down on New Orleans. Never had so many ancient cars of all makes been seen on the road. In the city, Perdido and all the colored sections were overflowing with visitors. Restaurants ran out of food and drink. The police worked double shifts and had even asked the National Guard to lend a hand.

At dusk, Louis left in an automobile with Alpha and his sister. As they neared the base, they came on excited groups heatedly gesticulating and discussing something among themselves. Then they began to encounter a stream of people returning from the opposite direction, all howling furiously. What could be going on?

, Louis found out at the next intersection, where he was told that all these people had been denied admittance at the gate! But he was still puzzled, and drove on to the base, still passing knots of screaming people. As the car stopped at the main entrance, Louis and the others saw some soldiers standing guard with fixed bayonets.

"Keep moving!" cried one of the guards.

"But we're stopping here—they're all waiting for us."

"Well, you'd better clear out of here in a hurry!"

"I'm Louis Armstrong's manager," intervened Johnny Collins.

"Maybe you are, Mister, but the base is closed."

"What's happened?" asked Collins.

"We don't know a thing," replied the guards.

Collins got out of the car and went off to hunt enlightenment. The rest kept asking each other what it was all about. They saw the mob struggling to get in at a side gate, and some scattered shouts rang out: "Down with Louis Armstrong!"

When Johnny Collins came back, he shook his head in discouragement.

"Well?" questioned Louis.

"We're going back to town."

"What's happening?"

"Nothing! The base is closed—that's all. They decided this afternoon."

"Who did?"

"The same gang that had it fixed up with the announcer—probably the colored manager who was shut out wanted his revenge."

"But that's awful! I'm disappointin' fifty thousand colored folks tonight."

"Nothing we can do," Collins replied wearily. "The old prejudice has us licked."

Louis said no more, and Collins turned the car around to follow the hundreds of blacks who were streaming back to the city, grumbling and footsore. As the car swung into the suburbs, Collins turned his head and asked:

"What's the matter, Louis?"

Louis was sobbing, head in hands.

"Listen, Louis, we can stay two more days in New Orleans and maybe organize something."

"No, no! I'm ashamed for my own race. I want to get out of here. I'm leavin' first thing in the mornin' for Houston."

"Good! You know I've got an offer to go to Europe."

"That's fine . . . the sooner the better."

Alpha slipped her arm under Louis's and tried to console him. They drove along the avenues, turned to the left, slowed down for a bad street, and suddenly Louis exclaimed:

"Stop the car at the nex' corner! I'm gonna tell Grandma good-bye."

"We'll all go with you."

"No," declared Louis firmly. "I've gotta be alone. We're on Dupré, back o' town."

"How about me, Louis?" proposed Alpha.

"Nobody. You wouldn't understand. Go back to the hotel. I'll meet you all in an hour."

And Louis waved to them as the car's tail-light disappeared in the darkness. He paused for a moment under the catalpas. Small frame cottages were huddled together in the dark. A few groups still sat on the stoops and discussed the excitement.

"An' I'm tellin' you Louis done played us a dirty trick."

"But they say it wasn't his fault!"

He quickened his pace and lowered his head to escape notice. In this fashion he came to a small lane: Jane Alley. He followed the dirt path. In the distance he could discern the turpentine factory where his father had worked and where now his half-brother continued his life of sweaty toil. A clumsy trumpeter was improvising somewhere on his left. He reached the vacant lot enclosed by a fence; it was piled high with rubbish, just as it had been nine years ago. To the right, a shack had been torn down and a familiar odor warned him that the china-ball trees were close by. His nostrils were assailed by the foul smell of poverty that had not changed in thirty years. He walked carefully so as to avoid drunken couples. A little farther on, to the right, was the spot where he had often played Indians. It was there he had been struck by a flying piece of slate; his head still bore the scar.

What he chiefly wanted to locate was the house where he had been born. He turned to the right, expecting this alley to lead him to the house, and was astonished to find himself facing an empty lot. He retraced his steps for a short distance. No!—*That* was their neighbor's house. He retreated up the dark alley. Now he recognized the tree he had so often leaned against; he touched it now with his palm. He crossed the dirt sidewalk, identified a familiar clump of trees—and found himself on the same spot where he had stood puzzled a few moments earlier. There could be no doubt about it: he was in the right locality. An old stump he had always known blocked him for a moment; then he understood—the house was gone!

He hurried away. At the end of the lane he found the sprawling tenement with the outside staircases. His uncle lived on the second floor, to the right. He hesitated an instant, dreading a lengthy explanation if he stopped to call; then passed on and came out of the alley, turned to the left and walked as far as Dupré.

The narrow street was deserted. He climbed the creaky stairs and knocked at the door.

"Who's there?" came a querulous voice.

"It's me, Louis!"

The door opened and Armstrong was face to face with his old grandmother, who clasped him to her bosom.

"Well, my boy!"

"I'm leavin' tomorrow. I came to tell you good-bye."

"You comin' back soon?"

"Don't believe I will, Granny."

"Well, Louis, I ain't gonna be here when you gets back. I'm gettin' old, my boy."

Louis opened his wallet, extracted a roll of bills, and pressed them into his grandmother's hand. Then he kissed her and went off into the night. From afar he cast a final look at the sordid alley of his birth. At the next corner, a one-legged oldster was sitting on the curb. He recognized Louis.

"Hurray for Louis Armstrong! Three cheers for the King of Jazz!"

Louis, still smarting from the night's blows, hurried on. How should he return to town? By taxi? But there were none to be had in this quarter, of course. So he walked for several blocks until he reached an avenue where there were streetcars.

It was very late. He handed the conductor his fare and moved on to find a seat. The car was almost empty, its only occupants two or three tattered Negroes nodding behind the screen marked *For Colored Only*. And Louis slipped into a seat in that section. . . .

30

AFTER LEAVING New Orleans, the musicians made several one-night stands on the way back to Chicago, where they disbanded, and Louis was alone once again. When he totaled his earnings he discovered that he was very wealthy—perhaps the richest man of his race. He decided to go to California again.

On arriving there he looked up Lionel Hampton, drummer in Les Hite's orchestra, and for a time stayed with him, making a few recordings. He bought himself an eight-cylinder automobile, and on that very morning Johnny Collins turned up in a sleek Studebaker.

"Louis—look. I've got a bran' new Studebaker!"

"Me too—only mine's a Buick!"

"I've just signed us up for Europe."

"Swell! If I ain't got my divorce by the time we leave, I'll get it in France."

Returning to Chicago, they left for New York by automobile. And one fine morning, Mr. and Mrs. Collins, Alpha, and Louis sailed away on the luxury liner *Majestic*. All were a little worried: Louis Armstrong had achieved great things in America—but what was in store for him in Europe? Did his name mean anything at all across the ocean? Did Europeans know the first thing about jazz?

On their second day at sea, Louis received a glowing message from Nat Gonnella, leading English trumpeter, who was waiting to welcome them at Plymouth.

"Louis," said Gonnella as he shook hands, "how do you like being the new American Ambassador? Now we haven't much time. A suite is reserved for you at a big hotel, and this evening all the musicians in London are giving a banquet in your honor."

"What do you mean?"

"Just that! It's to be quite an affair . . . and I assure you that it's the first time we've done this for anybody."

"But, Nat, all my suits are packed away and they need pressin'."

As soon as the train reached the London station, Gonnella went off with a suit under his arm, and half an hour later Louis was dressed impeccably, ready to play his part as guest of honor at the huge party given by well-known makers of popular music who wanted to pay tribute to their American colleague.

On Friday of that same week, the Palladium presented Louis on the stage in person. He was overwhelmed by a tumultuous greeting. On Saturday, he went to the station to welcome some colored musicians arriving from Paris: Joe Hayman, Fletcher Allen, Charlie Johnson, and several others. Rehearsals began at once in the studio on Poland Street.

It was there that Johnny Collins, who had left America desert-dry, and was yearning to slake his thirst, arrived as drunk as a lord and quarreled with Louis. As he was leaving, he made the fatal mistake of trying to walk through a plateglass window instead of the revolving door, and flattened his cigar and his nose in almost equal proportions.

The news of Louis's arrival quickly spread to the Continent, and jazz-lovers in Paris, Brussels, Amsterdam, and other cities sent congratulations and flowers when they were unable to come in person.

Finally the day of the première arrived. It was still early in the afternoon and Louis was in his suite with Alpha when someone knocked on the door. He went to open.

"Why, it's Fanny Cotton! *God!*"

"Hello, Louis boy!"

She opened her arms and was about to kiss him when her eyes met Alpha's redoubtable gaze.

"What you doin' in London, Fanny?" asked Louis.

"Ha, ha, that's a hot one! When last time I saw you in the States you told me you'd look me up in Europe!"

Too appalled to make a direct reply, Louis hastened to introduce Alpha: "Meet my fiancée."

Fanny sucked in her breath. "How do you do!" she rasped. The situation was tense.

"Oh, all right, I get it," Fanny went on bitterly. "Too bad I made a special trip from Paris by plane! But don't worry— I'm leaving. May I use the 'phone?"

After a brief talk with some friend who seemed to be a countess, she airily bade them good-bye.

By an unfortunate coincidence, on reaching the Palladium a few minutes before opening time, Alpha—still boiling over the episode—noticed a taxi parked near by and through its open window discerned Fanny Cotton's silhouette. Her jealousy thereupon mounted still higher, and shortly before Louis was scheduled to appear on the stage she flew into a terrible passion and clutched Louis by the neck, determined to strangle him if she could. When he broke away, she grabbed the lapel of his tuxedo, yelling hysterically.

Now the manager was going from door to door.

"Are you ready, Mr. Armstrong? It's almost curtain time!"

Louis was still warding off Alpha with one hand, and doing his best to guard his trumpet with the other.

"No, no!" Alpha screamed. "You ain't goin' out there to make sweet eyes at that Paris gal! You ain't goin' on the stage alive!" She tore off his lapel, clawed at him furiously.

"Your cue, Mr. Armstrong! Curtain's rising," came the manager's final warning.

It was now or never.

Louis let go a short uppercut which caught Alpha flush on the chin and knocked her out on the spot. He opened the door. Already he could hear the opening bars. In a twinkling he put on another dark blue coat and rushed out. *Sleepy Time Down South* was the first number. He appeared wreathed in smiles, and a thunder of applause hailed him. He played *You Rascal You, Them There Eyes, When You're Smiling,* and *Tiger Rag.*

Never before had such an exultant feeling of triumph surged over him. After the fourth piece, he hurried back to his dressing-room. There he found the manager, Mr. and Mrs. Collins, and several others dashing water in Alpha's face in an effort to revive her.

But Louis was obliged to make a second appearance on the stage. For five minutes, the audience refused to subside, standing up to cheer him. He gave them *St. Louis Blues* as an encore. When he returned to his room, Alpha had regained consciousness. Nat Gonnella was talking soothingly to her. The critic from the *Melody Maker* dashed in to shake hands with the star of the evening. A delegation of London trumpeters who came to congratulate the great man asked diffidently if they might see the famous mouthpiece, half suspecting that Armstrong's power was due to some trick. Soon undeceived, they were unstinting in their admiration of this new trumpet of Jericho.

That night Louis, Alpha, and their friends visited Monseigneur's, where London's smart set gave a rousing ovation to the black trumpeter whose profile and name twinkled on the Palladium's front. Everywhere Louis was the chief topic of conversation.

During the next forenoon, Selmer's agent, Benny Davis (brother of the famous trombonist) came to greet Louis, and when it was time for the latter to go on the stage, the Englishman presented him with a magnificent gold trumpet as a token of Europe's admiration for the real King of Jazz.

Louis was now a star of the first magnitude in the brilliant constellation of music-hall celebrities. On his return to America he received fantastic offers.

In 1933 he left again for England. Some newspapers there devoted more space to his comings and goings than to Hitler's rise to power. The English were conquered by this new music which was the expression of America's soul. So absolute was the spell of Louis's jazz-playing that hundreds of jazz clubs sprang into being, all named after Louis and Alpha.

Then Louis crossed the Channel and arrived in Paris. An enthusiastic crowd had gathered to welcome him at the Gare St.-Lazare. Panassié, Delaunoy, and all the other jazz fanatics were on hand. That night he was given a special reception at Bricktop's. Facing Louis, a young violinist by the name of Michel Warlop could only stare at him and mumble a few adoring words in French.

Louis spent the next fortnight in England and when he returned, Warlop had crammed enough English into his head to be able to communicate verbally with his hero. Hundreds of jazz clubs showered Louis with invitations and played his records. Canetti took him under his wing and had him record two pieces: *New Tiger Rag* and *Sunny Side of the Street*.

Louis traveled through France into Belgium with a first-rate orchestra including Cap McCord who played tenor horn and Herman Chittison, the pianist. Two jazz organizations—one, the "Jazz Club," had brought out the first review on the subject, the other was the "Sweet and Hot"—had joined forces to stage a worthy reception in honor of the great exponent of America's new-found artistry.

This reception was held in the Palace of Fine Arts in Brussels. The gilded youth of Belgium came in droves, and eloquent speeches extolled the new music and its high-priest, Louis Armstrong. That same evening he was officially welcomed by the president of the "Young Barristers of Belgium," who presented him with a memento of Napoleon's military career.

That night Louis felt that a great change had come over the world. First among his race, he, the lowly coal-vendor of yesterday, was now moving in the highest aristocratic and intellectual circles of the white man's world. Had it not been for his departure two days later, the Minister of Belgian Arts and Sciences would have bestowed an official decoration upon him.

Next he sailed for Copenhagen. Indeed, he went from capital to capital like a visiting monarch. The youth of the Old World knew that he who was carrying a new musical message was truly an outstanding figure. Conetti was amazed at the fervent welcome that Europe lavished on his protégé.

"If the President of the United States came to Europe, he could hardly get a warmer reception."

"I'm just a plain American, tryin' to help my people out by playin' my own brand of music."

Horn of Plenty:

"Yes," declared the President of the "Young Barristers of Brussels" in an official message, "Louis Armstrong has brandished Jericho's trumpet and caused the moldy old walls of prejudice to crumble into dust. He will restore the sense of liberty and human integrity to his long-suffering people."

In Copenhagen, he was received by Impresario Skaarup. All the jazz clubs gave him a royal welcome. The best suite at the Palace Hotel was reserved for him. Erick Tuckson's orchestra and a crowd of ten thousand awaited his arrival at the station. Ten photographers aimed their cameras at him. He was dragged from his compartment and carried off in triumph. The orchestra played as people danced in the streets. A delegation approached the great man, at its head Baron Rosenkrantz. After the welcoming committee had delivered various addresses, and a bevy of young girls attired in native costumes presented to Louis a gigantic trumpet made of interwoven roses and lilies, the crowd began to push wildly—everybody wanted to catch a glimpse of the genius. Hundreds of eager people crowded round him to shake his hand. In five minutes, the symbolic trumpet was trampled underfoot as Louis was being hugged and kissed by scores of Danish damsels. At the hotel he was almost mobbed by autograph hunters.

In Stockholm the same madness. . . . By chance, Marian Anderson was there at the same time. Sweden's young nobles and intellectuals honored them both at a memorable banquet. In Norway's Oslo, two thousand students applauded Louis and Alpha at the University.

From Oslo, Louis returned to Paris. Life was wonderful in the City of Light. Montmarte went wild with delight at having the musician in its midst. He had never imagined that whites and blacks might meet and live amicably side by side without a question being raised about color differences. As twilight fell each day, Louis could be found at the famous sidewalk Café Boudon toying with a glass of champagne or an apéritif. Arthur Briggs and the colored musicians of Montmartre often came to pay their respects to the greatest of them all and chat with him. Louis could no longer keep pace with his invitations. Counts, princes, millionaires, Josephine Baker, Bricktop, Gene Bullard, Hugues Panassié—all sang his praises.

There followed receptions in Amsterdam, at The Hague, and in Rotterdam. In the last, a champion of classical music, son of the noted violinist Ysaÿe, came to hear jazz for the first time. After listening to *St. Louis Blues*, he climbed up on his seat and shouted wildly, tears streaming down his cheeks:

"Hurrah for Louis Armstrong! He's the greatest musican in the world!"

In Switzerland, specially chartered buses brought wealthy Europeans from the mountain resorts to the Geneva Casino to listen to the latest phenomenon. It was a glittering gathering in full dress, and all the delegates of the League of Nations were there to view this orgy of success, while the Jean-Jacques Rousseau statue on the island in the river contemplated a scene that justified at last the philosopher's belief in man's emancipation.

After every tour Louis always returned to Paris and his flat in the rue de la Tour d'Auvergne. He had been acclaimed everywhere except in Germany where jazz was now blacklisted. When the sun's dying rays gilded the dome of the Sacré-Coeur and he had finished his daily dozen at Bullard's Gym, he frequently relaxed at Boudon's, where from a sidewalk table he could watch the flow of pedestrians. All the leading exponents of jazz passed by sooner or later, artisans of a new craft who revolved around Louis.

"I'll take another Pernod," Bobby Jones would say—a re-nowned colored trumpeter who had married a Parisienne.

"Who's that guy?" Louis asked one day.

"That's Cricket, the original trumpeter. Came with Mitchell in 1915."

"And *that* fellow?"

"Joe Clarke. He came here around 1919 with his Ha-waiians."

"And over yonder?"

"Looks like Coleman Hawkins talking with Big Boy."

"I know Coleman, of course. I mean the other fellow."

"Oh, you mean Willie Lewis. He's bandleader at Flor-ence's."

White people sat at Louis's table and discussed the music that had taken the world's youthful intelligentsia by storm.

"Louis, you've spoken the language of your race," Delau-nay told him once.

"Oh, I dunno—I blow like I feel!"

"Tell me something, Louis, don't you find the freedom here in Paris positively amazing? Why, it's really a paradise for Negroes," exclaimed Arthur Briggs, married to a white wo-man and now thoroughly Europeanized.

"Oh, sure, Pops. It's great. Black or white, only one thing counts here—what you got in your heart!"

"What do you think about the race question in America?"

"Well, of course I feel sorry for my people, but I ain't holdin' no grudge against the white folks. They been mighty good to Louis."

"Do you think your people will have full freedom in the near future?" eagerly asked Delaunay.

"That's what we're all shootin' for."

"I'll tell you something, Louis," interrupted Arthur Briggs.

"Our poor people, whose only crime is their dark skin, will achieve equality and make some progress only when they produce such musicians as Louis Armstrong. That kind makes anybody proud he's an American!"

It was growing dark. The first strains of jazz broke out. Tuxedoed musicians sauntered by. Taxis were climbing up the hill. Louis did not answer but sat gazing up at the rosy sky. He shook his head dubiously and finally said:

"Listen, my friends, France is a beautiful country. Paris gives us colored folks more 'n we ever get in the States. I've seen all the big shots in Europe, been received by the King of the Belgians, the Crown Prince of Sweden, and Umberto in Italy. Even the Prince of Wales shook hands with me. It was great! Sometimes we take an awful beating in America . . . but it's my country and I love it. I've gotta go back there!"

A few weeks later Louis was "back there." Joe Glaser had his old job as manager, and they headed westward. He made a triumphant tour, his name displayed everywhere in huge letters. At last he was able to marry Alpha; but later he divorced her and married his present wife, Lucille, whom he adores. His life is now a round of extraordinary triumphs that take him from one big show to the next. It's the road to undying fame. A hundred and thirty million Americans know that Louis Armstrong is the real King of Jazz. A hundred and thirty million Americans are beginning to realize that Louis Armstrong is a great American, one of the greatest.

He does not know it. He just blows his trumpet, as he used to deliver milk. He has given a new form of art to his people and a new kind of music to his country. Yet not very long ago Louis Armstrong, unable to find a good hotel in Boston willing to accommodate him, was forced to lodge in a hovel. And in a Southern city recently, without a word of protest, he meekly took a seat in the colored section of a bus.

"How can you stand it, Pops?" asked a friend.

"It's my country, and I love it. If we don't love it an' fight for it, we'll never be free and equal!"